**NEW PHILOSOP
THINKING IMAGES**

Also available from Bloomsbury

Aesthetics and Film
Katherine Thomson-Jones

Aesthetics: Key Concepts in Philosophy
Daniel Herwitz

Aesthetics: The Key Thinkers
Edited by Alessandro Giovannelli

Deleuze and World Cinemas
David Martin-Jones

Introducing Aesthetics and the Philosophy of Art
Darren Hudson Hick

Terrence Malick: Film and Philosophy
Edited by Thomas Deane Tucker and Stuart Kendall

NEW PHILOSOPHIES OF FILM

THINKING IMAGES

ROBERT SINNERBRINK

BLOOMSBURY

LONDON · NEW DELHI · NEW YORK · SYDNEY

Bloomsbury Academic
An imprint of Bloomsbury Publishing Plc

50 Bedford Square	175 Fifth Avenue
London	New York
WC1B 3DP	NY 10010
UK	USA

www.bloomsbury.com

First published in 2011 by the Continuum International Publishing Group Ltd
Reprinted by Bloomsbury Academic 2013

British Library Cataloguing-in-Publication Data
A catalogue record for this book is available from the British Library.

ISBN: HB: 978-1-4411-2257-5
PB: 978-1-4411-5343-2

Library of Congress Cataloging-in-Publication Data
A catalog record for this book is available from the Library of Congress.
Sinnerbrink, Robert.
New philosophies of film: thinking images/Robert
Sinnerbrink.
p. cm.
Includes bibliographical references and index.
Includes filmography.
ISBN 978-1-4411-2257-5 (hardback)
1. Motion pictures–Philosophy. I. Title.
PN1995.S514 2011
791.4301–dc22
2011016505

Typeset by Fakenham Prepress Solutions, Fakenham, Norfolk NR21 8NN
Printed and bound in Great Britain

For Louise, my ideal movie companion, and for Eva and Mimi, film-philosophers of the future!

CONTENTS

PREFACE

At first blush, film and philosophy appear to be uneasy bedfellows. Going to the movies and having a philosophical conversation seem to share little in common. Philosophers feature very rarely in films, though it is usually intriguing when they do. In a memorable scene from Jean-Luc Godard's *Vivre sa vie* (1962), for example, the beautiful Nana [Anna Karina] engages a 'real life' philosopher [Brice Parain] in conversation at a café. They talk of the necessity to talk, the difficulty of saying what one means, the way speech and action conflict, whether one can speak and live at once. At one point during the philosopher's monologue, Nana turns to the camera, addressing us with her ambiguous, mesmerizing gaze. Her gesture is simple but poses many questions: What is this experience we call 'cinema'? How are film and philosophy related? Can their relationship be a true meeting of minds (and bodies)? Can films 'do' philosophy?

This book is dedicated to these questions, exploring, in particular, the film-philosophy relationship. From strangers in the night they have become more than good friends. Indeed, the recent flourishing of philosophical writing on film has been a very welcome surprise. What are these 'new philosophies of film'? Why have philosophy and film theory come together in such fruitful (and sometimes fractious) ways? *New Philosophies of Film* examines the new wave of philosophical film theory that has challenged the older paradigm (so-called 'Grand Theory'). These philosophical approaches are distinguished by their retrieval and renewal of some of the problems of classical film theory, including the ontology of film, the question of film as art, and how we understand and interpret film. In the chapters that follow I focus on three major currents: the analytic-cognitivist turn in film theory; an alternative stream (inspired by

Stanley Cavell and Gilles Deleuze) that explores how film and philosophy respond to shared problems (film-philosophy); and the idea of 'film as philosophy' (that films not only illustrate but can 'do' philosophy in their own way). Because it is better to show than to describe a way of thinking, the final three chapters of this book offer instances of 'film-philosophy' in action, focusing on specific films by three challenging contemporary filmmakers: David Lynch, Lars von Trier and Terrence Malick. In so doing, I wish to show how the relationship between film and philosophy has the possibility of becoming a mutually transformative encounter — an aesthetic experiment in new ways of thinking.

A book has many parents who contribute to the conception and maturing of ideas that eventually appear in written form. Among the many friends and colleagues who have encouraged me over the years, I owe a special debt of thanks to the following people, whether for inspiring conversation, constructive suggestions, or invaluable support: Louise D'Arcens, Michelle Boulous-Walker, William Brown, Romana Byrne, Havi Carel, Alan Cholodenko, Felicity Colman, Marc de Leeuw, Damian Cox, Jean-Philippe Deranty, Lisabeth During, Joanne Faulkner, the *Film-Philosophy* editorial crew, Gregory Flaxman, Daniel Frampton, Berys Gaut, Michael Goddard, Greg Hainge, Laleen Jayamanne, Fiona Jenkins, Noel King, Andrew Klevan, Tarja Laine, Adrian Martin, David Martin-Jones, John Mullarkey, Miread Phillips, Orna Raviv, Daniel Ross, William Rothman, Richard Smith, David Sorfa, Jane Stadler, Lisa Trahair, Greg Tuck, Thomas Wartenberg and Magdalena Zolkos. I would also like to thank David Avital, Tom Crick, Giles Herman, and Moira Eagling from Continuum for their encouragement in fostering this project and in preparing my manuscript for publication.

ACKNOWLEDGEMENTS

Some of the chapters in this book draw on material previously published elsewhere. I would like to thank the editors of the following publications for their kind permission to use material from the following texts.

For the Introduction and Chapter 1:
Sinnerbrink, Robert (2010), 'Disenfranchising Film? On the Analytic-Cognitivist Turn in Film Theory,' in Jack Reynolds, Ed Mares, James

Williams and James Chase (eds), *Postanalytic and Metacontinental: Crossing Philosophical Divides*. London/New York: Continuum, pp. 173–189.

Sinnerbrink, Robert (2011), 'Re-enfranchising Film: Towards a Romantic Film-Philosophy', Havi Carel and Greg Tuck (eds) *New Takes in Film-Philosophy.* Palgrave Macmillan, pp. 25–47.

For Chapter 4:
Sinnerbrink, Robert (2010), 'Cognitivism goes to the movies (review article): Paisley Livingston and Carl Plantinga (eds), *The Routledge Companion to Philosophy and Film*; Carl Plantinga, *Moving Viewers: American Film and the Spectator's Experience*; Torben Grodal, *Embodied Visions: Evolution, Emotion, Culture, and Film*;. *Projections: The Journal for Movies and Mind*, 4, (1), Summer, 83–98.

For Chapter 9:
Sinnerbrink, Robert (2009), 'From mythic history to cinematic poetry: *The New World* viewed'. *Screening the Past*, 26 http://www.latrobe.edu.au/screeningthepast/26/early-europe/the-new-world.html (accessed December 22, 2009).

Sinnerbrink, Robert (2011), 'Song of the Earth: Cinematic Romanticism in Malick's *The New World*, in Thomas Deane Tucker and Stuart Kendall (eds), *Terrence Malick: Film and Philosophy*. London/New York: Continuum, pp. 179–96.

I also wish to acknowledge the Australian Research Council (ARC) for funding support made available through a Discovery Grant on 'Film as Philosophy: Understanding Cinematic Thinking' (with Dr Lisa Trahair and Dr Gregory Flaxman). This grant made possible much of the research necessary for the writing of this book. Finally, I would like to thank my students in the Department of Philosophy, Macquarie University, whose enthusiasm and engagement while teaching my 'Film and Philosophy' course contributed a great deal to my thinking.

INTRODUCTION: WHY DID PHILOSOPHY GO TO THE MOVIES?

Over the last one hundred years or so, philosophy, on the whole, has been rather averse to the cinema. Among the great modern thinkers film barely rates a mention. In 1906, French vitalist Henri Bergson described the 'cinematographic mechanism' of consciousness, only to then criticize the 'cinematographic illusion' by which we compose (apparent) movement from a series of static images (Bergson 2005: 251–2). Despite an intriguing philosophical dialogue touching on Kurosawa's *Rashomon* (1950), German thinker Martin Heidegger denounced film and photography as part of the reduction of art to an aesthetic resource brought about by the essence of modern technology (Heidegger 1982: 15–17). French phenomenologist Maurice Merleau-Ponty is the exception proving the rule, having composed a short essay on film and (gestalt) psychology, and making significant remarks on cinematic examples in his phenomenological work (1964: 48–59; 2002). Despite Merleau-Ponty's evident interest in the movies, French phenomenology, on the whole, tended to ignore it. Indeed, it is only in recent years that phenomenology, both classical (Husserl) and French (Merleau-Ponty), has been brought to bear on the theorization of film (see Casebier 1991; Sobchack 1992). Even Walter Benjamin's enthusiasm for the culturally and politically emancipatory dimensions of film was tempered by concern over its role in the 'aestheticisation of the political' (see Benjamin 2006: 269).

Within modern culture, moreover, film has typically been presented as 'the other' of serious philosophy. Ludwig Wittgenstein, so the story goes, would rush from delivering his arduous Cambridge lectures to find solace in the front row of the local movie theatre. Stress release from the rigours of conceptual analysis is how Wittgenstein's passion for Hollywood musicals, Westerns and detective stories is often portrayed (see Gilmore 2005). Until recent decades, particularly within the Anglo-American (analytic) tradition, this has also been true of philosophy's relationship with film: an amusing distraction, aesthetic example, or theoretical resource, perhaps, but not something having intrinsic philosophical worth. That a philosopher such as Stanley Cavell feels compelled to explain his decision to take movies — like romantic comedies and melodramas — seriously *as* philosophy is telling in this regard. As Cavell remarks, the great mystery is to explain why philosophy has ignored film, and why their relationship has been so ambivalent. There is, on the one hand, philosophy's persistent avoidance of film, as though philosophy were aware of film's power to challenge it (Cavell 2008: xiv). On the other, there is an affinity between film and philosophy (Cavell 1999: 25), film presenting a 'moving image of scepticism' that philosophy both courts and attempts to dispel (Cavell 1981: 188–9). Such an encounter, however ambivalent, should not mean that philosophy can now rejuvenate itself by appropriating film. As this book will argue, the point is to show how the film-philosophy encounter can open up new paths for thinking.

New Philosophies of Film is intended both as an introduction to the dynamic new wave of philosophizing on film, and as an independent contribution to this emerging field of interdisciplinary engagement. It welcomes both passionate film enthusiast and dedicated philosophical reader (who may well be one and the same!) and aims to show how the emerging 'field' of film and philosophy is one of the most exciting in aesthetics today. This field, however, has not emerged in a vacuum. The rise of the new philosophies of film, which have drawn heavily on analytic philosophy, aesthetics and cognitivist psychology, has coincided with the decline of 1970s screen theory. It is also distinguished by the effort to recast many of the problems of classical film theory — concerning the ontology of film, the question of film as art, questions of narrative, character, authorship and genre — within a philosophically renewed and theoretically transformed paradigm (supplanting the older paradigm of psychoanalytic-semiotic film theory). Whatever one's view on this shift, this new wave of philosophical film theory, which I will call the *analytic-cognitivist* paradigm, is becoming increasingly influential today.[1]

At the same time, however, this paradigm is now being challenged by alternative philosophical approaches, which have also moved away from the earlier paradigm of screen/film theory. In later chapters, I explore this alternative way of approaching the film-philosophy relationship, namely the idea of 'film as philosophy' (see Mulhall 2002, 2008; Wartenberg 2007). In doing so, I argue for greater interactive engagement between the rationalistic style of traditional *philosophy of film*, and the minor, interdisciplinary tradition of what I call *film-philosophy*, an alternative approach that combines aesthetic receptivity to film with philosophically informed reflection. My aim is to elucidate the productive possibilities for rethinking the film-philosophy relationship that are opened up by the encounter between new philosophies of film and film-philosophy, as contrasting yet complementary ways of exploring the philosophical dimensions of moving images.[2]

A USER'S GUIDE TO FILM AND PHILOSOPHY

Interest in the film-philosophy relationship has burgeoned in the last three decades, with a striking surge of interest in philosophical responses to questions of classical film theory, and enthusiastic exploration of the idea of 'film as philosophy'.[3] While film theory has retreated from psychoanalytical and semiotic theorizing, philosophers have discovered the manifold pleasures of film. We can now speak of the 'philosophy of film' as an independent field with its own theoretical debates, competing schools and research programs.[4] Although Stanley Cavell published works on the topic during the 1970s (*The World Viewed* was first published in 1971), philosophy of film only emerges as a speciality area from the mid 1980s and 1990s.[5] Interestingly, this was also the period in which the prevailing paradigm of film theory — what Bordwell and Carroll dismissively dubbed 'Grand Theory' — began to enter what might be described as a theoretical and disciplinary crisis.

As D. N. Rodowick confirms, during the 1980s film studies was challenged on three fronts, suffering a 'triple displacement' by historical studies, cognitivist psychology and analytic philosophy (2007a: 94–5). Much of what is now dismissed as 'Grand Theory' — inspired by psychoanalytic theory, semiotics, French structuralism and post-structuralism — is better described as 'aesthetics' or 'film philosophy' (Rodowick 2007a: 100). Indeed, the philosophical approach in theorists such as Cavell and Deleuze — what I call film-philosophy — contributes to 'a philosophy of the humanities critically and reflexively attentive in equal measure to its epistemological and ethical commitments' (Rodowick 2007a: 92).

Unfortunately, as Rodowick remarks, the combined analytic-cognitivist attack on 'Theory' for its lack of scientific credibility and philosophical cogency has had the unwelcome effect of serving as 'a de facto epistemological dismissal of the humanities' (2007a: 98).

At the risk of generalization, contemporary philosophical work on film can be defined by a number of competing currents. While psychoanalytical and semiotic orthodoxies have entered a decline, other theoretical perspectives remain important (cultural studies, media theory, post-colonialism, gender studies, queer theory, reception studies, production histories, historical and cross-cultural approaches, film history, especially early cinema, and so on). On the other hand, 'post-Theory', cognitivism, analytic philosophy and, more recently, neuroscience and evolutionary biology have begun to coalesce into a formidable research paradigm. The latter maintains that film studies, ideally, should draw on the best available science, be compatible with philosophical naturalism, and demonstrate cumulative, testable results. We might define these, respectively, as the *culturalist-historicist* versus the *cognitivist-naturalist* approaches to film.[6]

Against these currents we can also point to the recent emergence of film-philosophy as a distinctive approach, the founding figures of which I take to be Cavell and Deleuze. Their path-breaking works treated film as an artform capable of engaging in a distinctly cinematic exploration of philosophically important themes, and one that could provoke philosophy to respond in its own way to what film allows us to experience (see Cavell 1979, 1981, 1996; Deleuze 1986, 1989). A number of important works, inspired by Cavell and Deleuze, have appeared in recent years — works that are distinguished by their critical performance of variations on the film-philosophy theme (Bersani and Dutoit 2004; Mulhall 2002, 2008; Frampton 2006; Peretz 2008; Mullarkey 2009). Such a perspective is distinct from the more conventional 'philosophy of film', which is usually, but not exclusively, affiliated with the cognitivist-naturalist approach, although there are also interesting crosscurrents between dominant traditions (see Mullarkey 2009: 133–55).

To anticipate the argument I develop in this book, what distinguishes Cavell and Deleuze from the prevailing Anglo-American philosophy of film is their questioning of the 'Platonic prejudice' against art, or what Arthur Danto has called the 'philosophical disenfranchisement of art' (1986): the attempt to subsume works of art into a philosophical discourse that enables us to master, comprehend and subordinate the work to theoretical or moral concerns. Along with Cavell and Deleuze, other film philosophers (such as Jacques Rancière 2004, 2006) have engaged in similar critiques of this Platonic prejudice (see Wartenberg 2007: 15–31), highlighting the significance of affect, pleasure and thought in our experience of film. What unites many of these thinkers is another anti-Platonic gesture: an ethico-political commitment to the inherent *egalitarianism* of the cinema as a genuinely popular technological artform that has inherently *democratic* potentials. By virtue of its technological capabilities of recording, cinema is uniquely able to make any subject or event worthy of audiovisual temporal presentation. It exercises a generous 'ontological equality' between persons, objects and events depicted on screen (see Cavell 1979: 37). Indeed, it belongs to what Rancière calls the *aesthetic regime of art*, which undoes the hierarchical orders of representation structuring more traditional regimes, opens up experience to a plurality of forms of presentation, and thus anticipates the possibility of an aesthetic critique of modern culture (2004: 20–30). It is this third philosophical approach to film — the emergence of *film-philosophy* — that I shall explore in later chapters of this book, as well as the possibility of a distinctive kind of 'cinematic thinking' that resists reduction to philosophical theory.

WHY PHILOSOPHY OF FILM NOW?

A brief look at the history of film theory shows that philosophy and film share a long-standing affinity. All the great classical film theorists — Münsterberg, Arnheim, Balázs, Eisenstein, Bazin, Kracauer, Morin, and the like — engaged in philosophical reflection: on film as an art, as a medium, in regard to its ontology, on the question of realism, on cinematic expression, and on its cultural-ideological significance (see Colman 2009). After this promising start, however, philosophical reflection on film remained more or less dormant.[7] Leading philosopher of film Noël Carroll cites both historical and intellectual reasons for this peculiar state of affairs (2008). Historically speaking, Carroll claims, it has taken a couple of generations for there to be enough philosophers conversant with film to create a 'critical mass' of philosophically minded film theorists (2008: 1–2). Intellectually speaking, film theory abandoned its traditional 'philosophical' concerns, seemingly in the late 1980s and 1990s, and embraced a 'culturalist' approach that left, in Carroll's words, an intellectual vacuum that philosophers have been eager to fill (2008: 2). By 'philosophy' Carroll means recent Anglo-American philosophy, rather than the broad sweep of European as well as Anglophone traditions. As for the 'intellectual vacuum' claim, Carroll must mean that the film theory produced during those decades was inherently vacuous and thus ripe for philosophical rehabilitation. On this view, philosophy's 'civilizing' mission, at least to its adherents, was to rescue film theory from intellectual and moral perdition. Unsurprisingly, sympathetic philosophers and film theorists have often met this 'humanitarian intervention' with a mixture of exasperation and irritation (see Frampton 2006; Brown 2010). So what was this crisis in film theory to which philosophy responded so enthusiastically?

I shall consider the critique of 'Grand Theory' in more detail in Chapter 1. In the meantime, we can sum up this critique as resting on the rejection of psychoanalytic, hermeneutic and ideological-critical approaches to theorising film. At the same time, the strongly political orientation of earlier forms of film theory — its explicit commitment to Marxist and feminist theory and politics — has been significantly neutered. Instead, the emerging paradigm of philosophical film theory went 'back to the future', seeking to retrieve some of the traditional problems of classical film theory, and addressing these by drawing on the resources of analytic philosophy, cognitivist psychology and related empirical disciplines (including neuroscience and evolutionary biology). It could be described as a *naturalistic* rather than *hermeneutic* paradigm (more concerned with explanatory theories based on the natural sciences rather than humanistic forms of reflection or interpretation). The new paradigm embraces empirical and cognitivist psychology, the argumentative techniques of analytic philosophy, rejects ideological-critical and politically committed approaches, and downplays the former paradigm's emphasis on film interpretation. Call this the *analytic-cognitivist* paradigm of film theory (an ungainly rubric that nonetheless captures shared features of the new paradigm).

But does this account tell the whole story? While there is a link between the dismissal of 'Continental'-style film theory and the rise of the new philosophy of film, the picture involves far more than a shift from 'Continental' to analytic-cognitivist paradigms. There are important thinkers, for example, who do not readily fit into this neat division (such as Stanley Cavell). There are 'Continentals' whose work on film is rationalist in orientation (such as Alain Badiou 2005); 'Continental' thinkers whose philosophy of film has certain 'cognitivist' elements (such as Deleuze); and theorists whose work crosses over between cognitivism, ethics, cultural theory and 'Continental' phenomenology (see Buckland 2009; Laine 2011; Sobchack 1992; Stadler 2008). As these remarks suggest, the most interesting work in this emerging field cuts across this divide in exciting and innovative ways, retaining what was most valuable in the older paradigm but sharpening its theoretical focus thanks to the new one. So how should we describe the competing contemporary approaches to philosophizing on film?

Here I would like to propose a distinction between two ways of doing 'film and philosophy': (1) *philosophy of film*, a theoretical explanatory approach to analysing the nature of film and of film experience; and (2) *film-philosophy*, an aesthetic, self-reflective, interpretative approach that puts philosophy in dialogue with film as an alternative way of thinking. In the 'philosophy of X' approach, philosophy conceptually analyzes and theorizes its object precisely because the latter cannot do so. Philosophy of film belongs to the traditional 'theories of X' approach that seeks to provide, variously, a conceptual definition of, empirical investigation into, or philosophical criticism of theories claiming to account for X (where 'X' means film, motion pictures, moving images, and so on).

The alternative position, 'film-philosophy', is a style of philosophical exploration that questions the common tendency to philosophically privilege conceptual theorization over film aesthetics. Film-philosophy argues that film should be regarded as engaging in philosophically relevant reflection via the medium of film itself, or as being capable of a distinctively *cinematic* kind of thinking (as I explore in Part III of this book). It is a way of aesthetically disclosing, perhaps also transforming, our experience of the modern world; one that prompts philosophy to reflect upon its own limits or even to experiment with new forms of philosophical expression.

Instead of mapping these competing approaches onto the dubious analytic/'Continental' divide, we would do better to rethink these as expressing a difference between *rationalist* and *romanticist* approaches to theorizing film. These categories better capture the pertinent differences between practitioners of the philosophy of film and advocates of film-philosophy. Rationalist approaches to theory seek to provide explanatory models of various aspects of film experience. They elaborate empirically grounded models of our experience of moving images, of film ontology, of how we understand film narrative, and so on. Romanticist approaches, for their part, seek to reflect upon, interpret, or extend the kind of aesthetic experience that film evokes. They seek not only to explain and comprehend but to question and understand the significance of film experience; they search for apt ways of expressing this aesthetic experience in a philosophical discourse that aims to elucidate and thus deepen our understanding of film.

We might think here of how this divide between these two ways of doing philosophical work on film reflects a deeper debate over how we conceptualize the relationship between science and art. Is art, including film, reducible to the kinds of explanatory theories provided by the best available science? Or does the art of film express forms of meaning that resist reduction to naturalistic explanatory accounts? How can we bring together what both philosophy of film and film-philosophy have to offer in order to broaden and deepen our experience and understanding of film? These are some of the key questions that inform the lines of inquiry and argument explored in this book. *New Philosophies of Film* offers an account of the emergence of these new approaches, maps out the conceptual terrain of debate that animates them, and offers a modest contribution to philosophical film theory by arguing for a more pluralist approach to the film-philosophy relationship. My suggestion, developed in the last four chapters, is that we shift our way of thinking (and writing) in order to allow film to communicate with philosophy in more aesthetically receptive ways; we might thereby open up new ways of *thinking with film*, and thus help ameliorate philosophy's traditional disenfranchisement of art.

DESIGN OF THIS BOOK

The aim of *New Philosophies of Film* is threefold: (1) to introduce major developments in contemporary philosophies of film, from both so-called analytic and 'Continental' perspectives; (2) to argue for new ways of thinking the film-philosophy relationship that have been opened up by theorists working between these two traditions, as well as by those concerned with the idea of film as philosophy; and (3) to explore the possibilities of a more transformative relationship *between* film and philosophy. Throughout the book I argue that we should move beyond the adversarial battle between 'Grand Theory' and 'Analytic-Cognitivist' paradigms, and attempt instead to understand these new approaches as expressing two traditions or styles of thought: the *rationalist* and *romanticist* strains of philosophical film theory. I characterize these traditions by drawing the distinction between a more conventionally theoretical and explanatory *philosophy of film* and a more aesthetic, self-reflective, even experimental *film-philosophy*. The challenge for contemporary practitioners, therefore, is to find ways of overcoming the rationalist-romanticist divide; not to reprioritize one side of the binary opposition over the other, but to synthesize the theoretical acumen of philosophy of film with film-philosophy's aesthetic receptivity to film's distinctive ways of thinking.

In Part I, 'The Analytic-Cognitivist Turn', I outline the shift from so-called 'Grand Theory' to the new philosophies of film, and suggest that this shift can be understood as recapitulating some of the classical problems of film theory within a renewed theoretical paradigm (the analytic-cognitivist turn in film theory). In Chapter 1, I present an account of the crisis in film/screen theory and the Bordwell/Carroll attack on ('Continental') 'Grand Theory' that led to the analytic-cognitivist turn. In Chapter 2, I examine the return of ontology in the new philosophies of film, which retrieve and renew problems that preoccupied early film theory (such as the nature of the moving image, or the question of whether film is art). In Chapter 3, I turn to questions of narrative, authorship, and 'identification' or character engagement. Contra psychoanalytic theories of identification, contemporary philosophies of film have developed sophisticated theories of narrative, authorship, affective engagement and genre. The question, however, is whether these new approaches have underplayed the role of pleasure, affect and thought that more challenging kinds of film can evoke (what I call 'cinematic thinking').

Part II, 'From Cognitivism to Film-Philosophy', examines the ways in which contemporary philosophers of film have developed a variety of theoretical responses to the problems of classical film theory. Chapter 4 examines the emergence of a variety of 'cognitivist' approaches, including Bordwell's and Carroll's respective accounts of narrative and Carl Plantinga's 'moderate' cognitivist theory of affective engagement and cinematic genre. I consider both the possibilities and limits of cognitivist philosophy of film in order to make a transition to my discussion of Gilles Deleuze and Stanley Cavell, two of the key thinkers of contemporary film-philosophy. Chapter 5 explores Deleuze's and Cavell's distinctive ways of doing film-philosophy as important alternatives to the predominant analytic-cognitivist trends in contemporary philosophy of film. Deleuze's version of film-philosophy focuses on conceptualizing cinema from the viewpoint of the problems of movement and of time, rather than exploring individual films or genres in depth. Cavell, by contrast, develops a 'classical' ontology of film and explores its implications — in particular, the problem of scepticism — by way of detailed philosophical 'readings' of individual films (belonging to genres such as the remarriage comedy or the melodrama of the unknown woman). Both thinkers share the view that film can be an important response to *scepticism* or *nihilism* — our loss of belief in the world — and thereby help us find ways of renewing a sense of connection with the world. Chapter 6 explores the provocative idea of 'film as philosophy', examining both proponents and critics of this approach to film-philosophy; I challenge some of these critiques and argue that the validity of this approach rests less on general theoretical arguments than on robust and detailed philosophical film criticism.

In Part III, 'Cinematic Thinking', I elaborate the potential of these new approaches by exploring films by three innovative and accomplished filmmakers: David Lynch's challenging meditation on Hollywood in crisis, *INLAND EMPIRE* (2006); Lars von Trier's controversial psychological horror film, *Antichrist* (2009); and Terrence Malick's poetic recasting of the Pocahontas myth, *The New World* (2005). Apart from being remarkable works in their own right, these films can all be said, in different ways, to 'resist theory': to resist reduction to a philosophical thesis, theoretical problem, or hermeneutic transparency, and in so doing to open up new ways of thinking that present a challenge to philosophy (of film). These films provide instances of what I call *cinematic thinking*, which demands a different way of thinking (and writing) philosophically with film. My exploration of the possibilities of film-philosophy concludes with a brief fragment on a wonderful scene from Orson Welles' unfinished work, *Don Quixote*, the subject of a lapidary meditation by Giorgio Agamben (2007). My hope is that, by staging the encounter between film and philosophy, and exploring different ways of performing film-philosophy, this book will suggest ways of rethinking and renewing the film-philosophy relationship.[8]

PART I: THE ANALYTIC-COGNITIVIST TURN

CHAPTER ONE

THE EMPIRE STRIKES BACK: CRITIQUES OF 'GRAND THEORY'

In Part I of this book I introduce some of the new approaches to philosophizing on film, which I have dubbed the analytic-cognitivist paradigm, analyzing the related strands of its critique of the preceding model of film theorizing, so-called 'Grand Theory'. This approach has produced a host of powerful theories addressing philosophical, psychological and aesthetic aspects of film (see Livingston and Plantinga, 2009). In Chapter 1 I examine the influential critique of 'Grand Theory' developed by David Bordwell, Noël Carroll, Richard Allen, Murray Smith, and a host of other theorists. Underlying this critique is a dispute between competing ways of doing philosophy, associated with the vexed analytic/'Continental' philosophy divide (see Sinnerbrink 2010). After addressing some of the basic elements of the critique of 'Grand Theory', I examine Carroll's philosophy of film (his 'dialectical cognitivism'), which argues against 'medium essentialism' (the idea that film has a definable medium that would determine aesthetic style and value); against interpretation (which conflates film theory with film criticism); and against the 'film as language' thesis (that language provides an appropriate model for theorizing film). I also consider Bordwell's related critique of film hermeneutics and of speculative film theory, suggesting that there are problems with Bordwell's critique of the hermeneutic (interpretative) approach to film. Although generating a rich array of new theoretical work, the analytic-cognitivist turn can also be challenged for its sometimes 'reductionist' approach to the complex aesthetic, hermeneutic and ideological dimensions of film. In good dialectical fashion, the challenge is to incorporate theoretical innovations in the new approaches, yet retain what remains valuable in the older paradigms. The aim, in short, is to avoid both *reductionism* and *dogmatism* (the bugbear of so-called 'Grand Theory').

THE PHILOSOPHICAL TURN IN FILM THEORY

As Adrian Martin observes (2006), every fifteen years or so film studies seems to undergo a distinctive kind of theoretical 'turn'. From the Psychoanalytic Turn of the 1960s and 70s through the Historiographic Turn of the 80s and 90s, we now find ourselves, Martin remarks, in the midst of a 'Philosophic Turn' that was sparked by Deleuze's Cinema books in France and Cavell's works in the United States (2006: 76). The Deleuzian turn was followed by 'various certified philosophers exploring their passions for cinema — Bernard Stiegler, Alain Badiou, Slavoj Žižek, Giorgio Agamben, and Jacques Rancière, among others' (Martin 2006: 76). To explain this 'philosophical turn' in film theory, some philosophers have cited the general cultural popularity of film, its pedagogical potential (particularly for teaching philosophy), and the rise of cognitivist approaches in psychology and philosophy of mind (see Carroll 2008; Gaut 2010; Shaw 2008). Although these are all relevant factors, the most obvious reasons for the turn were institutional and theoretical: the collapse of what Bordwell and Carroll called 'Grand Theory' — 1970s and 80s film theory that combined psychoanalytic, semiotic and ideologico-critical perspectives — and its replacement by historicist, culturalist, and media-oriented approaches (1996a). In the so-called 'theoretical vacuum' that followed the demise of 'Grand Theory' and the cultural-historicist turn, so Carroll claims, philosophy offered the kind of theoretical resources required to renew the 'classical' problems of film theory that had been left in abeyance (see Carroll 1988a, 1988b).

Whatever their theoretical orientations, the new wave of 'post-Theory' philosophers of film defined themselves against the older paradigm of institutionalized film theory of the 1970s and 80s inspired by psychoanalysis, structuralism, semiotics, cultural theory, and various strands of German critical theory and French poststructuralism.[1] The title of Noël Carroll's 1988 book says it all: *Mystifying Movies: Fads and Fallacies in Contemporary Film Theory* (1988a).[2] The new philosophical film theory challenging the prevailing models styled itself as analytic rather than 'Continental' in inspiration; cognitivist rather than psychoanalytic in approach; scientistic rather than hermeneutic in orientation; concerned with framing and testing empirical hypotheses rather than engaging in speculation or interpretation. It aimed at a 'rational' understanding of film rather than at plumbing unconscious desire, and was concerned to use plain language and theoretical arguments rather than what critics derided as metaphysical jargon. With its preference for analytical argument and empirically testable models, analytic-cognitivist film theory has become an increasingly dominant way of pursuing the study of film.

The story becomes rather intriguing at this point, for it is a very specific approach that the new philosophers of film were challenging. Noël Carroll usefully distinguishes between the then 'contemporary film theory' (semiological approaches that also drew on psychoanalytical and Marxist theories of ideology) and 'classical film theory', which included earlier theorists (such as Arnheim and Bazin) as well as more recent ones (such as V. F. Perkins and Stanley Cavell) (1988a: 1). According to Carroll, semiological film theory had a first wave (for example, Christian Metz), taking its inspiration from linguist Ferdinand de Saussure, and then a second wave (1970s Screen Theory), in which this semiological approach was combined with (Lacanian) psychoanalytic and (Althusserian) Marxist theories of ideology. This second wave of film theory was also given a political inflection during the later 1970s through the feminist analysis of gender and a critique of the ideological function of Hollywood film.

THE CRITIQUE OF 'GRAND THEORY'

Noël Carroll's critique of 'Grand Theory' targets its uncritical commitment to eclectic strains of 'Continental' philosophy (1996: 37–68). Carroll identifies what we might call 'five obstructions' to more rational ways of theorizing on film; difficulties which all stem, he claims, from the flawed foundation of 'Continental' theory:

(1) *A monolithic conception of film theory*, according to which a 'foundational' theoretical paradigm has to account for all relevant aspects of film; this is linked with an implausible 'medium-essentialism', which sought to explain all relevant phenomena in terms of the film medium.

(2) *The conflation of film theory with film interpretation*, in which film theorists adopt a theoretical framework (Lacanian psychoanalysis,

for example), and then 'confirm' the theory in question by finding its concepts or ideas instantiated in specific film examples.

(3) *Political correctness*, in which the progressive ethico-political claims of film theory are bolstered via solidarity with emancipatory social-political movements of the 1960s and 70s.

(4) *Charges of formalism*, in which ways of theorizing about film without a 'political' or ideological focus are dismissed as 'formalist' or as lacking substantive content.

(5) *Biases against truth*, which refers to the alleged postmodernist dismissal of truth as an ideological construct, a claim that rests on an untenable 'argument from absolute truth' (any truth claim about film presupposes an absolutist concept of truth; there is no such concept; *ergo* truth claims about film are 'ideologically suspect') (Carroll 1996: 38–56).

Taken together, these five obstructions hampered philosophical theorization of film, prompting the need for a 'paradigm shift' towards more analytic-cognitivist forms of theory (Carroll 1996: 56–68).

There are two features of so-called 'Grand Theory' deemed most suspect or troubling by analytic-cognitivist critics: (1) the 'decentred' conception of the human subject whose claims to rational autonomy are undermined by the role of the unconscious in psychic life, and by the shared background structures of language, culture, and ideology; and (2) the conviction that film, whether in its popular or modernist forms, is an important ideologico-political battleground over forms of social and cultural representation (in particular, of gender, sexuality, class, race and cultural identity). The upshot of these two theses — the challenge to rational autonomy (posited by psychoanalytic theory) and the ideologico-political function of film (posited by Marxist and feminist theory) — was to suggest that film theory provided a privileged site for the examination of psychic mechanisms of desire and for the related critique of social and cultural ideology.

Indeed, the paradigm of 'Grand Theory', whatever its theoretical shortcomings, clearly questioned two key assumptions of the new analytic-cognitivist paradigm: (1) that the human being is a rational autonomous agent whose cognitive powers are not subject to irrational 'unconscious' forces or to ideological manipulation; and (2) that film is a popular form of entertainment that does not have any pernicious ideological function, that operates using transparent visual and narrative techniques, and that can be analyzed and understood in broadly 'naturalistic' terms (with reference to physical, physiological, biological and evolutionary processes). In short, the battle between 'Grand Theory' and the analytic-cognitivist paradigm turned on our assumptions concerning *human nature* and the relationship between *subjectivity and culture*. To what extent are we rational beings, unperturbed by unconscious or ideological forces? And to what extent does film — *the* mass artform of the modern age — have the tendency to serve ideological ends?

Suffice to say, these are difficult and important philosophical questions that cannot be answered glibly here. I raise them in order to signal that there are deeper issues at stake in the dispute between competing paradigms in film theory. It is by no means obvious that these questions have been settled either way; the assumption that they have is closer to dogmatism than to criticism. This point has been forgotten in the fractious debates over 'Grand Theory' and its critics, and remains pertinent today given the analytic-cognitivist turn in film theory. For the pendulum swing from the 'hermeneutics of suspicion' practised by 'Grand Theory' to the analytic-cognitivist defence of a rational, commonsense approach to the movies has now reached the most extreme point of its amplitude.

The polemical character of Carroll's critique of 'Grand Theory' was intended to challenge the dogmas of a once-dominant paradigm in crisis, and to advocate in its stead a more rationally defensible model of film theorization. Despite its 'Culture Wars' rhetoric, it is worth making some critical remarks on this critique, which was crucial for the development of what we might call 'post-Theory theory'. I shall take each of Bordwell/Carroll's 'five obstructions' in turn.

Monolithic theory and 'medium essentialism'

One of the sharpest criticisms of 'Grand Theory' was that it adopted an all-encompassing theoretical paradigm — psychoanalytical, semiotic, and so on — that was used to account for the manifold aspects of film. There is some truth to the claim that 'Grand Theory' relied on what seemed like all-encompassing theories, even though they were not 'monolithic' in the sense of being homogeneous or univocal. It is worth recalling, moreover, that the motivation for so doing was to account for the two assumptions outlined above:

that human subjects are subject to 'irrational' forces that conflict with our rational capacities; and that film is not only an accessible medium of mass entertainment but also a complex instrument of ideological influence. That is why 'Grand Theory', far from being 'monolithic', was typically characterized by various theoretical 'fusions' (psychoanalytic-semiotic theory, psychoanalytical-feminist theory, structural linguistic-ideology critique, and so on). 'Grand Theory' may have struggled to find theoretically convincing ways of articulating these two assumptions, but it was at least concerned to question the view that human subjects are rational masters of their conscious experience, and that the medium of film need not be considered a powerful ideological force.

Conflation of film theory with film criticism

One of the most striking elements in this critique is the assertion that 'Grand Theory' conflated 'film theory' with 'film criticism', confusing theoretical claims about film with hermeneutic claims about the interpretation of particular films or genres (Allen and Smith 1997: 6). As a result, post-Theorists generally insist on a firm distinction between film theory and film criticism, arguing that the two should be kept well apart, lest we lapse into the kind of 'fallacy of exemplification' — 'proving' the claims of a theory via selective film interpretations — to which 'Grand Theory' was supposedly prone.

One consequence of this critique, however, has been the proliferation of theories about film that often remain aloof from the detailed analysis of particular films, save as useful illustrations of theoretical problems explored by the theory (see, for example, Carroll 2008; Gaut 2010).[3] It is one thing to say that theory should be general in scope and explanatory in nature; it is another to claim that such theorizing should avoid the anomalous or deviant cases studied in film criticism. Aesthetic theories, including philosophies of film, find their rigour and plausibility in the degree to which they illuminate our experience and understanding of singular works of art.

'Political correctness'

A regrettably pejorative phrase, it conjures up images of stoical cultural warriors fighting off the barbarians at the university gates.

18

Shorn of its unpleasant rhetorical aspect, it refers to the manipulating of theory or rejection of valid inquiry due to implicit ideological commitments (at least according to those making the criticism). To be sure, any attempt to stymie theoretical reflection in the name of ideological or political orthodoxy is rife for criticism; but then again so is political vacuity — or indifference towards the larger social, cultural, historical and ideological forces that also contribute to the context of film. Although some theorists deride attempts to explore the ideological dimensions of film, few would deny that film remains 'ideological' in some respects. Indeed, some cognitivists have begun to acknowledge that this remains an important topic to be addressed (see Plantinga 2009a: 12–14). The relationship between the empirical social, economic and historical circumstances of a film's production or reception within the broader cultural-ideological fields within which we live remains an important question, especially for those pursuing a methodologically pluralist approach.

(4) and (5) Formalism and biases against truth

The complaint concerning so-called 'biases against truth' is fair enough, assuming it is true that such theories have the kind of bias attributed to them by their critics. Here the classic critique of 'Grand Theory' sometimes runs afoul of caricature in its presentation of such theories, translating their claims in reductive terms, or else construing them as narrowly concerned with problems of interest to contemporary philosophers.[4] Nonetheless, Carroll and other critics of 'Grand Theory' were right to insist that questions of truth and falsity remain important, provided we do not assume that there is only one paradigm of knowledge — modelled on the natural sciences — that can provide a foundation for philosophizing on film. This is not to deny the importance of scientifically informed theorizing, but to point out that the relationship between philosophical naturalisms and the theorization of art remains a subject of debate. Indeed it is part of what we reflect on when we do philosophy of film.

The important question to be drawn from these remarks on the critique of 'Grand Theory' is how the new philosophies of film are to navigate the twin perils of *dogmatism* (stereotypically attributed to 'Grand Theory') and *reductionism* (stereotypically attributed to analytic-cognitivist theory). On the one hand, theorists within the analytic-cognitivist paradigm sometimes court the risk of assuming a too-narrow conception of what counts as knowledge, thus dismissing alternative ways of thinking about film as mere 'pseudo-argumentation'. On the other hand, 'Continental'-inspired theorists can court the danger of reproducing theoretical dogmatism in their assumption of a conceptual framework that is then applied uncritically to various aspects of film. The challenge for the new philosophies of film, therefore, is to steer a successful course between the Scylla of dogmatism and the Charybdis of reductionism. It is to find new ways of synthesizing, rather than dismissing, alternative theoretical frameworks and critical philosophical perspectives.

CARROLL'S DIALECTICAL COGNITIVISM

Perhaps the most paradigmatic of the post-Theory approaches to emerge in recent decades is Noël Carroll's 'piecemeal' or middle level theory. Carroll's approach, which he dubs 'dialectical cognitivism', draws on cognitive psychology and analytic philosophy and argues against three pervasive assumptions held within the 'Grand Theory' paradigm: (1) against *medium essentialism* (the view that there are essential features of film as a medium that both define it and determine its aesthetic possibilities); (2) against *interpretation* (the idea that the primary task of film theory is to provide critical inter-pretations of films drawing on an assumed theoretical framework); and (3) against the *'film as language'* thesis (the idea that language provides a privileged model for theorizing film). Carroll's approach is 'dialectical', in that it captures how competing theories attempt to dialectically supersede each other on the basis of correcting the errors of previous theories. It is also 'cognitivist', in that it shows how film-viewing involves cognitive phenomena amenable to rational analysis according to broadly empiricist psychologies or naturalistic theories of mind. Let us consider each of these three aspects of Carroll's critique of 'Grand Theory'.

Against 'medium essentialism'

Since the late 1980s, Noël Carroll has been arguing against *medium essentialism*: the pervasive assumption, part theoretical, part aesthetic, that 'each artform has its own distinctive medium' distin-guishing it from other artforms (Carroll 2006: 113–14). Such a view, moreover, claims that identifying this medium has important theoretical and aesthetic consequences (for example, extolling the virtues of cinematic realism as a proper realization of the possibilities of the medium). From Eisenstein's valorisation of montage, to Bazin's championing of deep-focus, philosophers of film have followed classical aesthetics in attempting to define a distinctive medium (in physical and material senses) proper to film, and on that basis to argue for the kind of aesthetic possibilities that film can realize. 'Grand Theory' too, for its part, made use of the medium-essentialism thesis, arguing, for example, that the nature of the cinematic apparatus determined both the nature of Classical Hollywood narrative and the ideological capture of spectators' desire (see Baudry 2004a, 2004b; Metz 1974, 1982).

According to Carroll, received versions of medium-essentialism display a number of questionable assumptions, such as the view that each artform has a distinctive medium; that the medium is also the (teleological) 'essence' of the artform, realized in appropriate works; and that the medium determines the style and/or content of the artform (2006: 113–14). Carroll's assumption here is that the 'medium' refers to the artform's underlying physical or material basis — the materials necessary for the creation and constitution of works of art within that artform. Such a view, however, is clearly open to criticism. V. F. Perkins offered such a critique already in the early 1970s, challenging Bazin's and Kracauer's claim that cinematic realism, with its long takes, 'naturalized' *mise-en-scene*, and unity of space and time, was therefore best suited to realize aesthetically the (photographic) nature of the medium (1972: 28–39). As Perkins argued, this orthodoxy privileged one aspect of the filmic medium at the expense of the rest, drawing implausibly rigid aesthetic conclusions from the 'realist' ontology of the moving image: 'Despite Bazin's careful qualifications and disclaimers, realist theory becomes coherent only if we identify the cinema's "essence" with a single aspect of film — photographic reproduction' (Perkins 1972: 39). It seems the 'sins of the Fathers', to quote one of Perkins' chapter titles, need to be redeemed by each new generation of film theorists.

Carroll has taken up this task with gusto, developing the most comprehensive critique of medium essentialism. How are we to define the distinctive 'medium' of a given artform? We might be tempted to nominate as 'essential' the distinctive physical basis of the artform, say celluloid film strip bearing 'certain photographic emulsions' (Carroll 2006: 115) in the case of (pre-digital) film. Here we can cite numerous counter-examples, however, that give the lie to the idea that the medium has a unique material basis (or even that it uniquely involves movement). Consider Derek Jarman's *Blue* (1993), a film consisting of a deep blue visual field, mesmerizing voiceover narration, and carefully composed soundtrack, presenting the narrator/filmmaker's reminiscences, experiences of increasing blindness, and preparation for his impending death.[5] There is no movement, no montage, no image, save for the 'colour field' of azure that serves as a pure phenomenological background; one that attunes us to the poetic reflections of the narrator and evocative soundscape presenting his life, memory and thought. One is hard-pressed to identify the relevant 'medium' in a film such as *Blue*.

From a technological point of view, new digital video technology may eventually become indistinguishable from traditional film stock; the digital basis for moving images is now shared with musical and sound recordings. Implements used to make films are also inadequate to distinguish the medium, since films can readily be made without the use of cameras (for example, flicker films, scratch films, and painted films, where the film strip is directly modified, inscribed, or marked). As these counter-examples suggest, the attempt to identify a unique medium for film, in any physical or material sense, is problematic.[6] Rather than deny the existence of (physical) media as such, the point is to show that there are various media at play in works of art, including cinema.

A similar criticism can be made concerning teleological attempts to prescribe appropriate aesthetic forms for a given medium. If artforms possess a plurality of media, then there is no reason to assume that they will converge on a specific style or subject-matter. Media underdetermine the aesthetic uses to which they can be put; artforms are open to technological transformations and new artistic uses. Artistic innovation involves inventing ways in which technological and practical developments can be given meaning and significance; think, for example, of the incorporation of handheld camera movements into fictional film, the integration of CGI animation into live action film, or the simulation of 'analog' effects (lens flare, for example) within digital filmmaking practices. Does this mean that one should abandon all attempts at defining what the media of film/cinema/the moving image might be? Not at all; but it does mean that we ought to acknowledge that film/cinema/ the moving image remains a dynamic artform, open to technical, aesthetic and practical innovations. It may be that this fluidity is what 'defines' film as an artform in perpetual flux.

For all its influence in contemporary film theory, Carroll's rather severe dismissal of 'medium-essentialism' seems something of a 'straw-man' argument. Do film theorists assume as rigid and prescriptive a concept of the 'medium' as Carroll avers? Surely one can regard the medium (or media) as important to understanding and appreciating film, without thereby being committed to an untenable 'medium-essentialism'. Consider Stanley Cavell's alternative version of the medium of film, which is hardly essentialist in this sense (1979: 68–74). For Cavell, contra Carroll, a 'medium' is not to be confused with the physical, material or technical means by which works of art are constituted. Rather, the 'medium' names the manner in which an artform is invented and transformed; the ways found to constitute enduring works, new means of expression, and uses of technique, conventions and style that are creatively explored, inherited and renewed. Cavell's anti-essentialist concept of medium avoids reducing film to its material or physical basis, is open to a plurality of uses, and eschews aesthetic prescriptivism about conforming to a given medium's alleged 'essence'. Indeed, Cavell's conception of a 'medium' corresponds with Carroll's requirements for media plurality. The 'medium' of film is what remains to be invented by putting to work the inherited traditions, conventions and aesthetic possibilities of film in an open-ended manner.

Against 'interpretation'

A second major criticism is that film theory (especially 'Grand Theory') dogmatically assumes a strongly hermeneutic model of theory: that film theories aim to provide interpretive frameworks (templates) that generate multiple interpretations of films and genres, and that such interpretations can even 'confirm' theoretically one's chosen framework. Having assumed a hermeneutic model that equates theorization with interpretation, coupled with the assumption that film theory was ideology-critique pursued by other means, the way was paved for a dogmatic recycling of 'theoretical readings' of favoured films as a means of unmasking ideological, gender or cultural-political biases. 'Grand Theory', according to Bordwell and Carroll, remained captive to this hermeneutic paradigm, resulting in the retardation of empirically contestable forms of film theorization.

While I shall address later how film theory and criticism might enter into a mutually beneficial relationship, it is worth commenting here on the relationship between theory and criticism, that is, the difference between *hermeneutic* and *explanatory* theories. These are distinct theoretical approaches that do quite different things: hermeneutic theories attempt to describe, interpret or analyze with reference to other interpretative communities; explanatory theories seek to present causal explanations that solve theoretical problems or integrate with established bodies of empirical knowledge. They should not be conflated as though they were essentially pursuing the same theoretical tasks or practical ends. Does this imply that we should therefore avoid hermeneutic in favour of explanatory theories? In fact, the reverse is more pertinent than ever — enhancing film theory through philosophically informed film criticism.

One problem that arises here is what we might call the 'hermeneutic gap' — how to account for the relationship between a high-level explanatory theory (providing a causal account of X, couched in empirical/naturalistic terms) and the use of a particular film/film genre as an 'example' of this theory. Even strongly cognitivist film theories depend upon tacit hermeneutic models of theory when they appeal to 'film examples' to help illustrate a theoretical point or bolster a theoretical claim.[7] In such cases, a hermeneutic gap opens up between the level of general theoretical explanation and the illustration of such claims with reference to a particular film or film genre. How do we bridge this gap? One response is to erect a theoretical firewall between film theory and film criticism; but doing this leaves unanswered how we move from the general theoretical claims to our aesthetic experiences of particular films. Interpretation, however, is precisely a way of mediating between general explanatory claims and singular aesthetic experiences of particular works of art (see Gadamer 2004). This is another important challenge for the new philosophy of film — how to heal the sundered link between theory and criticism via philosophical film interpretation.

Against the 'film as language' thesis

The third decisive element of the older paradigm of film theory, challenged by Carroll's dialectical cognitivism, was the attempt to draw an analogy between film and language. From the more commonplace metaphor of film as a language, theorists such as Christian Metz developed full-blown theories of film as a species of semiotic utterance, whose character, meaning and modalities were modelled on the rules and structures governing the linguistic sign (see Metz 1974). This semiotic assimilation of the image to language was coupled with a linguistically inflected psychoanalytic account of desire and of the unconscious (structured like a language, according to Jacques Lacan). The result was a theory that tended to reduce the image to a linguistic sign; composition, montage and visual style to literary narration; the multiform aesthetic of the movies to a structural matrix 'suturing' visual identification and ideologically manipulating narrative pleasure. This orthodoxy has been subjected to sharp critique, from Deleuze's criticism of the application of linguistic semiology to film (1986), Carroll's dismissal of the claim that understanding movies depends upon assimilating culturally constructed semiotic 'codes' (2006, 2008), to Gregory Currie's attack on the very idea of film as language, and the correlated view that interpretation involves 'reading' a film (1995). Carroll's and Currie's critiques are the most powerful of these recent challenges to the 'film as language' thesis, so I shall take these as paradigmatic of this particular line of argument.

The analogy between film images and language has a long and venerable history. Soviet filmmaker and theorist V. I. Pudovkin, for example, claimed that individual shots play the same role as words in the composition of a film 'sentence': '[Film] editing is the language of the film director. Just as in living speech, so one may say in editing: there is a word — the piece of exposed film, the image; a phrase — the combination of these pieces' (quoted in Carroll 2003: 14–15). From this analogy a whole body of theory was constructed, drawing initially on Saussurean linguistics and later on structuralist linguistics (Roman Jakobson). Roland Barthes' cultural-semiotic analyses of ideological myths (in bourgeois popular culture), as well as of literary and cinematic texts (in his later works), offered an influential semiological approach to film language (Barthes 1972).

But how plausible is the comparison of a shot to a word, an edited sequence to a phrase, or a 'grammar of film' that would encompass conventional codes of representation enabling us to understand what we see? For one thing, images are more complex than words; it takes many sentences to describe even a very simple shot. For another, the relationship between a word and its meaning is dependent upon arbitrary conventions (we use the word 'dog' for canines but could have used something else). The relation of an image to its referent, by contrast, is less a matter of applying arbitrary conventions than of using our capacities for natural or 'untutored' perception in order to understand what we see (see Carroll 2003). The word 'leg' has an arbitrary relation to the limb in question, whereas a shot of Barbara Stanwyck's ankle in *Double Indemnity* (Billy Wilder, 1944) does not. It may require some cultural knowledge to appreciate that Phyllis Dietrichson [Stanwyck] is a *femme fatale*, but not to recognize that I am seeing an arresting female character.

As Gregory Currie points out, moreover, language depends upon the use of recursive grammatical operations to compose sentences from words and phrases (once we are familiar with them, we can apply them to ever-new cases); but no such recursive operations are evident in film images or the way in which they are edited together to tell a story (1993: 209–15). Perhaps we might want to say that the conventions in question apply at the level of the combination (montage or editing) of images; that these are the arbitrary conventions that lend weight and plausibility to the film-language analogy. We might hold, for example, that the shot-reverse shot conventions of Hollywood narrative cinema are a culturally constructed 'code' that has been adopted — or even imposed — as a 'universal' film language. Comprehending the meaning of such a sequence would therefore require an act of 'decoding' it according to the relevant cinematic 'code'.

The problem with this approach, however, according to Carroll, is that it ignores the *pictorial* character of moving images: a shot of Walter Neff speaking, followed by Phyllis Dietrichson's facial expression in responding to him, are images that do not require 'decoding' in order to be understood. Rather, we grasp what we see using the same perceptual abilities that enable us to perceive faces and expression (not to mention speech) in ordinary experience. The shot-reverse shot 'rule' is a pragmatically effective way of showing the interaction and communication between two characters, but it depends upon the same kinds of perceptual abilities we ordinarily use in order to communicate with each other. Learning a language, with its arbitrary conventions and complex rules of grammar, is an arduous and time-consuming process. Understanding moving images, however, is relatively easy (young children have no difficultly following animated as well as live action movies), as well as being cross-culturally intelligible (similar cinematic conventions are used the world over). This is best explained, Carroll argues, by the fact that moving images are parasitic upon our capacities for natural perception, and hence that such images do not require 'decoding' in order to be understood.

While it is true that the facility of understanding moving images points to the way our comprehension of them is parasitic upon our shared capacities for embodied perception, there is more to understanding movies than simply recognizing figures moving on a screen. It is one thing to criticize a dogmatic conception of cinematic codes; it is another to argue that there are complexities of meaning that require some familiarity with cinematic conventions. Films in both the Hollywood tradition and in European cinema thematize the conventional and representational character of narrative cinema — think of Preston Sturges' *Sullivan's Travels* (1941), Wilder's *Sunset Boulevard* (1950), Renoir's *The Rules of the Game* (1939) or Fellini's *8½* (1960). There is more to understanding Lynch's *Mulholland Drive* (2001), Wong Kar-wai's *In the Mood For Love* (2000) or Kiarostami's *Shirin* (2008) than relying on 'untutored perception', or having an elementary grasp of the various images (and sounds) composing the narrative that one is perceiving on the screen. Such films are also concerned to render explicit, play with, or undermine a variety of conventional devices used in mainstream narrative cinema; moreover, to articulate a critical perspective on dominant (whether Hollywood or European or Asian) models of filmmaking. *This* is the critical dimension of most interest in claims made concerning the 'language of film'; but this dimension — the ideologico-critical significance of narrative conventions — is underplayed in critiques launched by 'post-Theory' theorists. In the rush to abolish any vestiges of the former paradigm, the ideological dimensions of narrative film have been left in abeyance. Having broached this dimension of film, however, a more basic question beckons: what *is* cinema?[8]

CHAPTER TWO

THE RULES OF THE GAME: NEW ONTOLOGIES OF FILM

Despite its attack on the older paradigm ('Grand Theory'), the new philosophical approaches to film have returned to key questions of classical film theory. The original question that animated much early film theory was the question of film as *art*. Was the new medium of film merely a clever technical gadget, suitable for recording works of artistic performance? Or was it a new artform with its own creative possibilities? With its novel combination of technological, industrial and collaborative production, the medium of cinema challenged traditional concepts of art. The question of film as art has therefore also returned as a topic of debate in contemporary philosophy of film, especially given the erosion of the distinction between high art and popular art. In what follows, I consider some of the key problems of the new ontologies of film: the question of how to define the 'medium' of moving images; the problem of defining 'movement' in moving images; and the return of philosophical debates over film as art. Despite the plethora of attempts to 'define' the medium, the ontology of the image, or the nature of film as art, cinema seems to resist any such attempts at conceptual definition. This inherent ambiguity of film reflects its irreducibly hybrid character — at once a traditional form of narrative representation and an expression of the freedom of modern aesthetics.

ONTOLOGIES OF THE IMAGE

The new philosophy of film has returned to investigating some of the classical problems of film theory: the nature of the moving image, the question of film as art, the problem of genre, how to understand narrative, questions of film style, and so on. These interconnected lines of inquiry constitute a *new ontology* of the moving image. What distinguishes the moving image from the photographic image? How is film to be distinguished from painting, theatre and photography? What is distinctive about the way narrative film works? As we have seen, Noël Carroll has argued against the idea of a distinctive medium of film, which medium would provide aesthetic criteria for particular styles of filmmaking (see 2008: 35–52). Other philosophers, however, have defended modified versions of a 'medium' approach to film, arguing that considerations of the medium remain important ontologically and aesthetically (Gaut 2010: 282–307). The advent of digital images and widespread use of CGI in contemporary filmmaking, moreover, have raised anew the traditional questions concerning the ontology of the moving image. Do these technological transformations mean that we need to rethink what we understand by 'film'? Is cinema essentially a form of animation? (see Cholodenko 2008). For some thinkers, such as D. N. Rodowick (2007b), not to mention filmmakers such as David Lynch (see 2006: 149–156), the advent of digital film images means that we are witnessing the 'end of film', its transformation into something rich and strange.[1] This is not only because of the novel aesthetics of the digital image, its flatness, immediacy and manipulability, or because of the ways in which digital photography breaks the ontological link between image and referent, opening up a digital regime of quasi-animated 'hyperimages' (as readily connectible and synthetic as hypertext); but also because the portability, immediacy, speed and diminished costs of DV film production promise a redemocratization of the medium, opening it up to new narratives, filmmakers and otherwise marginalized perspectives. For others, however, technological transformations in the way moving images are produced or communicated do not warrant such radical claims, yet they do demand philosophical reflection on the significance of new forms of digital cinema (Gaut 2010: 43–50).

One of the earliest tasks of film theory was to identify the nature of this new medium. Coupled with this was the cultural demand to defend its artistic value against criticisms that it represented merely a photographic recording of dramatic performances, hence was not an artform in its own right — a view recently rehearsed by Roger Scruton (1981). To this end, early film theorists (Münsterberg, Arnheim, Balázs, and Kracauer, for example) devoted much energy to arguing the case for the distinctiveness of film, articulating its relative strengths in comparison with photography, painting and theatre. While this is no longer something film theorists need to defend, questions concerning the ontology of film have returned thanks to the philosophical rethinking of classical film theory. Arthur Danto (1979) and Noël Carroll (2006), for example, have both offered important contributions to the ontology of the moving image (a category more congenial to the plural character of the image than the more conventional term, 'film'). Interestingly, however, they have abandoned any strong claim to have enumerated necessary and sufficient conditions for defining the moving image.[2] Their more modest definitions point, rather, to necessary conditions (elements that are necessary for something to count as a moving image), while acknowledging that moving images will continue to evolve, hence that any definition must remain plural and open-ended.

Despite his criticisms of the 'medium essentialism' thesis, Noël Carroll has recently offered a definition of the moving image that articulates some of its 'necessary, general features' in relation to other arts (2006: 113). Taking up Bazin's famous claim concerning the photographic basis of film (1967: 9–16), Carroll challenges the photographic realist approach, a view that has recently been described (by Scruton (1981) and Walton (1984)) as the 'transparency thesis': the claim that, due to their automatic, photographic recording, moving images are direct presentations (rather than visual re-presentations) of what they depict (Bazin 1967, Scruton 1981, and Walton 1984). According to this view, there is an *identity* relation between image and referent; the cinematic image is 'transparent', presenting us with an image of 'the object itself'. According to photographic realists, moving images can therefore be seen as akin to prosthetic images — telescopes, microscopes, convex mirrors, and the like — that involve an extension or enhancement of our natural perception (think of the remarkable scene in *Blade Runner* (Ridley Scott, 1982) in which Deckard [Harrison Ford] deploys a visual device enabling him to peer around corners *within* a photographic image). On this view, photography and cinematic images are similarly prosthetic devices that give us access to things, persons and events from the past. Such images, moreover, are counterfactually dependent upon their referents; had these referents been different, so too would the images (had Paulette Goddard been cast as Jean Harrington in *The Lady Eve* (Preston Sturges, 1941), as originally intended, we would have been deprived of Barbara Stanwyck's brilliant performance of Jean/Eve).

A simple objection that can be raised at this point is to question the photographic basis of contemporary moving images: CGI and digital image technology, for example, throw the identity between image and referent into question (such images are not linked to a referent as their model, and so are a class of images that need not refer to an actual object). Photography does not, strictly speaking, serve as a constituent element of such images, which are nonetheless included in what we understand by 'film'. Does this mean that cinematic images, especially computer-animated ones, are more akin to paintings than to photographs? This remains an intriguing question. A traditional distinction that is relevant here is between the *automatism* of film images (thanks to mechanical recording) and the *intentionalist* character of paintings or drawings (in the sense of including only those elements intended by the artist who created it).[3] One should note that such a contrast immediately raises critical questions: despite the automatism of film, photographers and cinematographers clearly intend to create certain aesthetic effects, and compose their shots accordingly, including manipulated photographic images; the view that paintings are the expressions of an artist's intentions, on the other hand, flies in the face of the 'automatism' of much modern art (in surrealism, in conceptual art, in pop art, in hybrid installations, in industrially produced works, and so on). Whatever the case, Carroll deploys the (rather simplistic) distinction between film images that are made by means of an automatic recording process involving the camera, and paintings that require deliberation and execution of the work by an artist. There can be unintended elements in a film shot that are recorded inadvertently (in Hitchcock's *North by Northwest* (1959), a young boy can be seen covering his ears just seconds before a gunshot rings out in the diner on Mount Rushmore). Traditional paintings and drawings, by contrast, include only those elements intended by the artist (a painting that extends beyond its own frame is clearly intended to do so).

Does this traditional distinction between the automatism of moving images and the intentional character of pictorial depiction capture what is distinctive to each? Carroll's rejoinder to this distinction is curious: 'there is no principled difference between film shots and paintings here' (2006: 122), he argues, since it is still possible to find 'unintended' figures even within a painting (Picasso, for example, claimed to have found the shape or relief outline of a squirrel within one of Braque's paintings). Even if one granted Picasso's claim to have 'found' (rather than simply seen) a squirrel in Braque's painting, it is not clear that this is the same kind of 'unintentional' effect that occurs within a film shot. The point of the contrast, rather, is to show that a typical film shot (involving a recording of profilmic action) may include 'mistakes' occurring during the recording that do not seem possible in the same way for a painting. That Picasso found a 'squirrel-like' shape in Braque's painting may add to its aesthetic interest, but it hardly constitutes a 'mistake' like the jumpy boy's precautionary ear-blocking in *North by Northwest*. Braque's 'squirrel' exists, so far as it does, as an accident of form or line more or less discernible on the canvas (thanks to Picasso's lively visual sense), whereas Hitchcock's jumpy extra was an ineliminable element within a recorded scene of live action. To blur the ontological distinction between these two cases — between accidental patterning of form and constituent element of the recorded image — seems to beg the question against the distinction between film images and paintings.

What of the claim that film images are prosthetic in the way the telescopic, microscopic, and other perceptually enhanced images are? Carroll makes an important criticism here that draws on similar arguments made by Arthur Danto (1979) and Francis Sparshott (1975). The difference between 'prosthetic' images and those in a (fictional) film involves the discontinuity between the latter and my own bodily orientation in space. According to Carroll, I can always orient my body towards what the prosthetic image reveals (whether supernova or bacteria), whereas I cannot do so with a film image (say Rick's bar in *Casablanca* (Michael Curtiz, 1942) or even the film set where these scenes were shot), since these both remain, 'phenomenologically speaking, disconnected from that space that I live in' (Carroll 2006: 123). Strictly speaking, this description is ambiguous and misleading, since the phenomenological space in which I live enfolds the various contexts in which I happen to watch films; moreover, such phenomenological connection with the space in which I view films is essential to my bodily, perceptual and aesthetic engagement with them (the wrong lighting, seating, noise levels, background features or image size will ruin my experience of the film). Phenomenological orientation within space is a condition of my bodily and perceptual engagement with film.

Be that as it may, Carroll, following Sparshott, dubs this feature of cinematic viewing 'alienated vision', claiming that what we see on the cinema screen is a *disembodied view* or 'detatched view' that disallows us any bodily or kinaesthetic orientation towards it (2006: 123). Here again one might question this claim on phenomenological grounds: it is hard to see how I can have the kind of bodily visceral responses of fear, panic or nausea to a horror film unless there is some possibility of bodily or kinaesthetic orientation towards the visual display — and what it depicts — before me.

One can take these criticisms further. Using unaided embodied perception as a phenomenological criterion for bodily orientation seems as dubious in the case of microphenomena (bacteria) or macrophenomena (supernovae) as in the case of an absent space or location (such as a film set). On the other hand, one can nonetheless imagine orienting one's body towards a film set that is nearby, or doing so while watching a film screening that takes place 'on set'.[4] The matter is further complicated by the fact that what we see may no longer exist (the film set, the distant star); how can I orient my body towards past events? Carroll is clearly right to say that I cannot orient my body towards *fictional* persons, places or events. While we generally do not watch narrative films in order to work out how to get to the fictional world in question (but think of *The Wizard of Oz*! (Victor Fleming, 1939)), we can nonetheless orient ourselves imaginatively *in relation* to the diegetic world of the film. In many cases this involves a distinctively phenomenological sense of bodily-perceptual orientation *within* the world of the film: in Hitchcock's *Rear Window* (1954), for example, we quickly orient ourselves in relation to Jeff Jeffries' [James Stewart's] apartment, his neigh-bours, the facing courtyard, and opposing apartment block with its interesting residents.[5] In Demme's *Silence of the Lambs* (1991), I could not experience the bodily fear and panic that Clarice Starling [Jodie Foster] experiences groping in the dark before a murderous 'Buffalo Bill' [Ted Levine] unless I could orient myself imaginatively (and phenomenologically) within the darkened cellar in which he stalks her wearing night goggles.[6] While I am obviously discon-nected from any fictional world from the perspective of my body, I am nonetheless perceptually, affectively and imaginatively engaged *within* the complex virtual world I perceive on the screen.

MOVING IMAGES

David Lynch tells the story of contemplating one of his paintings and wondering what it would look like if it could move, a thought that sparked his remarkable career as a filmmaker (quoted in Rodley 2005: 37). Animation is precisely the giving of movement — of life — to images that would otherwise be still, without life in the sense of self-movement. Here we seem to have an undeniable element of the ontology of the moving image (as distinct from other images or 'still images'). But what does it mean to say that moving images *move*? Are we enjoying merely the illusion of movement? Or do the characters we see on the screen 'really' move?

We know that the impression of movement in moving images is due to the psycho-physiological phenomena of the flicker fusion threshold and phi-phenomenon (an updated version of the older 'persistence of vision' idea): the point at which a rapid succession of static images is perceived as fused into a continuous image with 'flicker free' movement (slow the rate of image succession and one begins to perceive flickering of the image and a breakdown in one's perception of continuous movement).[7] Does the phenomenon of movement in movies give us an assured criterion to distinguish moving images from images in painting or photography? It might seem so, yet one can readily give counterexamples of films that eschew any movement of, or within, the image. Carroll (2008: 59), for example, provides an impressive list, ranging from Nagisa Oshima's *Band of Ninjas* (1967) (a film of a comic strip), Michael Snow's *One Second in Montreal* (1969) (a film of photos), Hollis Frampton's *Poetic Justice* (1972) (a film of a shooting script), to Godard and Gorin's *Letter to Jane* (1972) (another film of photos).

The most famous example, however, is Chris Marker's *La Jetée* (1962), a mesmerizing reverie and time-travel narrative composed of a series of projected still images, photographs one wants to say, with no movement (bar one) throughout the entire film. As Carroll notes, one could imagine an idealised version of *La Jetée* (with no movement at all), and ask the question whether this is a film, a work of cinema, or something else. A similar question is posed by Jarman's *Blue* (1993), which presents a film without a moving image or arguably any image at all (in the sense of being an image *of* something). If we accept *Blue* as a moving picture, then we have to ask if films need be composed of moving images in the conventional sense. Similarly, if we accept *La Jetée* as a work of cinema (indeed a revered and memorable one), then we have to question whether movement need be a necessary condition of film. Or we could question on what grounds we would count *La Jetée* as a work of cinema, but not an identical slideshow installation of just these enigmatic photographs telling the story of a lost soul 'haunted by an image'.

Carroll's response is to argue that it is not actual movement but rather the 'technical possibility' of such movement that is a necessary element of film. Because we have the reasonable expectation that we *may* see movement at some point, we can classify *La Jetée* as an unconventional cinematic work. This could never be the case with a slideshow of all the relevant still images screened in a comparable manner (say, an installation in an art gallery consisting of a slideshow of just the images used in Marker's film). So the ontology of the moving image does not depend on actual so much as *potential* movement within such images. Agreeing with Arthur Danto (1979), Carroll concludes that is the technical possibility, hence reasonable expectation, of potential movement that distinguishes the 'moving' image, even if we are confronted by a cinematic work, like *La Jetée*, in which images may not actually move.

A difficulty arises here, however, with Carroll's preferred term for film ('moving images'). For if a film can be a film without having any images that move (*La Jetée*), or even any images in the conventional sense (*Blue*), why insist on the term 'moving images' as the proper designation for works of cinema? Indeed, we could also query Carroll's assumption that *La Jetée* is 'indisputably a motion picture' (2008: 59). Why so? A number of alternative hypotheses are equally possible. Perhaps *La Jetée* shows that our assumptions concerning what is 'indisputably a motion picture' are open to question. Perhaps it is a slideshow masquerading as a work of cinema; perhaps it suggests that, under certain circumstances, slideshows can be construed as films; or that the kind of expectation we bring to our interpretation of images depends upon what we take them to be, even on their context of presentation. Imagine an art gallery photographic slideshow of images from *La Jetée* presented by a postmodern artist. One might respond quite differently to the slideshow than to a conventional screening of the film version. Imagine that we are in the gallery, and that we share a knowledge of Marker's film; we would now be perplexed as to whether we are seeing a version of 'Marker's film' or a clever 'simulation' of it by means of the slideshow exhibit. What if no discernible physical difference distinguishes my viewing of the slideshow from my viewing of the film? What, ontologically speaking, distinguishes the slideshow version from the film version? Would the means of exhibition, or the material 'medium' being used, or the context of performance, change the meaning of the work? Here it is the expectation that is important, rather than any ontological features of the images. *La Jetée* thus is a 'cinematic' work that remains ambiguous between still and moving image, slideshow and motion picture, and thereby challenges us, philosophically and cinematically, to ponder the differences that we usually assume to exist between them.

Whatever the case, it is undeniable that movement, in most cases, describes what moving images typically show. Is this movement, however, merely illusory, an apparent movement due to the animating effect of perceiving related images in rapid succession? Or is it, rather, a 'real' movement that we perceive when we watch movies? This question was addressed in classical film theory, with Münsterberg and Arnheim both arguing that the movement we observe arises as an effect of the psychological and cognitive operations of our own minds (Münsterberg 2002: 69–71). Münsterberg and Arnheim make the familiar phenomenological point that, while we are aware that we are watching 'flat' two-dimensional images, we nonetheless *experience* the impression of depth and movement on the screen (Münsterberg 2002: 71; Arnheim 1957: 20). They take the further idealist step, however, of imputing this experience to our 'inner mental activity' uniting separate phases of movement in the 'idea of connected action' (Münsterberg 2002: 78).[8] Depth and movement on the screen, according to this view, are a mixture of 'objective' perception and the subjective construal of this perception, which we do not even notice once perceptually and psychologically immersed in the complex visual world of the film.

Henri Bergson offered (back in 1907) one of the paradigmatic criticisms of the illusory character of the movement we perceive in cinematographic images. Because the appearance of movement in moving images depends upon the projection of a series of static images at a rapid rate of succession (through a projector), cinematic images can only ever deliver the 'illusion' of movement based upon the animation of a series of static poses. Bergson even argued that ordinary perception and consciousness also operate according to the 'cinematographic illusion', composing apparent movement out of the synthesis of successive static images (2005: 251–2). It is fair to say that this has remained a persistent view in much film theory, although it has recently been challenged by a number of contemporary philosophers (such as Deleuze 1986, Currie 1995, and Carroll 2008). As Deleuze argues, Bergson's error was to assume that, because moving images were composed of a succession of static images, the movement they depicted could only ever be illusory (1986: 2). This is to confuse, however, the mechanical genesis of moving images with the experience of what they depict.

Deleuze's criticism is elaborated by Currie and Carroll, who both agree that, although our impression of movement depends upon static images, we can still hold that the moving image really does move for us (see Currie 1995, Carroll 2008: 87–93). This is not to say that we need assert that this movement is 'real' in some deep metaphysical sense. Rather, it means that the movement is 'objective', in the sense of being intersubjectively verifiable by others, hence that we need not accept that the movement we perceive is merely illusory (Carroll 2008: 88).[9] Both Currie and Carroll draw the analogy with colour perception: even though the colours we ordinarily perceive are merely apparent (dependent upon our capacity for vision as much as the wavelengths of light reflected from particular surfaces), this does not mean that they are 'illusory' (otherwise how could we distinguish genuine colour illusions such as colour blindness?). In the same way that we take colours to be real but response-dependent properties (intersubjectively perceived, under normal conditions, by other human subjects), we should also take movement to be a real but response-dependent property of moving images (Carroll 2008: 89–93). From this point of view, 'movies' are precisely what we see!

The argument over movement in the movies is polarized between critics who point to the way movement is generated by 'illusory' means, and defenders who argue that the onus is on critics to explain why we should not accept that the movement we perceive on screen is 'real' movement. Part of the issue here, I suggest, is a confusion between phenomenological and causal levels of explanation: critics argue that, because the causal process involved in generating moving images involves the perceived fusion of static images, the movement can only be illusory; defenders claim that we need not posit any metaphysical kind of reality to the movement we perceive since it is experienced, in a subjective or response-dependent way, like any other movement we perceive in ordinary experience.

A way out of the impasse is to clarify that we *do* perceive movement on the screen — within an image, between images, unfolding in time — from a phenomenological point of view. There is nothing in the phenomenal experience of movement in a cinematic image to distinguish it from movement perceived by the unaided eye. We can even consult movement presented in cinematic images in cases where our perception is doubtful or deceived; consider the use of visual tracking and trajectory simulation technology in television sporting coverage of cricket and tennis. There is no reason to question the phenomenological reality of such movement perceived, since it accords with the kinds of experiences of movement we have within ordinary perception. Indeed, the movies rely on such emulation (and manipulation) of natural perception in all sorts of ways — and it is why we do not need to absorb elaborate cultural codes in order to perceive and understand movement in movies.

To make a familiar phenomenological point, theoretical questions concerning the ontological status of movement in the moving image can arise only once we (consciously or deliberately) interrupt the immersive experience of watching a movie and reflect on the mechanisms — technological, psychological, physiological — that causally generate the movement that we perceive.[10] Rather than questioning our phenomenological experience, we need only distinguish what we might call the primacy of cinematic perception — what we experience, phenomenologically, when we watch movies — from the theoretical or explanatory accounts of the various causal mechanisms that generate this phenomenological experience of movement in time. Our phenomenological and aesthetic experience of movement is a perceptible expression, rather than illusory distortion, of the causal mechanisms generating what we perceive on screen (see Merleau-Ponty 1964, 54–9).

FILM AS ART REDUX

The other striking feature of contemporary philosophy of film is its renewed interest in the question of film as *art*, a question traditionally tied with the ontology of film. Münsterberg's *The Photoplay* (2002 [1916]) and Arnheim's *Film as Art* (1957 [1930]) inaugurated the tradition of commencing theoretical reflection on film by addressing the question of film as art. Like Arnheim, Münsterberg argued that film ('the photoplay') is an artform distinct from theatre and photography, yet aesthetically superior in having becoming (artistically) freed from the constraints of space and time (2002: 129).[11] Anticipating a line of inquiry that continues today, Münsterberg and Arnheim argued that film artistically transforms, rather than merely passively records, dramatic performance and visual display. Far from simply recording interesting objects or events (like the early cinematic *actualités* depicting everyday scenes) or dramatic performances (like the earliest narrative films), cinema gives artistic expression to how things, events, performances are depicted. In doing so, moreover, cinema can emulate psychological acts of consciousness (perception, attention, imagination, recollection), thus suggesting an intriguing film/mind analogy that has continued to fascinate theorists of film from Münsterberg and Jean Mitry to more contemporary cognitivist philosophers of film.[12]

The questions that animated early film theory were at once technological and aesthetic, ontological and evaluative. What was the nature of this new medium? Was it an artform akin to photography or theatre, or something with its own artistic possibilities? Early reflection on film as art underlined not only its technological character but also its cultural legitimacy. Given the clash between technical and evaluative issues, however, it was paramount to establish the nature of the new medium. Cinema emerged out of experiments with animation that attempted to create the image of movement through the rapid projection of successive images (late-nineteenth century devices such as the zoetrope, praxinoscope and kinetoscope). Film was also subjected, however, to the same sceptical arguments that had been made against photography as an art. The new artform was often derided by critics for simply mechanically recording actions and events, and hence as lacking the kind of deliberate skill and expressive power required for art (see Arnheim 1957: 8–9). Early theorists thus developed a defence of film as not merely recording but as *artistically transforming* our perception of reality. From here it was but a short step to ally the filmmaker, typically the director, with the author of a work whose artistic vision, thematic concerns and aesthetic style comprise an oeuvre belonging to what was later baptised the cinematic *auteur.*

The debate at issue here concerns the contrast between the medium of film construed as a technical recording of an artistic performance (and so not an artform in its own right) and film as expression of an artistic point of view, using compositional and stylistic devices to evoke aesthetic meaning (and so an artform expressing artistic intentions on the part of an artist). This debate crystallized the polarity between *realist* (film captures reality thanks to its mechanical recording of images) and *expressivist* positions (film expresses subjective states and the artistic intentions of a director) regarding the medium of film. Indeed, this intersection between ontological and aesthetic concerns — does the medium of film shape its artistic possibilities? — continues to play a role in contemporary philosophical debates. The most striking instance of such a return to the question of film as art is Roger Scruton's revisionist critique (1981).

Perhaps because of its deeply counter-intuitive character, Scruton's critique of the idea of film as an independent artform has generated a host of critical responses (see Abell 2010; Gaut 2002; Lopes 2005). For all its contemporary influence, however, Scruton's critique rehearses arguments that were prevalent in the early days of film theory. Indeed, Scruton begins, in the traditional manner, with an investigation of the question of photography and representation (1981: 578–81). Contra most conventional accounts, Scruton claims that photography, due to its mechanical nature, cannot be regarded as representational (it simply records or shows us the subject, not how the photographer regards the subject). Paintings, on the other hand, *are* representational, since they are intentional artefacts that reflect how the artist intended to portray something: a painting displays only those elements an artist intended to portray; a photograph, as a recording of its subject, displays unintentional elements that bear no relation to the photographer's artistic intentions (Scruton 1981: 578–84). Assuming one accepts this strongly intentionalist account of art (about which one can raise serious doubts), Scruton goes on to distinguish painting as a representational art from photography as a presentational recording of reality. On this view, Rembrandt's *The Night Watch* (1642) is a work of art, whereas Peter Greenaway's *Nightwatching* (2007), a complex cinematic reflection on Rembrandt's painting, is not!

Scruton then extends this critique, arguing that film, as dependent upon photographic recording of its subjects, similarly fails to qualify as a representational art. Rather, a 'film is a photograph of a dramatic representation' (Scruton 1981: 598). Scruton concludes that the common assertion that there are cinematic masterpieces rests on a confusion between dramatic art and its photographic recording: 'It follows that if there is such a thing as a cinematic masterpiece it will be so because — like *Wild Strawberries* and *Le règle de jeu* — it is in the first place a dramatic masterpiece' (1981: 577).

Again echoing criticisms from the early days of film theory, Scruton goes further in his attack on the aesthetic status of film, arguing that its unintentional recording of a plethora of extraneous detail and unfocused jumble of visual information detracts from the aesthetic form of the image and is apt to confuse the unfortunate filmgoer (1981: 599–600). Indeed, our aesthetic interest in film, Scruton claims, concerns only its subject; we cannot take an aesthetic interest in it as such because it is essentially a photographic recording, rather than an aesthetic presentation, of a performance. Repeating a pattern that has unfortunately become rather familiar, in this kind of prescriptive critique the philosopher feels little need to acknowledge the rich history of theorization over precisely the question of film (or photography) as art. The idea that there might be philosophical film criticism that argues precisely for the artistic achievement of film (or photography) barely rates a mention.

In any event, Scruton's critics have rehearsed sophisticated defences of film as art using arguments that go back to Münsterberg and Arnheim. As Katherine Thomson-Jones points out, one can either challenge Scruton's claim that photography cannot be an artform in its own right, or one can challenge Scruton's extension of his claims concerning photography to cinema, arguing that film has its own distinctive aesthetic possibilities (2008: 8–9). Another strategy is to argue that Scruton is simply wrong in construing cinema as a photographic — that is, non-representational — art, either because his account of photographic art is questionable (Lopes 2005), or because of his account of cinema as non-representational (Abell 2010). From an aesthetic point of view, surely the burden of proof, one might argue, falls on the sceptic who claims that we cannot entertain a genuine aesthetic interest in photographs (and by extension films), but are merely satisfying our intellectual curiosity while mistakenly believing that we are enjoying art. As we shall see, everything depends, of course, on what we understand here by 'art': indeed, what kind of aesthetic theory of the work of art we entertain (for example, that art is the object of a disinterested aesthetic pleasure; or an expression of cultural-historical meaning;

or a unity of significant form; or whatever the relevant art institutions of the day count as belonging to the 'artworld', and so on). Suffice to say that these aesthetic questions are deeply contested. Although Scruton refines Bazin's claims concerning the photographic character of film, it is ironic that the aesthetic conclusions Scruton draws are quite opposed to those that inspired Bazin.

BACK TO THE FUTURE: BAZIN AND ARNHEIM ON FILM AS ART

Contemporary critics of Scruton repeat more sophisticated versions of the defence of film as art that began with Münsterberg and Arnheim, arguing either that photography can sustain aesthetic interest and involves a variety of intentional artistic effects; or that the extension of claims made concerning photography cannot be simply extrapolated to film, since film has its own aesthetic potentials that contribute to its artistic significance. Alexander Sesonske, for example, argues that the aesthetics of film can be articulated via the affordances of the medium itself: film has its own ways of representing space, time and movement that are novel in relation to the other arts, as are the ways of experiencing space, time and movement that film affords us as viewers (1974: 53–5). Film offers a way of representing and of experiencing space as two-dimensional, yet as creating the impression of depth in which action and movement can occur. It reveals a new way of representing time, both within the world of the film and for the viewers who experience a complex narrative spanning different times and places all within a 'real time' span of two hours. It represents a new way of framing and depicting movement that incorporates natural perception as much as the complex artistry of camera movement, framing and montage, with rhythms of movement and shot sequencing that can heighten meaning as well as intensify our affective responsiveness. All of these novelties of representation and aesthetic experience are opened up by cinema as an artform that partakes of all the rest, yet is unique in its own possibilities of aesthetic expression. As Carroll remarks, the main service performed by Scruton's arguments against film as art is, ironically, to clarify our reasons for defending film's aesthetic significance!

An alternative position that has emerged in recent years involves an uncoupling of ontological and aesthetic questions. The ontology of film, according to Carroll, does not have normative implications concerning aesthetic questions of film as art, or at best leaves open the question of the aesthetic uses to which the (pluralistic) medium of film can be put. For all the sophistication of the philosophical debate, however, what we might call the *aesthetic question* still persists: granted that film is a (mass) art, what is it that qualifies a particular film as art? Philosophers of film, when they acknowledge this question, tend to respond by presenting a theory of film as art or by invoking criteria of aesthetic evaluation. Carroll, for example, argues that we should remotivate a traditional (Aristotelian) categorical approach that would distinguish differing genres and styles, each with their own aesthetic qualities and excellences (2008: 192–225). Such an approach, with its laudable emphasis on pluralism, nonetheless raises the question of the way in which we should decide the relevant criteria of aesthetic evaluation: what are the criteria for choosing our aesthetic criteria? This question is complicated further by the technological-industrial character of film. Even if we refrain from drawing normative conclusions from the physical or technical aspects of the medium, the technical, collective, commercial and cultural-ideological dimensions of film still present filmmaker, critic and audience with a unique set of aesthetic questions and challenges.

Part of the problem, I suggest, is that the aesthetic criteria that we use either derive from 'the medium' or from our shared horizon of cultural practices; and here we find both a plurality of criteria and a plurality of ways in which film can be understood. As Jacques Rancière has argued (2004: 20–30; 2006: 1–19), film is a hybrid artform that cuts across the three main historical regimes of art: (1) the *ethical* regime (going back to Plato), which grasps images in regard to their truth content and the ethical uses to which they are put; (2) the *representational-poetic* regime (emerging with Aristotle's poetics), which grasps images in terms of their representational character and the ways in which they are composed into narrative forms; and (3) the *aesthetic regime* (Kant and beyond), which links the autonomy of art with the theme of freedom, sunders the link between hierarchies of representation and social hierarchies, and posits an 'egalitarianism' of subject-matter and plurality of aesthetic forms (Rancière 2004: 20–30). From this point of view, film belongs principally to the modern *aesthetic* regime of art; it introduces an ontological egalitarianism (all objects are 'equal' from the viewpoint of the cinematic image) and an aesthetic pluralism that has long been linked to film's inherently democratic potentials (see Cavell 1979: 35).

Film shares the freedom of aesthetic art, the 'premodern' concern with the ethical use of images, and the representational conventions of narrative fiction. This is why arguments over the ontology of the moving image and the question of the aesthetics of film remain so intractable: film is inherently plural, hybrid, with myriad, sometimes conflicting, aesthetic possibilities. As for the question of what makes particular films works of art, this can only be addressed by way of aesthetically responsive philosophical film criticism. Given that the vast majority of films made, viewed and criticised, however, are instances of narrative cinema, the obvious question which follows is that of narrative, its related features (character, genre), and aesthetic effects (affective engagement and varieties of meaning). What *is* narrative film and how does it work?[13]

CHAPTER THREE

ADAPTATION: PHILOSOPHICAL APPROACHES TO NARRATIVE

In my previous chapter I discussed the renaissance of classical questions of film theory within the new philosophies of film, in particular the question of film as art and the ontology of the moving image. Other elements of classical film theory that have been renewed within contemporary philosophy of film include narrative, character and 'identification' — our psychological and emotional engagement with film. Here again analytic-cognitivist philosophers have sharply criticized the theoretical models developed within the previous paradigm of film theory (structuralist and semiotic theories of narrative, psychoanalytic theories of identification, and so on). Theorists such as Bordwell, Carroll, Wilson and Gaut have proposed alternative accounts of narrative, character and emotional engagement that draw on debates in analytic aesthetics, philosophy of literature and cognitivist psychology. What post-Theory theorists generally dismiss, on the other hand, is the critical theory-inspired claim that popular film narratives are also vehicles of ideological manipulation. Whatever the case, a host of contemporary film theorists have developed complex theories of narrative, character engagement and affective responsiveness to film (Branigan 1984: 1992; Bordwell 1985; Elsaesser and Buckland 2002; Buckland 2009). Far from being a neglected area in film theory, narrative studies have been flourishing in recent decades, with philosophical theories of narrative adding a significant contribution to current debate.

In this chapter, I shall consider some of the most significant recent philosophical contributions to theorizing narrative film, canvassing topics such as the differences between literary and cinematic narrative, the significance of plot, story and style, the problem of cinematic authorship, and the vexed question of whether films have narrators — more specifically, an 'implied narrator' — as the agent responsible for the images comprising the narrative. I shall focus on Bordwell's and Carroll's highly influential problem-solving or question-and-answer models, which hold that film narrative activates the same cognitive capacities for making inferences, testing hypotheses and drawing conclusions as we use in ordinary experience. The question I shall pose in conclusion is whether such theories have an overly intellectualist view of narrative engagement. Does the close analysis of the mechanisms of narrative understanding (and of emotional and affective engagement) do justice to aesthetic dimension of narrative film?

PLOT, STORY AND STYLE

Although movies are among the most accessible of narrative artforms, the cognitive tasks of understanding, interpreting and evaluating them are far from simple. As Metz famously quipped, '[a] film is difficult to explain because it is easy to understand' (1974: 69). It is the sheer obviousness of narrative film that is so puzzling and perplexing. There is our perceptual engagement with the image, which relies on the same cognitive operations as ordinary, 'untutored' perception. The images we perceive in a film, however, are linked in an orderly sequence depicting a meaningful series of interconnected events. Despite some notable exceptions (the early cinema of attractions, experimental and modernist art film), movies have remained overwhelmingly narrative-driven. In the simplest terms, narrative refers to the temporally and/or causally ordered representation of meaningful actions and events, presented from particular points of view, within an overarching structure with an intelligible meaning. In this respect, narrative is a very general phenomenon, found not only in fictional works (novels, plays, films) but also non-fictional ones (journalism, documentaries, scientific investigations and historical accounts). For these reasons, we need to ask what distinguishes narrative film from other narrative forms and to investigate how it works.

Here David Bordwell's deployment of the Russian formalist distinction between *plot* [*syuzhet*] and *story* [*fabula*] has proved very useful (1985: 49–53). The *plot* refers to the ordered structure of what is (visually or linguistically) narrated; it is literally what we see on screen, a selection of images composed in a certain sequential order. The *story*, on the other hand, is the narration (the telling or showing) of what happens chronologically, which viewers understand by reconstructing an account of events from the visual and narrative cues composing the plot. On Bordwell's view, viewers are therefore active participants in the construction of narrative, whereas plot and style are 'objective' features that can be identified by historico-critical analysis. Viewers frame their interpretation of the narrative from the visual and narrative elements comprising the plot, applying various culturally and historically acquired interpretative schemata (familiarity with narrative patterns, historically shaped forms of style, relevant genres, tropes, and so on). Individual viewers may draw different inferences, hence hold different versions of the story, depending on which interpretative schema he or she has applied to the plot. On the other hand, we can also have formal film criticism that conforms to norms of interpretation, focusing on formal generic elements, relevant historical context, a filmmaker's development, generic features, comparisons between relevant works, hermeneutic insights derived from the skilled use of interpretative heuristics, and so on. To this duality, Bordwell also adds cinematic 'style': the historical evolution of norms and cinematic techniques used to order and structure (that is, to plot) the manner in which the story is narrated (for example, the use of certain camera angles, point-of-view, lighting, editing, montage, *mise-en-scène*, performance, production techniques, and so on). Style, which is how plot is articulated, can also be the object of formal analysis from a historical point of view, according to which we discern and comprehend style by testing its elements and techniques against already familiar, 'classical' norms (Bordwell's 'historical poetics' (see 2008)).

To take a familiar example, let us consider Christopher Nolan's *Memento* (2000). Its complex 'puzzle plot' (Buckland 2009) centres on Leonard Shelby [Guy Pearce], who is suffering from anterograde amnesia and so cannot form new memories. The film consists of short, seemingly disconnected sequences, which unfold both forwards (in black-and-white) and backwards in time (colour). The viewer is thus placed in a position much like Leonard; both are forced to reconstruct the story in piecemeal fashion, relying on the various visual and narrative clues presented in each out-of-order episode (scrawled notes, annotated photographs, tattooed messages, ambiguous conjectures, and so on). The visual style, using black-and-white images for the 'real time' events in Leonard's current situation and colour for the reverse chronological presentation of his investigation sequences, combines elements of the action/crime film, neo-noir, psychological thriller and art film genres, with the addition of various literary and philosophical references (not only to Nolan's brother Jonathan's short story *Memento Mori*, but also Oliver Sacks' remarkable literary medical narratives (1986)).[1] It is not surprising that *Memento* has become a philosophers' favourite (possibly trumping *Rashomon* and *The Matrix*!), for it not only deals with personal identity, the relationship between memory, identity and moral agency, and our experiences of trauma and grief, but also enacts the kind of rational reconstruction of meaning that renders conscious experience coherent. *Memento* therefore chimes with cognitivist theories of narrative that emphasize the roles of rational inference-making, the testing and adjusting of beliefs, and the cognitive matching of affective tone with perceptual awareness.

VISUAL SEQUENCING AND NARRATIVE TECHNIQUE

Noël Carroll (2008) has developed a similar theory of narrative, arguing that narrative is a means of patterning information that requires cognitive processing in order to grasp and resolve the various cognitive puzzles that a narrative poses. His 'erotetic' (question-and-answer) model is an attempt to explain the basic elements of film narrative that dominate contemporary filmmaking (the Hollywood style). As Carroll points out (2008), most films involve *visual sequencing*, the assembling of images into meaningful sequences, most commonly, though not exclusively, used for narrative. Having rejected the 'film as language' thesis, Carroll proposes an alternative model, involving 'attention management', to account for our ability to make sense of visual sequencing (2008: 122 ff). Movies manipulate audience attention, directing our attention to salient aspects of the image, visual sequence, or narrative episode; filmmakers carefully select what we see, from which point of view, in which style, and with what narrative purpose. Our attention is guided by the composition and sequencing of images, which direct us towards the film's intended narrative meaning. We do not require culturally complex competences in decoding film conventions in order to make sense of such sequences; rather, we need only respond using the same perceptual and cognitive abilities that we use in ordinary experience. There are a number of ways in which a director or filmmaker can guide our attention. As Carroll suggests (2008: 124), images can use *scale* to emphasize salience (a close-up of a showerhead, for example, as a woman showers alone), and they can be '*variably reframed*' to draw attention to relevant connections between images that we are encouraged to make (the shadow of a raised knife behind the shower curtain; the woman's face, screaming). More specifically, Carroll identifies three variables that can be used to direct audience attention: *indexing* (bringing the camera closer to a salient object or tracking relevant movements or actions), *bracketing* (screening out irrelevant details, objects, or spaces, and thus emphasizing relevance by selective framing), and *scaling* (altering the scale of the object that is the focus of our concern, thus underlining its significance for the story) (2008: 123–8). To be sure, directors can deviate from all three variables (misleading uses of indexing, bracketing that draws attention to what is off-screen, and avoiding obvious forms of scaling); yet most narrative films, even non-standard ones, use all three devices to direct audience attention and thus communicate narrative meaning.

CARROLL'S 'EROTETIC' NARRATIVE

How, then, do meaningful cinematic sequences fit together in a coherent narrative? Carroll's (2008) cognitivist account of '*erotetic narration*' shares similarities with Bordwell's neo-formalist approach. The first feature of the erotetic model Carroll identifies is narrative '*closure*': unlike soap operas with their indefinitely expanding plot lines, movies are supposed to conclude in such a way as to 'tie up' their various narrative lines. Agreeing with Aristotle's classic definition — stressing the importance of plot as a unity of action with a beginning, middle and end — Carroll highlights the sense of finality for which most mainstream narrative films aim: a fitting conclusion that leaves nothing left for the film to reveal or explain. Why do viewers find narrative closure so satisfying?

Drawing on Hume's essay 'On Tragedy', Carroll points to the way narrative films typically set up a series of questions that pique our curiosity, and then delay their resolution until the film's conclusion. The appropriate 'ending' for the film is one in which all relevant narrative questions posed have been addressed or resolved. Within shorter narrative sequences, smaller 'micro-questions' can be posed and answered. In Brian de Palma's *Body Double* (1984), for example, we want to know whether voyeuristic protagonist Jake Scully [Craig Wasson] will reach his beautiful neighbour Gloria Revelle [Deborah Shelton] before she is killed by the drill-wielding killer hiding in her apartment. In regard to the whole film, however, the larger narrative 'macro-questions' remain unanswered until the film's conclusion. What is the nature of the murderous plot in which Jake has been cast? Who really killed Gloria? Will Jake be able to rescue Holly Body [Melanie Griffith] from the driller killer's clutches? Whereas plots are generally networks of events and situations held together by various forms of causation, movie narratives are typically 'a network of questions and answers, where the questions are self-generated but then finally resolved' (Carroll 2008: 136). Resolving these self-generated questions is what drives the narrative forward and affords us the satisfaction of a conclusion.

Narrative film manipulates time in order to select and order the various sequences for the purpose of guiding viewer attention. Flashbacks and flashforwards, for example, are conventional ways of organizing and manipulating time; they allow the film to provoke questions or answer puzzles and help solicit audience attention until the resolution of salient questions at the end of the film. *Memento*, for example, uses both devices to great effect, posing (and answering) micro-questions about particular narrative sequences (should Leonard [Guy Pearce] trust Teddy Gammell [Joe Pantoliano]?) and macro-questions (was Leonard responsible for his wife's death?). The desire to pose questions and seek answers to narrative puzzles, for Carroll, is an extension of the 'natural' forms of cognition we deploy in everyday experience. Such questions can involve the significance of details, objects or contexts (what is the significance of the key and of the cellared wine bottles in Hitchcock's *Notorious* (1946)?); of character knowledge, belief, affect or motivation (does Devlin [Cary Grant] really love Alicia Hubermann [Ingrid Bergman]?); or concern the broader project of the characters or indeed of the film narrative as a whole (will their plot to expose Nazi collaborator Alexander Sebastian [Claude Rains] succeed?).

Alternatively, art films can refuse to resolve all narrative questions in order to frustrate viewer expectation, provoke thought about narrative conventions, pose questions of a more philosophical nature, or intensify associative aesthetic experience. Michael Haneke's *Hidden* [*Caché*] (2005), for example, does all of the above in its refusal to reveal the 'source' of the mysterious surveillance videotapes left on the doorstep of Parisian couple Georges and Anne Laurent [Daniel Auteuil and Juliette Binoche]. The narrative combines elements of the psychological thriller with reflections on the effects of colonialism, our consumption of media images, and the traumatic experience of guilt. It concludes with a further unresolved question in the film's final enigmatic shot — perhaps from another surveillance video? — of students leaving school at the end of the day, which reveals (to attentive viewers) George's teenage son Pierrot [Lester Makedonsky] and Algerian Majid's older son [Walid Afkir] in animated conversation before they walk off together ...

'JUSTE UNE IMAGE': THE AESTHETIC DIMENSION

Both Bordwell and Carroll propose enlightening cognitivist models to explain our ability to reconstruct the story of a film from its plotted images and narrative cues, or to resolve narrative questions by drawing inferences and framing hypotheses that will be resolved at the conclusion of the film. As I shall discuss in the next chapter, however, Bordwell's constructivist model has been criticised by Gaut (2010: 173–4) for sharply opposing the *construction* to the *discovery* of meaning in the film's various cinematic structures; for its undervaluing of naturalistic and cultural-historical constraints on interpretation (2010: 176–7); and for positing an overly rigid distinction between comprehension and interpretation.

Before we consider these objections in more detail, there is another criticism worth exploring: namely, whether Bordwell's and Carroll's cognitivist models of narrative account adequately for our *aesthetic* experience of cinema. Not all films conform to the canonical narrative style of Hollywood, or are amenable to the 'erotetic', question-and-answer model. Such cases, however, Bordwell and Carroll classify as 'parasitic' on the norms of conventional, narrative films. Art films with 'parametric' styles of narrative — Bordwell mentions classic examples such as Resnais' *La guerre est finie* (1966), Bresson's *Pickpocket* (1959), Resnais' *Last Year at Marienbad* (1961) and Godard's *Vivre sa vie* (1962) — present deviant or abnormal cases that refuse the question-answer format and frustrate our desire for narrative coherence or closure, and in so doing provoke reflection on the conventional norms and expectations we bring to narrative film. As other cognitivist theorists have argued, on this view canonical narrative models remain the source of norms and conventions that are violated, challenged or transformed by non-mainstream narrative films (see Plantinga 2009a: 86–7).

As Daniel Frampton points out, however, one can equally argue that cognitivist accounts of film narrative fail to do justice to the sensuous, affective, aesthetic dimension of film (2006: 106–7). Are images simply there to provide information for the cognitive reconstruction of the story or to resolve narrative puzzles set by the film? On the Bordwell/Carroll view, a narrative film appears akin to a giant Sudoko puzzle designed to satisfy our intellectual curiosity. Although viewers no doubt do understand and interpret images as sources of narrative information and cues for reconstructing the story, there are also other ways in which we engage with images in narrative film — ways that are not principally concerned with narrative meaning. This is what we could call the image's *'aesthetic dimension'* — those features which contribute to, but also remain independent of, narrative meaning: the images' sensuous qualities, their visual rhythms and tempo, their use of colour, texture and form, their dramatic (and undramatic) moments of singularity in gesture and performance, their mood-disclosing capacities, their orchestrating of aural and visual patterning, their ability to reveal and conceal nuances of expression in the human face and body, their capacity to express movement and time in novel ways, and so on. To be sure, Bordwell develops a theory of film style, grounded in the appropriation of historically acquired stylistic norms, which can be revealed through formalist analysis of such conventions; but even here the point is to avoid 'impressionistic' interpretation in favour of formalist analysis, generic classification and historical contextualization. Does this intellectualist account of narrative do justice to the receptive viewer's aesthetic experience of cinema?

Cognitivist theories assume that it is our intellectual satisfaction in reconstructing meaning and solving narrative puzzles that accounts for our pleasure in a film. On this view, however, it becomes difficult to explain our aesthetic delight in being misled or deceived by a work of art. Why do we enjoy narrative deception? If our engagement with narrative film were primarily about processing and resolving narrative puzzles, one would expect to experience displeasure at having one's desire for cognitive closure thwarted. My response, however, to the discovery of the duplicitous narrative presentation in M. Night Shylamalan's *The Sixth Sense* (1999) or the 'impossible' narrative paradoxes in David Lynch's *Mulholland Drive* (2001) is not anger or embarrassment, but pleasure and fascination. That said, a cognitivist might respond that the pleasure lies in the attempt to process the narrative puzzles, not in whether such puzzles are actually resolved by film's end. 'Puzzle films' (Buckland 2009), for example, often seem to intentionally thwart cognitive closure via the resolution of narrative puzzles, which then prompts the engaged viewer to reconstruct or 'replay' the narrative in imagination (or even to see the film again) in order to explore alternative interpretations or to analyze how the narrative puzzles work.[2] A cognitivist might add that 'parametric' films (such as *Mulholland Drive*) are principally directed towards this kind of cognitive processing, satisfying the more reflexive viewer, or soliciting the critic's ability to engage in formal analysis or symptomatic readings. All of which makes good sense of the cognitive pleasures that such puzzle films can afford.

Nonetheless, this kind of cognitivist approach overlooks the varieties of 'non-cognitive' affective response, cognitive dissonance and visual fascination that such films can also powerfully evoke. Cognitivist accounts of narrative are not incorrect, but they do not always acknowledge the role of our 'non-cognitive' aesthetic responses to film — the multifarious sensuous and affective ways in which film can provoke altered states of mind, body and thought. As Deleuze points out, in addition to canonical narrative (defined by what he calls the 'sensory-motor action scheme'), there are also 'pure optical and sound situations' that are not principally concerned with revealing the plot or developing narrative through action (1986: 141–51, 205–15; 1989: 1–24). Rather, these are images concerned with eliciting affect and thought; images that resist familiar interpretative schemata, and thereby open up different ways of experiencing time, movement and the body.

We might gloss Deleuze's point by saying that cognitivist theories risk missing the 'excessive' aspects of the visual image: those dimensions that resist rational reconstruction or cognitive comprehension. To borrow a term from an earlier generation of film theorists (such as Edgar Morin), we could call this aesthetic dimension of images '*photogénie*': the 'magical' aspect of images, their specifically cinematic 'charm', what Morin described as ' "that extreme poetic aspect of being and things" (Delluc), "that poetic quality of beings and things" (Moussinac), "capable of being revealed to us only through the cinematograph" (both Moussinac and Delluc)' (Morin 2002: 15; see also Andrews 2009). We could gloss this specifically 'photogenic' dimension of images as that which exceeds cognitivist narrative functionality, and thereby exposes the viewer to an intensive experience of aesthetic singularity. There is, of course, a great tradition of films that remain fascinated by this aesthetic or 'photogenic' dimension of images: Falconetti's suffering visage in Dreyer's *The Passion of Jeanne D'Arc* (1928); the traumatic fascination elicited by Buñuel's *Un Chien Andalou* (1929); the unbearable pathos of Nadine Nortier in Bresson's *Mouchette* (1967); the wind blowing mysteriously over grass in Tarkovsky's *Mirror* [*Zerkalo*] (1975), the sublime fields of wheat being harvested in Malick's *Days of Heaven* (1978) ... Any account of our affective and intellectual engagement with narrative film remains incomplete without some acknowledgement of the aesthetic or 'photogenic' dimension of moving images. It is what we allude to, as Morin observes, when we talk of the 'magic of movies' (2002: 13–17).

AUTHOR, AUTHOR

But who (or what), we might ask, is the source of these wonderful images? Or, more prosaically, who (or what) is responsible for the plot and visual style of a film? It is not surprising that narrative film raises the question of authorship, especially given the influence of literary theory on the theorisation of film. The topicality of authorship, however, has waxed and waned in the history of film studies. The concept of film author or, later, the *auteur* was part of the campaign to legitimate film as art; an organising centre whose artistic vision, authorial control and signature motifs guaranteed the artistic legitimacy of certain films. As the traditional argument goes (despite being subjected to various critiques), works of art are the expression of an artist's intentions; hence films that aspire to the status of art must have their provenance in the intentions of an author. The rise of structuralist, psychoanalytical and critical theories of film, however, challenged the individualist assumptions that underpinned auteur theory. The figure of the *auteur* nonetheless survived, if not as a particular individual, then as a postulated construct unifying the cinematic text. Although *auteur* theory has waned, reports of the death of the (cinematic) author are greatly exaggerated.

The question of authorship reflects a curious state of affairs. On the one hand, it is common to question the plausibility of *auteur* theory; on the other, it is also common to refer to films by their directors, which is to say, their authors (we talk of Sirk's mastery of melodrama, Wes Craven's self-reflexive irony, the visual daring of Gaspar Noé ...). Even Berys Gaut (2010), incisive critic of the doctrine of single authorship, refers to films by the proper name of the director with artistic responsibility for the film.[3] Perhaps precisely because of this ambiguous state of affairs, authorship has returned as a major issue in philosophical film theory.[4]

Indeed, the debate over authorship in the new philosophies of film owes much to debates over authorship in the philosophy of literature (see Chatman 1990). Literary narratives can have narrators, who are usually part of the fictional world being narrated (like Philip Marlowe in *Farewell, My Lovely*); they also have authors, whether actual (Raymond Chandler, the empirical individual who wrote this novel) or implied ('Chandler' as the authorial persona or agent postulated as responsible for the composition of this text). Both actual and implied authors are external to the fictional or diegetic world of the narrative (Philip Marlowe takes as real the events he relates truthfully, more or less, whereas for the actual/implicit author Chandler, they are mandated as fictional, which is how they are understood by the reader). Do the same distinctions apply to cinematic fictions?

As a collaborative and industrial art, film introduces a number of complexities to the debate over authorship. Indeed, as Gaut points out (2010: 99–102), there can be a number of distinct claims and senses relevant to the concept of an author in film. We can make *existential* claims concerning the existence of film authors, who are responsible for the creation of films as works of art. We can postulate an author in order to make *hermeneutic* claims about the interpretation of a film (which is taken to express the author's artistic intentions), or *evaluative* claims about its artistic merit (where a film is compared with others in an author's body of work, or with works by another author, or with relevant works in a genre). We can make *ontological* claims concerning the author as a *real person*: Charlie Chaplin, the great filmmaker and comic genius, or Chaplin as a '*textual construct*' unifying various filmic texts (*City Lights* (1931), *The Great Dictator* (1940), *Modern Times* (1936), and so on). The author can be construed as an *artist* (Welles, Hitchcock, Ozu) or as a *textual author*, the composer of a film text analogous to a literary text (Welles as author of *Citizen Kane* (1941), Ozu as author of *Tokyo Story* (1953)). Different candidates can be forwarded for the role of cinematic author: most commonly, the *director*, but also the screenwriter, cinematographer, star actor, or the producer and/ or production studio (*Finding Nemo* (2003) as a Pixar animated film). And finally, there can be *solo authors* (Errol Morris as author of *The Fog of War* (2003)),[5] or *multiple authors* (Michel Gondry/ Charlie Kaufman as authors of *Eternal Sunshine of the Spotless Mind* (2004)). As Gaut observes, variable combinations of these dimensions of authorship are possible; claims for cinematic auteurs generally posit at least one, sometimes several, of these claims, in varying permutations (2010: 102).

As we have seen, the construction of a cinematic auteur (typically the director), whichever combination of elements is selected, remains part of the process of legitimating film art (works of art require an author who intentionally creates them). Whereas some forms of cinema are collaborative enterprises, with shared authorship, defenders of the solo author model, such as Paisley Livingston (2009b), claim that only some films are authored: those in which an individual artist — the director — exercises sufficient control over the relevant aspects of the filmmaking process (for example, Bergman writing the script for, and then directing, *Winter Light* (1963)). Even in cases where there are significant artistic contributions by other collaborators — say, Harriet Andersson's performance of Monika in Bergman's *Summer with Monika* (1953), or the indispensable role played by Bergman's cinematographer Sven Nykvist — these contributory sub-plans, while meshing with Bergman's intentions, are still subordinate to Bergman's creative control over the film. For Livingston, screenwriters, cinematographers, actors or producers can contribute to, but not define or control, the cinematic realisation of the whole; hence they cannot be co-authors.

According to Gaut (2010: 118 ff), however, such a model, which acknowledges contributors but not co-authors, has difficulty explaining how the artistic whole of a film can be realized. Moreover, it overlooks the decisive and often independent role played by the various collaborators involved in making a film. Actors frequently argue with directors over the interpretation of a role or presentation of a character in the script. In cases where an actor persuades a director to follow their lead, there is no good reason to deny him or her co-authorship, even if the director retains primary artistic control over the film. Gaut cites the case of Spike Lee's *Do The Right Thing* (1989), in which Lee saw pizza parlour proprietor Sal [Danny Aiello] as an unambiguous racist; Aiello disagreed, however, and in the end portrayed him more sympathetically, thus adding nuance and complexity to the film's dramatic treatment of the climactic race riot. Another interesting example is Sigourney Weaver's arguments with Ridley Scott, director of *Alien* (1979), over the interpretation of her character, Ripley (Gaut 2010: 130). Scott wanted Ripley to 'hate' the alien, whereas Weaver argued that Ripley couldn't possibly 'hate' a creature driven by instinct; the end result of their dispute, according to Scott, was 'this incredibly modulated performance' (quoted in Gaut 2010: 130–1), the happy result of the creative tension between actor and director. The same point can be made concerning scriptwriters, cinematographers, editors, producers, and other collaborators in the filmmaking process. Thus, films can be co-authored, with many creative contributions to the film as a whole, even if these artistic contributions vary in degree and kind, and even if they are subsumed under the director's authorial accomplishments (praising 'Welles' deep focus camera', for example, rather than the artistic contribution of his cinematographer, Gregg Toland).

Film is a collective and collaborative enterprise, with multiple authors, whose contributions often mesh (and sometimes clash) to produce unanticipated creative achievements. Contemporary practices of criticism and interpretation, moreover, still require the attribution of authorship, whether individual or collective, so the question is how this might best be done. One plausible candidate is a critical concept of authorship that admits of multiple authors, that relates filmmaking practice to its broader cultural-historical contexts, but also aims to capture the shared intentionality — between a number of co-authors — that we often need to acknowledge in order to deepen our understanding of a film. By knowing about Nykvist's collaboration with Bergman, or Lee's conflicts with Aiello, or Gregg Toland's contributions to Welles' direction, we gain a more nuanced and complex understanding and critical interpretation of the film. But how widely should we construe film authorship? Should all significant contributors be acknowledged as co-authors? The concept of authorship, after all, is discriminating as much as evaluative. It distinguishes individual films within a coherent body of work, enabling comparisons to be made, parallels to be pursued, and interpretations to be ventured. At the same time, a too-narrow concept of authorship can constrain our understanding of film, its contexts of production and of reception, as well as its broader cultural, historical or ideological meaning.

Perhaps, then, we should understand the proper name of the author as naming an artistic event (like the 'Hitchcock' event), analogous with the way we name complex natural phenomena (Hurricane Katrina, the Doppler effect). The proper name 'Hitchcock' would thereby unite the actual/implied author with a distinctive innovation in film style, an 'event-like' contribution to the 'historical poetics' of cinema. One problem with this analogy, however, is that artworks are intentional artefacts whereas natural phenomena are not. On the other hand, one can use the proper name of the author to designate a body of work and stylistic innovation within a history of cinema; this helps preserve a concept of authorship that strives to reconcile the intentionalist sense of the concept with its more functionalist and historicist senses. This unresolved ambiguity — we recognise that films are co-authored, a collaborative enterprise, part of a shared cultural practice, yet usually name them according to their solo director/author (or even their lead star or production house) — suggests that the concept of authorship is continuing to evolve. We need not vacillate between taking film, on the one hand, as the expression of impersonal semantic structures, of economic-industrial or ideological-cultural forces; and film as the expression of individual psychology or the mythology of genius, on the other. Instead, we can posit a plural and hybrid concept of authorship that accommodates the multiplicity of aspects we need to take into consideration in understanding and interpreting narrative film.

IS THERE A NARRATOR IN THIS FILM?

Another puzzling situation arises when we consider the nature of film narration. Perhaps because of the perceived affinities between literary and cinematic fiction, philosophers of film have been exercised by the question of whether films have (implicit) narrators (Chatman 1990; Branigan 1992; Wilson 1997; Carroll 2008; Gaut 2010). To be sure, there are narrative films with explicit verbal narrators, characters within the diegetic world who narrate events, usually via voiceover (Walter Neff's confessional narration in Billy Wilder's *Double Indemnity* (1944), dead screenwriter-narrator Joe Gillis in Wilder's *Sunset Boulevard* (1950), the indeterminate character narrators of Malick's *The Thin Red Line* (1998)). What of narrative films in which there is no explicit narrator? According to Seymour Chatman's 'a priori' argument (1990), narrative is a kind of *activity*, which thus requires an *agent*, namely the *narrator*, who performs this activity; where there is no explicit narrator, there must be an *implicit* one, the agency responsible for (our access to) the particular images composing the film.

This argument might strike the reader as rather peculiar. Ordinarily we would say that Hitchcock was the author (whether explicit or implied) of the images comprising the shower scene from *Psycho* (1960). Why postulate such exotica as 'implied narrators' when an (implied) author will do the job? As we shall see below, this is a persuasive response. The interesting point here, however, concerns the ontological status of fiction: how do we viewers gain access to the diegetic (fictional) world of the film? We might think of this implicit narrating agent, for example, as what is often called 'the camera', which is generally identified with the agency of 'the director'. Obviously the director (and cinematographer) decides on camera setups and how to frame particular shots; however, neither 'the camera' nor the director is part of the diegetic film-world. I might say, 'Hitchcock's camera rotates on its axis as it zooms out slowly from the open eye of Marion Crane's corpse'; but neither Hitchcock nor his camera are part of the fictional world of the Bates Motel, with its creepy proprietor and famous shower recess. When we talk of directors and cameras in this fashion, we are describing the artistic decisions and stylistic techniques evident in the film, rather than what happens within the fictional world of the narrative. We are doing (low-level) film criticism rather than recounting the story.[6]

There are cases, of course, where the camera and director *are* included within the diegetic film-world, which happens in narrative films that incorporate a 'film-within-a-film' (the film theorist's *mise-en-abyme*). We might think here of Fellini's *8 ½* (1963), de Palma's *Body Double* (1984), or Lynch's *INLAND EMPIRE* (2006), which all feature directors as characters, and reveal the cameras used for making the film-within-the-film. In conventional narrative cinema, however, we do not see 'cameras' or 'directors' within the diegetic film-world since they do not exist within that world. Yet the narrative is portrayed through the composition and arrangement of certain images, with a particular visual style, selectively showing salient details necessary for our understanding of the story. So who (or what), we might ask, is the source of the images showing us these objects, characters, actions and events?

One answer is to posit an *implied narrator*. This is distinct from a verbal narrator, who may also be a character within the fiction (as in Fincher's *Fight Club* (1999); but which character is the narrator here?) or else an impersonal, omniscient narrator (as in P. T. Anderson's *Magnolia* (1999)) (see Thomson-Jones 2009: 75). As Bordwell points out, early film theorists frequently posited the visual narrator as 'witness' or 'guide' to what is relevant in the narrative (1985: 9–12). Such an approach to film narrators, however, strains credulity once it is taken as more than a suggestive metaphor (What kind of entity have we in mind here? How does this guide manage to gain access to a character's private thoughts? How can they witness, and reveal to us, say in Kubrick's *2001: A Space Odyssey* (1968), a spaceship's balletic movements in space?). While suggestive as a metaphor, the narrator as invisible witness or guide suffers from the difficulty of explaining 'impossible' shots or points of view, as well as how we can have access to the images being presented by the implied narrator (see Gaut 2010: 204–5). Do we personally imagine seeing these characters and events from within the fictional world (I imagine being in the shower alongside Marion Crane), or do we perceptually imagine them, impersonally, from outside the fictional world (I imaginatively perceive Marion's stabbing within the shower, but from a viewpoint outside the fictional world)? The difficulty with suggesting that we 'make-believedly' imagine the events on screen through the narrator's eyes is that it implausibly personalizes the narrative point of view, and demands that we inhabit the diegetic fictional world ourselves (which viewers cannot do).

Another kind of implied narrator is described by George M. Wilson (1997). Using a term borrowed from Christian Metz, Wilson describes the *'grand imagier'* or grand image-maker as implied narrator, the imputed source of the images composing the narrative film. The grand image-maker is an intermediary between fictional and non-fictional worlds; it is thanks to her/him/it that we have access to the images composing the fictional narrative. On this account, however, the implied image-maker sounds suspiciously close to an implied author (director). The relevant difference here, however, is that the narrated events are *fictional* for the implied author but *'real'* for the implied narrator who is part of the fictional world. How, then, do we distinguish between implied author and implied narrator? Indeed, why postulate an implied narrator distinct from the implied author? (Why not just say that 'Hitchcock', as implied author, is responsible for the images in the shower scene from *Psycho*?)

The question gains urgency in cases involving unreliable narration, a phenomenon well known in literary fiction. Cinematic narrative, however, creates interesting possibilities for unreliable narration due to film's capacity for both visual showing and verbal narration (telling). The visual representation of the narrative shows us the events comprising the story; the verbal representation (dialogue or voiceover) conveys a character's (or narrator's) perspective on the story's events. In some cases, however, there is a conflict between the visual showing and verbal telling of the story. In Bryan Singer's *The Usual Suspects* (1995), both the visual showing and verbal telling are unreliable for most of the film, since we eventually learn that Keyser Soze, whose story is both shown and told, does not exist (or rather, that he is revealed to be 'Verbal' [Kevin Spacey], the master teller of the tale!). Hitchcock's *Stage Fright* (1950) is another famous case of unreliable narration in that it visually suggests that a dubious account of events is correct; when Johnny [Richard Todd] tells his friend Eve [Jane Wyman] how he came to be on the run, his false version of events (that Johnny's lover, rather than Johnny, killed her husband) is shown in flashback, thereby suggesting its veracity (since the visual showing of events is usually given credence over a character's verbal telling). Verbal narrators, on the other hand, can be unreliable in revealing the limitations of their own perspective or their inability to grasp the significance of what is visually shown in the narrative (for example, Linda's [Linda Manz's] lyrical, naïve voiceover in Malick's *Days of Heaven* (1978) suggests her inability to grasp the nature of the relationship between her sister Abby [Brooke Adams] and Bill [Richard Gere]). By positing an implied narrator, so the argument goes, the clash between visual showing and verbal telling in unreliable narration can be explained by attributing the unreliability, where appropriate, either to implied visual narrator or explicit verbal narrator.

Does the case of unreliable narration warrant the postulation of an implied narrator? As Currie argues (1995: 269–70), we are better off postulating an implied author, rather than implied narrator, as the agent responsible for the unreliable narration. For an implied author (which is not the same as an actual author, be it the director, screenwriter, lead actor, or all three) can intend for a film narrative to have two (or more) levels of hermeneutic complexity: a superficial version that gives a seemingly accurate account of events (in M. Night Shyamalan's *The Sixth Sense* (1999), child psychologist Dr Malcolm Crowe [Bruce Willis] treats young Cole Sear [Haley Joel Osment], a traumatized child who claims that he can see the ghosts of dead people) and a more complex level that reveals the unreliability of the account given of certain events or even of the narrative overall (the narrative is selectively presented such that we only ever see Cole [Osment] speaking directly with Crowe [Willis], even though Crowe appears in various shots with other characters, such as his wife Anna [Olivia Williams] or Cole's mother [Toni Collette], but without ever being directly addressed by those characters). Whoever the actual author of the film turns out to be, the implied author of *The Sixth Sense* can be understood as the agent responsible for the ambiguity between visual showing and verbal telling.[7]

Novels can give us access to a fictional world by way of a third-person omniscient narrator (as in George Eliot's *Middlemarch*). We might ask whether fictional films do the same, although an interesting problem arises at this point. As we have seen, only the author can present events as fictional; the narrator, ensconced within the fictional world, presents these events as being true. If we take the images we see on screen as direct presentations of the characters and events within the fictional world (that is, as 'true' images), then the 'camera' is indeed akin to an implied narrator. If, however, we take the images we see to be representations of fictional characters and events that we *imagine* composing a narrative (that is, as 'fictional' images), then the 'camera' is more akin to an author (implied or actual). Arguably, it is the latter that is more plausible to describe our experience of narrative cinema. In watching Mankiewicz's *All About Eve* (1950), I both perceive Bette Davis and imagine Margo Channing, a dual perspective allowing me to relish the play of senses in her famous warning: 'Fasten your seatbelts, it's going to be a bumpy night!'

Given the paradoxes that arise once we start to postulate implied narrators, we are probably better off ignoring him or her (or it). Indeed, there is no need to postulate such an entity unless the film explicitly directs us to do so (presumably by way of its author). It certainly behoves philosophers, however, to study more carefully what intelligent and accomplished films have done with the concepts of narrator, author and character. In *All About Eve*, narrator and character Addison DeWitt [George Sanders] not only has the power to guide us verbally through the story of Eve Harrington's [Anne Baxter's] rise to fame, he can also 'direct' the film — acting momentarily as its implied author — by showing us certain things, avoiding showing others, even having a say over the film's diegesis (as when he decides not to show this scene or speech but to show something else).

In Pasolini's version of Geoffrey Chaucer's *The Canterbury Tales* (1972), the paradoxes are dizzying. Pasolini directs the film and also features in it as a character, one 'Geoffrey Chaucer', who appears in the literary text of *The Canterbury Tales* (which he authored) as a hapless pilgrim who tells the worst tale. Pasolini's film is a cinematic 'adaptation' of Chaucer's famous tales, in which Pasolini interprets 'Chaucer' less as pilgrim than as author (Chaucer/Pasolini is seen composing the written text of the separate tales that are depicted cinematically). Chaucer/Pasolini is at once author of *The Canterbury Tales* and author (explicit and implied) of the cinematic tales that we see, playing his authorial role as a character in the film that he has himself authored (as a cinematic adaptation).

In Haneke's *Funny Games* (1997/2007), one of the two tormentors is shot by the unfortunate woman being tortured in her family summer house; but he has the authorial power of the filmmaker (to direct the images) as well as that of the spectator willing the tormentors to be killed (to 'rewind' the image); he can not only interrupt the narrative but also rewind the film/video and 'replay' the scene so that the shooting never takes place (thus implicating the viewer in the consumption of images of violence that is the subject of the film).

In Spike Jonze/Charlie Kaufman's *Adaptation* (2002), we see a cinematic adaptation of a non-fictional text (Susan Orleans' *The Orchid Thief*). The film takes as its subject the travails of blocked screenwriter Charlie Kaufman [Nicolas Cage] (the actual screen-writer, if not part-author), as Charlie struggles to adapt *The Orchid Thief* into a cinematic screenplay. Resolving to break his block by writing a screenplay precisely on his experience of failing to adapt *The Orchid Thief*, Charlie's ironic failure turns the film — thanks to the wit and irony of Kaufman/Jonze — into a self-referential meditation on authorship, on adaptation, on screenwriting, and on the mysterious alchemy between text and image. In an amusingly ironic twist, Charlie finally succeeds in having his script made into a high concept blockbuster with Gerard Depardieu to play Charlie! *Adaptation* thus turns a potentially ponderous literary-philosophical thought experiment into a self-referential but charming 'puzzle' narrative. In such cases, far from determining who has authorial status or narrative authority, the philosopher-theorist struggles to adapt the creative cinematic thinking of inventive films.[8]

PART II: FROM COGNITIVISM TO FILM-PHILOSOPHY

The new philosophies of film are characterized by their critique of the older paradigm of film theory — so-called 'Grand Theory' — and their recasting of some of the 'classical problems' of film theory (concerning the ontology of film, film as art, understanding narrative, character engagement, authorship, and so on). What I have called the analytic-cognitivist turn is the dominant strain in this new wave of philosophical film theory, but there are other ways of philosophizing on film that have also become prominent; alternative paths of thinking that also move away from the older paradigm but draw on hermeneutic, romantic and aesthetic approaches to film (particularly in the 'Continental' tradition). In Part II of this book, I consider three of the most significant and original developments in the new wave of philosophical film theory: cognitivism, Deleuzian and Cavellian film-philosophy, and the idea of 'film as philosophy'. While Chapter 4 on cognitivism continues the discussion of narrative film developed in the last chapter, Chapter 5, on Deleuze and Cavell, introduces 'film-philosophy' as an alternative way of philosophizing with film. This discussion explores both convergences and divergences between Deleuze and Cavell, and thus prepares the way for my elaboration of the idea of 'film as philosophy' in Chapter 6. The latter chapter analyzes the claims made by critics and advocates of the bold thesis that films do not simply reflect or illustrate philosophical ideas but can be said to philosophize, by cinematic means, in an independent manner. I conclude with an argument to show that the film-as-philosophy thesis is best supported by acts of philosophical film criticism.

CHAPTER FOUR

A.I.: COGNITIVISM GOES TO THE MOVIES

In a number of survey essays that introduce 'cognitivism' as a new way of theorizing film, it is common to find remarks lamenting its relatively marginal status in film studies (see Bordwell 1989a; Currie 1999; Carroll 1996). The same point, however, could not be made today. In the last twenty-five years, analytic philosophies of film and cognitivist theory have combined forces in a formidable research paradigm. Bordwell (1985, 1989b, 1989a) and Carroll (1985) pioneered the wave of film theory that based itself on analytic philosophy and cognitive psychology. Having attacked 'Grand Theory', Bordwell and Carroll's follow-up collection of essays, *Post-Theory* (1996a) showcased the kinds of analytic-cognitivist approaches they hoped would define future research in the discipline.

Whatever tensions persist, cognitivism has rejuvenated film theory on key questions of affective engagement, narrative understanding and the role of genre. Here again we find a vigorous theoretical revision of the problems of classical film theory. Challenging 'psychosemiological' accounts of unconscious desire, cognitivist theories focus instead on everyday forms of affective and perceptual experience, arguing that the same processes are also activated in our engagement with movies. There are three main areas that cognitivism has revised most thoroughly: the question of interpretation and our (cognitive) understanding of film; the problem of 'identification' or our affective engagement; and the issue of genre, in particular the relationship between genre and the emotion-cueing structure of narrative. The challenge facing cognitivist accounts of emotion, understanding and character engagement, however, is how to deal with films that resist the kind of cognitive mapping invited by mainstream narrative film. How do we explain our affective and aesthetic responsiveness to films that thwart narrative expectations and disrupt routine cognitive reasoning processes? How would a cognitivist approach deal with a film like *Mulholland Drive* (2001)? Such questions (and films) suggest that we need to consider 'non-cognitive' affective responses as part of any nuanced account of our affective, emotional and aesthetic engagement with film.

THE CRITIQUE OF PSYCHOANALYTIC 'IDENTIFICATION'

As Bordwell (1989b), Currie (1999) and Plantinga (2002) all observe, cognitivism in film theory emerges during the late 1980s and 1990s as an alternative to psychoanalytic theories of film identification. As is well known, the starting point for psychoanalytic film theory was Lacan's famous theory of the 'mirror stage' (2006 [1936]: 75–81). For Lacan, the developing infant begins to identify with a unified (mirror) image of its own body (between six to eighteen months), but misrecognizes itself in so doing due to the disparity between its unified ideal image and its underdeveloped sensory-motor capacities. This condition of misrecognition distorts and deflects the development of our imaginary psycho-sexual self-image, and thus motivates our (unconscious) tendency to restore a sense of psychic unity by identifying with idealized ego surrogates (such as movie stars). Drawing on Lacan, psychoanalytic film theories thus distinguished between *primary* identification (with the point of view of the camera) and *secondary* identification (with a character as a psychological surrogate or ideal ego type). According to Baudry (2004a, 2004b) and Metz (1974: 1982), for example, the primary identification with the all-seeing viewpoint of the camera offered the spectator an illusory sense of mastery over the film's visual field. Feminist theorists such as Laura Mulvey (1975) famously extended this analysis to include *secondary identification* with a character, aligned along gendered hierarchies that privileged a masculine 'gaze' (identifying with a male character as source of narrative action, while taking female characters as objects of the character's, hence spectator's, 'masculinised' gaze).

This concept of 'identification' has generated a plethora of criti-cisms by analytic-cognitivist theorists (Bordwell 1996b: 15–17; Prince 1996). Such criticisms can be summarized under two heads: (1) the lack of clarity in the concept of identification, which covers a multitude of often conflicting meanings; and (2) the lack of empirical evidence for psychoanalytic theory, or its selective use of evidence in order to make sweeping generalizations about human psychosexual development. According to critics such as Carroll, it is unclear, for example, what it would mean to 'identify with the camera', since the camera is not a character. Moreover, the psychoanalytic concept of 'identification' posits a kind of numerical identity relation or 'Vulcan mindmeld' (Carroll 1990: 89) that is supposed to hold between my perception and that of a character or camera. According to the second criticism, psychoanalytic theory ignores commonsense intuitions, offering a speculative account of 'identification' that remains under-supported by empirical evidence (Prince 1996). Secondary identification, for example, rests on a dubious account of psychosexual development, a politicized critique of gender bias in cultural representations, coupled with an implausibly 'deterministic' account of the manipulative ideological power of narrative film. Pathological or deviant cases — fetishism, voyeurism, sadism, and so on — are taken to be paradigmatic of the general processes of spectator 'identification'. Psychoanalytic theory, on this view, is prone to taking the exceptional case as revealing the general rule.

These key points of the analytic-cognitivist critique, however, can of course be questioned. Take the distinction between our commonsense intuitions concerning 'identification' and the theoretical concept developed by psychoanalytic theory. The latter concept is explicitly different from the commonsense notion, and indeed questions whether we can assume that our commonsense intuitions are psychologically reliable or ideologically neutral. Psychoanalytic 'primary identification' does not refer to identifying with characters but to the process enabling the spectator to enjoy an illusory mastery over the visual field of the film. To cite commonsense intuitions as evidence against a claim that such intuitions may be specious is to beg the question. Indeed, the issue at stake is whether commonsense intuitions *are* reliable, or truthful, or ideologically untainted sources of knowledge or evidence. The same point applies to the question of gender: to assert that we are not subject to ideological manipulation in respect of cultural representations of gender because we do not believe ourselves to be so manipulated is again to beg the question (since the kind of ideological influence at issue is that which would infect our commonsense intuitions about 'normal' gender identity). This, again, is the matter to resolve in such disputes, and so cannot be cited as evidence settling the debate. Suffice to say, this dispute is far from over; some aspects of cognitivist psychology may even turn out to help reform, rather than refute, psychoanalytic theories.

Whatever the case, the growing dissatisfaction with psychoanalytic film theory prompted a variety of alternative cognitivist theories. Currie identifies two related themes characterizing the cognitivist approach: (1) that we take films to be rationally motivated, and thus endeavour to make sense of a work at each of its various levels of presentation (as sensory stimulus in light and sound, as narrative, and as cultural object expressing higher-order meanings); and (2) that we approach the process of making sense of film as one that deploys the same cognitive and perceptual resources that we also deploy 'in making sense of the real world' (Currie 1999: 106). The corollary to these two themes, we might add, is that cognitivists assume that 'irrational' processes — as thematized in psychoanalysis — are of marginal interest in accounting for our experience of film; and that we can rely on ordinary processes of cognition — including commonsense intuition — as evidentiary sources for claims about our experience of film. Cognitivism as a research program, furthermore, applies scientifically informed 'theories of perception, information processing, hypothesis-building, and interpretation' in tandem with an analytical, problem-focused philosophy oriented towards the natural sciences (Currie 1999: 106). How does this cognitivist map relate to cinema?

MAKING MEANING: BORDWELL'S COGNITIVISM

Bordwell's 'constructionist' cognitivism (1985) combines elements of cognitivist theory with a theoretical framework borrowed from the Russian formalists. By 'constructionist', however, Bordwell means an account of cognitive processes that emphasizes the active role of the subject in hypothesizing, making inferences, and drawing conclusions that go beyond what is immediately 'given'. This kind of *cognitive* constructionism applies not only to ('bottom-up') processes of perception and affective engagement, but also to higher-order ('top-down') processes of comprehension, interpretation and evaluation. We do not passively perceive or automatically understand the world; rather, we apply concepts and cultural schemata to sensory inputs in order to 'construct' coherent and meaningful cognitive experience.

So how *do* we understand movies? Bordwell (1985: 48–62) distinguishes between our *comprehension* of the film narrative (understanding the referential meaning of the images pertaining to the narrative world); our more complex *interpretations* of the film (grasping implicit meanings, themes, symbolic motifs, and so on); and the critic's *symptomatic* readings of a film's 'suppressed' psychological or ideological meanings (which reflect deeper psychic or cultural-historical forces). Take Welles' *Citizen Kane*, for example: we can comprehend the narrative film-world of Charles Foster Kane [Orson Welles], successful media tycoon, unhappy husband and failed politician, whose life reporter Jerry Thompson attempts to investigate. We can interpret the implicit meaning of key scenes or narrative elements (for example, the meaning of Kane's dying word, 'Rosebud', and hence the tragic significance of his forgotten sled as it is consumed by flames). The critic can also posit a symptomatic reading of the film, elaborating its suppressed or indirect meaning (*Citizen Kane* as an allegory of the Oedipal self-destructive drive for phallic power, or an expression of the capitalist ideology of individual genius, and so on). Film theory and criticism, Bordwell claims, focus on implicit and symptomatic interpretation, thus generating a variety of 'readings' that draw on favoured 'semantic fields' (discourses or theoretical frameworks) and which conform to institutionalized hermeneutic routines.

Although widely influential, Bordwell's cognitivist account of narrative has also been subjected to various critiques. Berys Gaut (2010: 164–179), for example, argues that Bordwell overemphasizes the role of what Gombrich called the 'viewer's share' (as well as institutional routines) in the construction of film meaning. Bordwell's concept of 'construction' encompasses quite distinct cognitive processes, only some of which may involve a degree of construction. Gaut identifies three relevant senses of the term that are operative, if not thematic, in Bordwell's account. First, *conceptual* construction, which refers to the application of concepts to visual arrays guided by shared background knowledge (Gaut 2010: 170). Secondly, *normative* construction, which refers to how film, like other artworks, is 'incomplete', and requires 'fleshing out' by the viewer (Gaut 2010: 172). Examples here would include the way in which we extrapolate from 2D images in order to 'construct' a film-world of 3D objects (we perceive 2D objects but visually imagine that they are 3D). 'Construction', however, can also refer to the way interpretations and evaluations are generated by practitioners mapping concepts from 'semantic fields' onto relevant narrative cues, following the established routines and norms of institutions of criticism. This third, more radical sense is what Gaut calls 'critical school constructionism' — a radical constructionism that 'really does entail that meanings are made, not found' (2010: 173–4). If a new school arises, or applies different semantic fields to the film, different meanings are attributed to the film, which are accepted as legitimate or not by the relevant critical school.

The problem, according to Gaut, is that Bordwell's model conflates these distinct senses of 'construction', and thus relativizes understanding and interpretation either to the viewer or to a critical school. To overextend the concept in this way, however, is to risk conflating conceptual, normative and institutional senses of construction. It is one thing to 'construct' perceptual experience by making inferences that go beyond immediate sensory inputs; it is another to map concepts drawn from a particular 'semantic field' (or what Foucault called a 'discourse') in order to produce, say, a psychoanalytic reading of a film. If everything is 'construction', then nothing really is, since the term loses conceptual specificity and therefore explanatory precision.

Rehearsing a criticism that has also been made of 'social constructionism', Gaut argues further that a constructionist account should not imply that whatever we perceive, understand, or interpret is therefore a 'construct' (2010: 170). Perception can be 'constructed' in that the cognitive processing of sensory inputs goes beyond what is immediately given; but this does not mean that the objects we perceive are 'constructions', hence a matter of cultural convention or subjective invention. On the contrary, there are both naturalistic and cultural-historical constraints on interpreting film that question the view that such interpretations are simply 'constructed' by institutionalized film theorists. If we take the 'semantic fields' and institutional norms governing practices of criticism as authoritative, then we lose the hermeneutic constraints that formalist and historicist approaches to criticism can provide.[1] The result, over time, is a relativistic proliferation of interpretations, which fail to provide 'an independent brake' on whether they are 'valid' for the work in question (Gaut 2010: 175). How do we know, in other words, when we are 'making meaning' or just making it up?

The counterexample Gaut cites against Bordwell's constructionism refers to the significance of cross-cultural differences for interpreting film style. Welles' use of low-angle shots, Gaut points out, might well signify power and stature in *Citizen Kane*, but the same kind of shots do not have this meaning in Japanese cinema (2010: 176). This is because low-angle shots in such films can reflect a culturally specific vantage point: the view one might have while seated on a traditional *tatami* mat, as one finds, for example, in Kurosawa's *Rashomon*. Such counterexamples, Gaut argues, suggest that practices of interpretation and evaluation are not simply 'constructed' but are subject to various normative constraints, be they cultural, historical, or 'institutional' (2010: 177–9).

In response, however, one could argue that Gaut's contrast between the use of low-angle shots in *Citizen Kane* and in Japanese films is itself open to question. Welles' celebrated low-angle shots do not straightforwardly signify 'power' or 'authority' but work ironically as well: Welles/Toland both deploys and subverts this conventional assumption, showing at once the stature and superficiality of Kane's self-image as leader destined for power and glory.[2] Gaut's example, moreover, echoes Bordwell's own insistence on historical specificity and attention to style.[3] Indeed, Gaut's point about placing the low-angle shots from *Rashomon* in their proper historical, and hence cinematic, context inadvertently supports Bordwell's claims for his 'historical poetics': a practice of critical interpretation and evaluation that analyzes formal elements with regard to historically shared norms of film style.

COGNITION, AFFECT AND EMOTION

One of the primary motivations for the analytic-cognitivist turn was many theorists' increasing dissatisfaction with reigning forms of psycho-semiotic film theory. One of the most contested concepts in this dispute is that of 'identification', a concept that many cognitivists have been at pains to criticize (see Carroll 1990: 88 ff). Identification, within psychoanalytic theories (Metz 1982), was construed as a kind of fusion with the point of view of the camera (primary identification) yielding an illusion of visual mastery, accompanied by a secondary identification that aligned the spectator with the active (masculine) gaze of the protagonist, fascinated by the passive feminine object of the gaze (Mulvey 1975). Together these forms of primary and secondary identification implied a psychological-discursive positioning of the subject into dominant forms of ideological discourse (concerning gender, sexuality, race, class, and so on). In what follows, I sketch some influential critiques of the concept of 'identification' and canvass some of the more significant theoretical alternatives that have been proposed. Much of the debate on emotions has been dominated by the so-called 'paradox of fiction' (how can we be moved emotionally by fictional characters that we know are not real?). In recent years, however, the problem of emotion itself has become a favoured topic in cognitive film theory. I conclude, therefore, with some remarks on the question of emotion, in particular the relationship between cogni- tivist and phenomenological accounts of mood in film. Cognitivist theories of emotion can explain many aspects of our emotional engagement with more conventional forms of narrative cinema. They encounter their limits, however, in dealing with films that thwart these more familiar kinds of cognitive mapping, and which open up varieties of aesthetic experience that are not 'cognitive' in the narrow sense.

It may seem obvious that narrative film works dramatically by eliciting and modulating affect and emotion. Yet until recently, emotion was a relatively neglected topic in film theory and philosophy of film. Today, however, studies of emotion, affect, character engagement and genre are flourishing (see M. Smith 1995; Plantinga and Smith 1999; G. Smith 2003; Coplan 2006; Plantinga 2009a; Grodal 2009; Laine 2011). To ask an obvious question, why does emotion matter? Carl Plantinga identifies five ways in which affect and emotion are essential for narrative film: (1) because of the pleasure, value, or emotional significance (personal and social) that they afford; (2) because they provide narrative information by drawing the spectator's attention to salient features of the narrative situation, creating sympathy and antipathy for various characters; (3) because they intensify the phenomenological experience of the film, both bodily (accelerated heartbeat, tensing of muscles, laughing or moaning) and aesthetically (lending significance, quality and imaginative power to particular scenes); (4) because they are connected with various cognitive processes, such as inferences and evaluations, which are essential to the understanding of film; and (5) because they have rhetorical and ideological significance, influ- encing how we feel and think about the world and others (Plantinga 2009a: 6; 2009b: 86). The polymorphous pleasure in movies flows from a combination of cognitive play (solving narrative problems, puzzles, enigmas), visceral experience (thrills and spills), sympathy (for multiple, often conflicting characters), narrative satisfactions (cueing emotional, visceral and cognitive experience), and reflexivity (where cultural awareness of film genre, style, history, and so on, meets social communication and sub-cultural belonging) (Plantinga 2009a: 39).

What do we mean, then, when we talk of 'affect' and 'emotion' in film? Although commonly used as synonyms, philosophers and psychologists usually distinguish affect and emotion depending on whether these have a definite object or cognitive content. Feeling nausea is an (unpleasant) affective-bodily state; feeling pride in having accomplished a difficult task is an emotional-cognitive state. Human emotions are complex phenomena, but speaking generally we can define them as mental states accompanied by physiological and autonomic nervous system changes, subjective feelings, action tendencies (where emotional responses prime us towards certain kinds of action), and outward bodily behaviours (facial expression, bodily posture, gestures, vocalizations, and so on) (Plantinga 2009b: 86). Affect, on the other hand, can be defined very broadly as 'any state of feeling or sensation' involved in conscious cognition (Plantinga 2009a: 29). Affect differs from emotion in being without a definite object, whereas emotions are directed towards intentional objects (Gaut 2010; De Sousa 1987; Plantinga 2009a; Roberts 2003). I feel the warmth of the sun and enjoy the sensation of water as I swim; but I suddenly feel panic and fear at the dark submerged shape moving rapidly towards me beneath the waves.

Arguments abound, however, over the precise nature of emotion. Carroll (2008), for example, distinguishes between affects, which are structurally more primitive, and emotions, which are affects with a complex structure integrating feeling with 'computation' or a cognitive construal (Plantinga 2009b: 86). For a strong cognitivist like Carroll, emotions have a definite cognitive content such as a thought or a belief; emotions just are affective responses coupled with the relevant belief or thought. Emotions thus provide important cognitive information concerning our environment by combining feeling with cognitive appraisals (my anger at a reckless driver depends upon my conviction that people should drive safely, that this driver has endangered me, and so on). For other theorists (such as de Sousa 1987; Roberts 2003; Prinz 2004; Plantinga 2009a), emotions involve cognitive appraisals but these do not have to be beliefs; emotions can involve concern-based construals that are largely perceptual in nature (my anger expresses a concern-based construal of a situation that I perceive as dangerous, threatening, or provocative). Finally, for some theorists, such as Robinson (2005), emotion is not necessarily cognitive, but can be understood as primarily a bodily, physiological phenomenon, activating a variety of neurological and bodily processes that prime us for responsive action.

Plantinga (2009a) offers a pluralist approach, arguing that emotions are bodily-mental responses that span perceptual, affective and cognitive registers. Cinematic emotions, in particular, are elicited by our immersive (bodily, affective and cognitive) experience of narrative film. Following Robert C. Roberts, Plantinga defines emotions as *concern-based construals* (2009a: 55–6 ff) that are at once perceptual and cognitive, intentional and embodied. They can be understood as encompassing an agent's judgements or perceptions of 'how a situation affects her or his concerns', where such construals are also relationally defined with regard to those of other agents (Plantinga 2009a: 9; 49). Emotions, on this view, express 'a mental state that is accompanied by physiological arousal' (Plantinga 2009a: 54), a heightened perceptual, affective and cognitive receptivity towards our situation as well as that of others.

So how do emotions figure in our experience of film? For many theorists, mainstream Hollywood seems to offer an ideal opportunity for the study of the relationship between emotion and cinema. On the one hand, as Plantinga remarks, it is clear that Hollywood films are 'packaged experiences, commodities designed to engage audiences affectively and emotively', yet they also provide a clear case study of filmmaking practice specifically designed for eliciting emotional engagement (2009a: 6). Hollywood is 'a particularly emotional cinema', according to Plantinga, avoiding the distantiation or intellectualism of much European or international art cinema (2009a: 7).[4] Such films typically fall into three broad classes: (1) 'robustly sympathetic films' that encourage emotional congruence with sympathetic characters; (2) 'action films' dedicated to eliciting sensation, excitement, or spectacle; and (3) 'humorously ironic' films that replace distance with humour and irony (Plantinga 2009a: 6–7). Mainstream narrative films typically emphasize emotional engagement and strive to avoid boredom, whether through action and spectacle or by sympathy and humour. They therefore display a variety of visual and narrative techniques designed for eliciting and modulating affective and emotional responses to film. These include the elicitation of sympathy for characters, the elaboration of proto-typical or 'paradigmatic' narrative scenarios, and 'prefocused' cueing of appropriate affective responses to stylized narrative situations.

THE 'PARADOX' OF FICTION?

We are all no doubt familiar with our affective and emotional responses to film. Although the kinds of emotions elicited by fictional film are similar to those experienced in ordinary life, they are clearly accompanied by an awareness of the *fictionality* of what we are seeing (Plantinga 2009a: 77). In Almodóvar's *All About My Mother* (1999) I feel shock, pain and sympathy for Manuela [Celia Roth] as she cries out, reaching for the head of her dying son Esteban, who has just been hit by a car; but I also know that I am seeing a fictional scenario and that neither Manuela nor Esteban actually exist. Nonetheless, I find myself choking with tears. How so?

The fact that we can experience emotional responses to fictional characters has perplexed a number of philosophers. Does it confirm the traditional (Platonic) philosophical suspicion of emotions as conflicting with reason? Or are the emotional responses we experience in response to fictions still 'rational'? This question has become important for cognitivist film theorists, and answering it has tended to track the so-called 'paradox of fiction' (how can I be emotionally engaged with fictional characters that I know do not exist?). This paradox, first articulated and pursued by Colin Radford (1975), can be stated in the following form: (1) we respond emotionally to what we believe to be actual; (2) fiction presents us with scenarios and characters that we do not believe to be actual; (3) yet we nonetheless do respond emotionally to such fictional characters and scenarios. According to Radford, we cannot hold all three propositions without falling into contradiction; hence our apparent capacity to respond emotionally to fiction is 'irrational, incoherent, and inconsistent' (1975: 78).

Radford's conclusion does not seem very appealing or persuasive to many philosophers or theorists of the arts. What purpose, other than to disenfranchise art, is served by arguing that it is 'irrational' to appreciate it? Whatever our response to this question, our enjoyment of fiction does seem to present a puzzle: if we do not believe that fictional characters exist, how can we be moved by the depiction of their plight? Three competing responses have emerged as ways of accounting for our emotional engagement with fiction: 'pretence theory', 'illusion theory', and 'thought theory' (see Carroll 1990: 60–88). Kendall Walton (1990) is the best-known exponent of 'pretence theory', which claims that we have 'quasi-emotional' responses to fictional characters, where cinematic images serve as props within an elaborate game of fictional 'make-believe'. In effect, Walton denies the third premise, namely that we *do* respond emotionally to fictional characters or scenarios. If our emotional responses were real, I would feel moved to take some kind of action in response to an emotionally stirring scene. Since I do not, they are not.

This approach seems rather dubious from a phenomenological point of view, relying again on the philosopher's appeal to common-sense intuitions about emotion and fiction. Walton's paradigm case is the child's game of make-believe: when we play such a game, we pretend to be in a (genuine) emotional state (the child pretends to be really afraid of his father pretending to be a monster). Likewise with fiction, Walton claims, which is the adult version of a game of make-believe. The problem with this analogy, however, is that such games are entered into and enacted voluntarily, whereas our emotional responses to fictional scenarios are largely involuntary (I cannot will myself to laugh at a comic scene or cry at a tragic one). Do I really engage in a game of make-believe, pretending to be 'really' sad, as I witness Manuela's crying grief for her dying son? Consider the kinds of affective and emotional responses one experiences in witnessing a violent fight, a moral injustice, or a sex scene: do I merely pretend to be viscerally revulsed, morally indignant, or erotically excited? Can one be 'make-believedly' aroused? These kinds of 'quasi-emotions' do not account for the sorts of involuntary responses that we frequently experience with fictional films (like horror): nausea, disgust, revulsion, and the 'startle effect' suggest that, at least for some emotions, there are significant involuntary, bodily-physio-logical responses that are hardly 'make-believe'.[5] Moreover, the idea of 'quasi-emotions' seems peculiar, since it requires us to distinguish real from fictional emotions, which seem to differ from each other principally in their object. As Carroll argues, however, having a genuine emotional reaction to someone telling us terrible news does not suddenly change into a fictional emotion if it turns out that the person was telling us a lie (1990: 61).

'Illusion theory' denies Radford's second premise, namely that fiction presents us with characters and scenarios that we do not believe to be real. Variants of this view include the traditional 'suspension of disbelief' idea (Coleridge), Freudian concepts of disavowal within psychoanalytic film theory (Metz), and so on. This approach, not much in favour today, maintains that we do come to believe (or partially believe) fictional characters or scenarios to be in some sense real. The standard objection to this view is that, if this were the case, even partially, we would be moved to act or react in some way to what we take to be actual. The fact that I do not feel moved to act on my belief suggests that I do not literally believe the fiction or its characters are real. However moved I am by Manuela's pain, I do not find myself calling for an ambulance.

The most promising response is to deny the first premise — that we respond emotionally to what we believe to be actual — and that is the path taken by the 'thought theory'. According to this view, it is the thought of the character in that particular situation that generates the relevant emotion (Carroll 1990: 79–87). We do not need to believe in the literal existence of vampires in order to feel frightened by the thought of Nosferatu bearing down upon his hapless victim. Rather we can mentally represent this idea, entertain the unasserted thought, or propose in imagination the idea of a vampire; and that is all we require in order to feel fear, dread, but perhaps also awe, at the shadow of Nosferatu's claws silhouetted in the dark.

A recent variant of 'thought theory' is Greg Currie's account of 'simulation theory', which maintains that the viewer mentally simulates — in imagination — the relevant state of mind (beliefs, desires, and so on) of the character within that fictional scenario, and by allowing this simulation to (mentally) run we arrive at an understanding of the character's subjective states (Currie 1995). As Carroll put it, we simulate a character mentally by 'being immersed in a virtually continuous process of replicating the emotions and desires of (especially) the protagonists' (2008: 172). Simulation theory, however, seems to imply a rather rigid alignment between viewer and character, such that I need to simulate his or her attitudes and responses in order to experience an appropriate affective or emotional response. It does not account well for the variability of our engagement with characters, the fact that we can have a different view or attitude to the situation from that of the character, that we can sympathize with characters with whom we do not share attitudes or beliefs, or that we can interrupt this simulation in order to reflect on the character's predicament, or the actor's performance, or the cinematic presentation, all of which contribute to our affective and emotional responses to film.

Once again, we can question the kind of phenomenology of emotions that 'thought theory' seems to assume. 'Thought theory' makes affective and emotional response dependent on having the appropriate thought or belief, which does not account well for affective responses in cases where such a thought may be absent or obscure (when I cannot identify or name what 'thought' is being expressed in one of the many anxiety-inducing sequences in David Lynch's films). Nor does it really address the bodily, sensorial, visceral dimension of our affective engagement, which also depends upon various non-conscious neuro-physiological processes (see Robinson 2005). My feeling of helpless horror (in de Palma's *Carrie* (1976)) as I watch fragile Carrie White [Sissy Spacek] about to be drenched with a bucket of pig's blood just as she is being crowned Homecoming Queen is not just a matter of entertaining the thought of such a scenario and finding it unpleasant or disagreeable. Nor is it a matter of my simulating in imagination how I would feel, standing on the stage, with a feeling of cautious pleasure, having finally overcome my fear, shyness, and religiously abusive mother, only to be humiliated in the most abject and appalling manner. (The scene is a good example of how we do not have to be aligned with a character's mental state in order to feel a (moral) allegiance with that character; we feel appalled about what is about to happen to poor Carrie, who is unaware of the impending catastrophe, as well as feeling sympathy for her friend, Sue [Amy Irving], who does realize what is about to happen but is powerless to prevent it.) My affective and emotional engagement with a scene such as this involves, rather, a complex interplay of bodily, visceral responses, sympathy and emotional attunement, reflection on the parameters of the narrative situation, and acknowledgement of de Palma's skilful heightening of tension and suspense.

To return to our earlier example, Almodóvar's cinematic presentation of Esteban's death and Manuela's grief is not simply a matter of the characters' actions or narrative content. It depends as much on the aesthetic mood and cinematic mode of presentation of the scene. There are a number of elements that are significant here. We might list the pounding rain, the striking colour palette, Esteban's pleading expression against the car window, the silencing of the underscore to heighten our affective attunement, the tilting image from the perspective of the dying Esteban, the expressiveness of Celia Roth's face, Manuela's harrowing cry of grief, the raw sound of her pain. Our affective and emotional engagement with this scene cannot be reduced simply to the thought being expressed, or to simulating the emotional responses of characters, but involves sensuous, bodily and aesthetic elements that heighten our receptivity to, and resonance with, the emotions portrayed on screen.

These remarks suggest that the most promising way of resolving the paradox of fiction is to question the assumption that we can only have emotions towards what we take to be real. As Thomson-Jones remarks, we can maintain that emotions are cognitive in nature, but question whether emotions always require beliefs (2009: 108). The cognitive dimension of emotions, we might argue, involves having the relevant perceptual construals (Plantinga), or thought and beliefs (Carroll), which relate to the fictional character or scenario in question. Alternatively, we can deny that emotions are cognitive, and argue that they are primarily bodily and neurophysiological, priming us, through 'unconscious' bodily and physiological processes, for heightened perception and relevant action (Robinson 2005).

An attractive pluralist approach that combines elements of both these strategies has been developed by Carl Plantinga (2009a), who likewise denies that we can only have emotional responses to what we believe to be actual. The paradox of fiction can be dissolved provided one adopts a 'moderate cognitivism' denying that emotion depends on belief (Plantinga 2009a: 77). It may be that we require some kind of evaluative belief concerning the specific character-istics of the character or situation in question; for example, that a certain character is frightening, or fascinating, or pitiable (I have to entertain the notion that vampires have frightening characteristics, even if I do not believe that they actually exist). Nonetheless, if we can entertain 'unasserted thoughts' concerning the character, as Plantinga argues, then we can resolve the apparent paradox of our emotional engagement with him or her. If I imagine the character thus and so, I can respond emotionally to him or her, without being committed to any definite beliefs concerning the character's existence. The so-called paradox of fiction is merely apparent — an indication of the confusing assumptions we bring to our experience of emotion in response to fiction.

To return to our example, the emotional effect of Celia Roth's performance in *All About My Mother* is dependent upon my construal of her situation perceptually, cognitively and aesthetically. I can imagine or entertain various 'unasserted thoughts' concerning Manuela's character (thanks to Roth's performance and Almodóvar's direction), and thus enjoy an affective and emotional engagement with her, independent of any definite beliefs about her existence. Imaginative emotional engagement thus offers one way of dissolving the paradox of being moved by fictional characters that we believe do not exist.

More generally, we can extend Plantinga's point and argue that the phenomenological experience of emotional response is too complex to be reduced to a simple cognitive stance (a propositional content, entertaining a thought or belief, imagining that such and such is the case). Emotional response orchestrates different levels and layers of affective attunement, bodily responsiveness, and psychological cognition (sympathy and empathy). The so-called paradox of fiction arises only if we ignore this complex phenomenology and make the 'intellectualist' assumption that emotions either presuppose beliefs or they do not. The experience of affective attunement and emotional resonance that primes us for and intensifies our aesthetic engagement with film shows us that we need an appropriate phenomenology of emotions if we wish to theorize them aright.

IDENTIFICATION, SYMPATHY AND CHARACTER ENGAGEMENT

How does our complex emotional engagement with character work? Film viewers frequently describe their enjoyment of narrative film as a matter of 'identifying' with the characters. One common view is that films which elicit such identification are absorbing and moving, whereas films that do not are somehow unengaging or even boring. A conversation between film fans might run thus: 'I loved *All About My Mother*; I could really identify with Manuela, but also with Huma and Agrado!' 'Did you like *Inception*?' 'No, I couldn't relate to Cobb at all. He seemed more like a computer game avatar than a real character, and his relationship with wife Mal wasn't very convincing.' For the first speaker, it is all about emotional engagement with the characters; for the second, it is the lack of such emotional engagement that is the problem.[6] How, then, do we account for the more familiar 'folk' sense of identification as emotional engagement with characters?

As mentioned above, the concept of 'identification' operative in psychoanalytic accounts has been criticized by many cognitivist theorists. Some philosophers, such as Gaut (2010), however, have argued that the concept of identification at issue here requires refinement rather rejection. Carroll, for example, construes 'identification' as referring to an *identity* relation between viewer and character; moreover, that the strong alignment, even fusion, between viewer and character that identification implies cannot account for cases where the viewer's emotional attitude is at variance with that of the character.

The problem with Carroll's overly literal construal of 'identification', however, is that it underplays the role of *imagination* in our emotional engagement with fictional characters. Carroll assumes that to 'identify' with a character is to assume all of his or her relevant attitudes, beliefs, traits and responses, which is far too demanding a conception of the term. On this view — call it 'strong identification' — we are dealing with an empathizing that encompasses a multitude of relevant aspects at once. Construed in this fashion, Carroll concludes, unsurprisingly, that 'identification' is not only incoherent as a concept but untenable as a description of our emotional engagement with film. However, we can address Carroll's criticism by pointing out that the meaning of 'identification' is principally to do with imagining oneself in a character's situation, rather than as having precisely his or her affective and emotional responses. Such *imaginative* identification can be ambiguous and ambivalent; it may involve feeling sympathy for a character, but then again it may not (it is possible to identify with a character without feeling sympathy for him or her, while one can also feel sympathy for a character with whom one does not identify). Moreover, as Gaut argues (2010: 258 ff), if we construe the process of identification as involving a plurality of aspects (perceptual identification, affective identification, epistemic identification, and so on), which need not be activated all at once, then we can rehabilitate the term theoretically in a way that accords with the folk sense of 'identifying' with characters in film. All the same, it is clear that there are many aspects involved in such processes of identification, which require further specification than the concept of 'identification' generally affords.

STRUCTURES OF SYMPATHY

Murray Smith has taken up this problem of providing a more differentiated conception of emotional engagement — what he calls the 'structure of sympathy' — as an alternative to undifferentiated 'folk' as well as psychoanalytic concepts of identification. There are three levels of engagement that comprise the structure of sympathy: recognition, alignment, and allegiance (Smith 1995: 81 ff). According to Smith, *recognition* 'describes the spectator's construction of character', the way in which we individuate or pick out characters with definite characteristics and a coherent identity. For the most part, recognition occurs very readily in narrative film, being 'rapid and phenomenologically "automatic"' (1995: 82); yet there are cases where films block or undermine recognition such that the viewer struggles to identify a character as a coherent, individuated personage (Buñuel's *That Obscure Object of Desire* (1977) or Lynch's *INLAND EMPIRE* (2006), for example). The second level, *alignment,* describes 'the process by which spectators are placed in relation to characters in terms of access to their actions, and to what they know and feel' (Smith 1995: 83). It refers to the way films focus attention on, and grant us knowledge of, a character via two related processes: *spatio-temporal attachment* (restricting the narrative to a character's or characters' actions) and *subjective access* (granting us access to the character's subjectivity) (1995: 83). POV shots are one common way of doing this, but there are many other devices used as well (POV shots, moreover, can also serve other ends; for example, concealing the identity of a character in a horror film) (1995: 83–4). Finally, *allegiance* refers to 'the moral evaluation of characters by the spectator' (1995: 84); the way that various narrative, visual and aural cues grant us access to the character's state of mind, allow us to understand the context of his or her actions, and thus to morally evaluate the character on the basis of this knowledge and understanding (1995: 84). Taken together, recognition, alignment and allegiance comprise a 'structure of sympathy' that enables us to discriminate between levels of engagement. It can therefore help us to avoid the common confusion between alignment with a character's actions or state of mind, and allegiance with the character from a moral-evaluative point of view. In Demme's *Silence of the Lambs*, for example, we cannot be emotionally aligned with Buffalo Bill (his mental state remains a mystery), even though we momentarily share his point of view (watching, through his night goggles, the terrified Clarice Starling pointing her pistol blindly in the dark); whereas we can be both aligned with Clarice (share her state of abject fear) and feel allegiance with her (finding her courage and determination morally virtuous).

Let us consider another example of the complex ways in which alignment and allegiance can be articulated. Julian Schnabel's *The Diving Bell and the Butterfly* (2007) tells the story of Jean-Dominique Bauby [Mathieu Amalric], a former fashion magazine editor, husband, father, and would-be novelist, who falls victim to an almost complete bodily paralysis ('locked-in syndrome') following an unexpected stroke.[7] Large stretches of the film consist of POV shots from the perspective of 'Jean-Do', our paralysed 'protagonist', whose sole remaining voluntary movement is the capacity to blink his left eyelid. On the one hand, these strikingly vivid POV shots align us with Jean-Do's bodily, phenomenological and emotional states (showing us his eyelid blinking, his erratic visual focus, allowing us to hear his thoughts); on the other, they also merge into fantasy and memory images that are part of his convalescence as well as his creative process as a writer (the 'butterfly' images of creative imagination and recollection as compared with the 'diving bell' sequences of bodily paralysis and entrapment). At the same time, these POV shots are also strikingly expressive reaction shots that align us with the beautiful women characters — his wife, Céline [Emanuelle Seigner], and his therapist and emanuensis, Henriette [Marie-Josée Croze] and Claude [Anne Consigny]—who treat Jean-Do, attend to his most minute expressions, and painstakingly help him to compose his memoirs. These intimate combined POV/reaction shots not only align us with Jean-Do's bodily and psychic life, as well as the emotional responses of his carers; they also allow us to entertain dual allegiances, sometimes conflicting, towards Jean-Do, with his remarkable courage, humour and spirit, and towards the women characters' emotional commitment, patience and love. At the same time, the film maintains a respectful distance — an ethical acknowledgement — of the sheer otherness of Bauby's strange experience and his astonishing achievement in writing his memoirs. As Tarja Laine remarks of the film, it transcends the mere simulating of emotion, offering instead an 'emotional event' in which spectator and film meet each other halfway; haptic (tactile) image, bodily affect and emotional resonance come together to compose an experiential aesthetic process of mutual becoming (2010: 299).

IN THE MOOD

Most cognitivist theories of emotion, narrative and genre tend to focus on character engagement, narrative content and the cognitivist bases of film understanding. Carroll argues, for example, that we can explain the puzzle of emotional convergence in film — that viewers will typically respond in similar ways to particular movie scenes — by the 'criterial prefocusing' of narrative cues that ensure the appropriate affective/emotional responses are elicited and directed (2008). Even theorists like Plantinga (2009a), who emphasize the interplay of cognitive, emotional and generic factors, still foreground the role of character, action and narrative content in their analyses of affective and emotional engagement with film.

Here one could object, however, that this approach overlooks the broader aesthetic and cinematic setting of narrative drama. It is not just character action and narrative content that elicits emotion, but the entire repertoire of cinematic-aesthetic devices (lighting, composition, montage, rhythm, tempo, colour, texture, gesture, performance, music and sound). Emotion is elicited and communicated *aesthetically* as well as cognitively. Indeed, some cognitivist theories can be questioned for focusing too exclusively on discrete (cognitively) focused emotions, rather than on the background aesthetic attunement elicited by the film as a whole. Films do not simply present characters in discrete emotional states in order to convey narrative information. Rather, their aesthetic effect depends on the sensuous-affective background or encompassing 'mood' against which our complex flow of emotional responsiveness becomes manifest; the background against which we are able to recognise, align, and ally ourselves with particular characters within specific narrative scenarios.

As an alternative to Carroll's 'criterial prefocusing' approach, Greg Smith (2003) has offered a different account of how film narrative works to achieve emotional engagement — namely, by the complex evocation or cueing of *mood* rather than the triggering of discrete emotions based on objects or character alignment and allegiance. Indeed, 'the primary emotive effect' of cinema, Smith argues, 'is to create mood' (2003: 42). At the same time, mood cues the background affective dispositions that enable us to experience emotional engagement with characters in the narrative. More significantly, mood provides a sustained, low-level, indeterminate 'focusing' of affective attunement that is necessary for the successful 'convergence' of a particular viewer's emotional responses to specific scenes or narrative sequences. Expressed differently, mood provides the (phenomenological) background of aesthetic attunement against which certain features of the narrative, character, or situation can show up as salient, dramatically charged, or emotionally significant. It is because of the mood of anxiety and tension artfully evoked in Hitchcock's *Psycho* (through aural, visual and narrative cues) that the famous shower scene has such a powerful and dramatic effect. Consider the preceding parlour scene between Marion [Janet Leigh] and Norman [Anthony Perkins] sharing a sandwich, with its gloomy shadows, stuffed birds, stilted conversation, Norman's stammering speech, his denunciation of asylums, and the minor musical background score; all of these elements contribute to cueing the relevant moods of anxiety and suspense that prepare for the famous shower scene that follows. It is because we have been attuned to the mood of anxiety and suspense following Marion's flight after having stolen the money, her unsettling conversation with Bates in his gloomy parlour, her change of heart about the 'private trap' she stepped into back in Phoenix, that the sudden mutation of her (morally) cleansing shower into a watery death trap becomes so viscerally shocking and emotionally powerful.

Smith's account suggests that we should consider a richer phenomenological approach to the ways in which emotions are keyed by mood or affective dispositions that serve to disclose the narrative world in particular ways. Mood attunes us to being receptive to specific emotional cues and thus to the particular responses of characters that thereby take on a heightened emotional significance. Such an approach finds some confirmation in recent studies of the phenomena of mimicry (the way in which individuals tend to mimic each other's affective or emotional responses), affective contagion (the phenomenon of group or shared affects, where individuals 'catch' the emotional responses of others), and the affective basis of intercorporeal recognition (the way our basic cognitive and psychological engagement with others is dependent upon affective responsiveness) (see Smith 2003: 19–34; Copland 2006; Grodal 2009: 181–204; Plantinga 2009a: 112–29; Laine 2011). It also finds confirmation in the way in which narrative film uses a multiplicity of aesthetic elements and cinematic devices to cue mood in order to elicit and enhance the viewer's affective and emotional engagement.

Wong Kar-wai's *In the Mood for Love* (2000), for example, uses a haunting refrain, 'Yumeji's Theme' (composed by Shigeru Umabayashi), which accompanies the repeated gestures, poignant expressions and balletic movements of the main characters, the exquisitely elegant So Li-zhen [Maggie Cheung] and dashing Chow Mo-wan [Tony Leung]. The recurring use of this refrain, with its slow, sensuous sequences of everyday encounters between So Li-zhen [Cheung] and Chow Mo-wan [Leung], evokes the romantic moods of nostalgia and longing that make this poignant love story — achingly sustained but never actually consummated — so aesthetically charged and emotionally nuanced. The slowly unfolding temporal arc of the film is prepared by its subtle and sustained evocation of a variety of harmonically resonant moods. These moods are cued by Kar-wai's artful use of colour, décor, costume and music, and they are beautifully sustained by the graceful movements and repeated gestures of the characters as they sojourn through time and memory.

Another memorable mood sequence can be found in Almodóvar's *Talk to Her* (2002), a scene that Cavell might have described as a 'nothing shot' (2005: 182) — an image or sequence that serves no particular narrative purpose other than to evoke an aesthetic charge or affective mood. There is a brief musical interlude in the course of the film that features a large gathering of people seated together for an artistic social event, listening to a performer (Caetano Veloso), accompanied by a guitarist and two cellists, singing a beautiful song ('Cucurrucucu Paloma').[8] The scene, set in a delightful courtyard on a warm summer evening, lingers on the singer's performance, his expressive voice and features, the pleasure on the faces of the audience, including the lead characters. Everyone is enjoying the performance, which evokes a languorous ambience, a romantic mood, a poignant sensibility registered on Marco's [Mario Grandinetti's] melancholy face as he is moved, once again, to tears (a recurring motif in the film). The scene has little narrative significance other than as an occasion for Marco, the broken journalist, and Lydia [Rosario Flores], the broken matador, to talk, to recall (painful) memories. He leaves the performance, overcome with emotion (as we have seen him do several times already), with Lydia following him, captivated by his overflowing feeling, thus opening a space for their uneasy intimacy to unfold. The scene is a mood-cue that uses music, song, and our pleasure in performance to imbue the narrative situation with affective intensity. It expresses an aesthetic mood that celebrates the power and pleasure of performance, whether musical, dramatic, or cinematic, for no particular narrative reason, other than the aesthetic pleasure of watching narrative film.

In Lynch's *Mulholland Drive* (2001), mood-cueing is no longer a background feature to guide our engagement with characters, but a quasi-independent element within the cinematic world. In the 'Club Silencio' sequence, Betty [Naomi Watts] and 'Rita' [Laura Elena Harring] listen to an aching Spanish rendition of Roy Orbison's 'Crying', a performance that turns out to be mimed, the singer [Rebekka del Rio] suddenly collapsing and 'dying' on stage. This extraordinary mood-evoking performance, however, also communicates an intuitive affective or aesthetic understanding to both characters and viewers (that we are witnessing a performance while in the grip of cinematic illusion; and that the characters' fantasized love affair is not real but illusory). This complex cueing and evocation of mood, involving music, colour, visual patterning, gesture and performance, is often overlooked by more 'intellectualist' strains of cognitivist theory. Yet it clearly plays a vital role in our aesthetic, imaginative and emotional engagement with narrative film.[9]

CHAPTER FIVE

BANDE À PART: DELEUZE AND CAVELL AS FILM-PHILOSOPHERS

Cognitivists have developed an impressive array of theories dealing with a number of classical problems of film theory, including how we understand and interpret film, the problem of character engagement, and the relationship between emotion and genre. One important question that is not much addressed in cognitivist approaches is *why* film matters to us more generally. What is at stake in our aesthetic engagement with film? Is film just a clever cognitive puzzle to amuse a distracted public? Do films respond to our cultural anxieties or 'existential' concerns? Can cinema deal with problems such as nihilism and scepticism? These are some of the deeper questions animating the philosophical projects of Gilles Deleuze and Stanley Cavell, two of the most original and influential of the new film-philosophers. If Bordwell and Carroll are the founders of the analytic-cognitivist approach, we could cite Cavell and Deleuze as exemplars of the film-philosophy approach. What they share, beneath superficial differences, is a concern with *why* film matters philosophically. Their responses take different but related paths. For Deleuze, (modern) cinema is a way of inventing reasons 'to believe in this world' — a response to the problem of nihilism via the invention of new images (such as the time-image). For Cavell, film is an implicit response to *scepticism* that enacts a retrieval of the ordinary, and thus provides an image for what philosophy strives to overcome, but also sometimes struggles to express. Cinema is philosophical, for both Deleuze and Cavell, because of the way it retrieves the ordinary and fosters the creation of new perspectives or modes of existence.

Rather than presenting a philosophical commentary on Deleuze and Cavell's respective projects, of which there are many excellent examples (see Rodowick 1997; Rothman and Keane 2000), I shall explore their overlapping responses, at once creative and critical, to the philosophical and cultural problem of a crisis of meaning: how film can contribute to a rethinking of scepticism and nihilism in modernity.

IMAGE = MOVEMENT: DELEUZE

Gilles Deleuze published the first of his two books on film and philosophy in 1983, *Cinema I: The Movement-Image* (1986), followed by the 'sequel' in 1986, *Cinema II: The Time-Image* (1989). In their ambitious attempt to conceptualize the 'essential' concepts of cinema and to develop a conceptual taxonomy of cinematic signs, Deleuze's *Cinema* books would seem to qualify as prime examples of 'Grand Theory'. Yet there are some intriguing parallels between Deleuze and the Bordwell/Carroll critique of the older paradigm. Deleuze, for example, is critical of psychoanalytic film theory, as well as the dominance of linguistic models of the image that assimilate it to an utterance (1989: 25–8; 2000: 366). Deleuze also claims to be sceptical of simply applying philosophy to film, arguing that cinema has no need of an overarching explanatory framework, since it is capable of responding to problems in its own way, namely through images (2000: 367). Moreover, Deleuze was an early enthusiast of the way the 'sciences of the brain' might be able to open up new connections between film and philosophy, devoting a section in *Cinema II* to what he calls the 'cinema of the brain' (Deleuze 1989: 204–15).[1]

Whatever the parallels, Deleuze develops a quite different approach to the film-philosophy relationship, one that seeks to extract the concepts of cinema in a way that responds to problems shared by film and philosophy. Deleuze's project thus begins with a critical commentary on Henri Bergson's metaphysics of movement, which we may summarize in the following three theses:

(1) Movement is distinct from the space covered

Bergson's first thesis, according to Deleuze, holds that movement as such is qualitative, and so cannot be divided up without changing qualitatively (1986: 1). Space, on the other hand, is quantitative and so can be divided indefinitely. Space is homogeneous, movement heterogeneous (Deleuze 1986: 1). This implies that movement cannot be recomposed out of individual positions in space or instants in time; static sections (positions and instants) can only be synthesized in succession to create an 'illusory' movement. This is what happens in cinema, according to Bergson, which synthesizes static images, passing in rapid succession, in order to generate a 'false movement': the illusionistic impression of movement on screen. However, what we experience in film, Deleuze claims, is a 'mobile section of duration' — a genuine 'movement-image' that moves in itself, enabling movements to be captured and extended over time through the cinematic devices of framing, editing, cutting, montage, and so on (1986: 2–3).

(2) Ancient versus modern conceptions of movement

According to Deleuze/Bergson, there are two ways of composing 'illusory' forms of movement (that is, recomposing movement from static instants or 'poses').[2] For the Greeks, movement was composed via intelligible elements or eternal Forms; for the moderns, following modern science, movement refers to generic temporal instants or what Deleuze calls the 'any-instant-whatever' (1986: 3–4). Time is taken as an independent variable, which allows movement to be measured and quantified. Cinema inherits this quantitative conception of movement and of time, and can therefore be defined as 'the system which reproduces movement by relating it to the any-instant-whatever' (Deleuze 1989: 6).

(3) Movement expresses a quantitative change in the Whole

According to Bergsonian/Deleuzian process philosophy, what we take to be temporal instants are only 'immobile sections' of movement; movement itself, on the contrary, is a 'mobile section' expressing quantitative change in a larger Whole (Deleuze 1989: 8). From this holistic perspective, movement is an expression of qualitative change; it is an expression of what Bergson famously called *duration* [*durée*]. What we take to be static images are really 'frozen' movements or 'immobile sections' of movement, frozen moments of *durée* (Deleuze 1989: 8–9). As we shall see, a key distinction comes into play here: that between mobile sections of duration, which Deleuze calls *movement-images*, and direct images of duration (*time-images*), in which movement is no longer subordinated to time.

The key points that Deleuze derives from his analysis of Bergson on movement are these: (1) that cinema produces movement-images depicting movement *within* the image; (2) that film expresses movement *between* composed images (montage); and (3) that this composed series of images expresses duration *across the Whole* of the film (1986: 11). These three Bergsonian theses on movement provide Deleuze with a conceptual framework for analyzing and classifying cinematic images (namely as varieties of movement-image and time-image).

All the same, Deleuze challenges Bergson's critique of the way that cinema composes an 'illusory' movement out of a series of static images. Like contemporary cognitivists, Bergson underlines the selective and interest-driven character of perception — the way our brains select out cognitively salient objects or features of our environment that are relevant to our immediate practical ends or goal-directed actions (see Grodal 2009; Plantinga 2009a). As a process-philosopher, however, Bergson claims that the selective nature of perception shows how we thereby *distort* the processual character of reality. As for the cinema, Bergson (like Gaut) takes an *illusionist* view of cinematic movement: since the impression of movement is generated by the animation of a series of static images or poses, cinematic images can only reveal an *illusory* movement that remains dependent on 'real' movement (like of the film strip through the projector).[3] Deleuze, however, in a manner echoing Currie, argues that this Bergsonian criticism confuses the mechanistic process by which movement is generated with the immediate movement perceived in the image. Rather than reduce the immanent movement in the image to an illusory representation, Deleuze argues that the movement-image depicts movement *directly* without being reducible to the mechanical process that generated it.

MOVEMENT-IMAGE

Deleuze's ontological project in his *Cinema* books is to define the specificity of cinema as depicting movement in relation to generic instants (the 'any-instant-whatever'), which allow for the measuring of movement against the succession of equidistant temporal instants $(t_1, t_2, t_3, \ldots)$. Contra traditional conceptions of movement, Deleuze follows Bergson in arguing that movement cannot be deduced from pre-existing 'transcendental poses', static positions, or privileged moments (1986: 4). Rather, cinema is a mechanical system of *animating* images that enables the reproduction of movement 'as a function of the any-instant-whatever' (equidistant temporal instants), which are selected and combined in order to 'create the impression of continuity' (Deleuze 1986: 5). Once the technical apparatus of creating movement-images via generic instants is taken over 'as a machine of synthesis for purposes of art and entertainment', we have, according to Deleuze, the cinema (1986: 6). As we shall see, it is this subordination of time to movement — time as *indirectly* presented via the composition (montage) of movement-images — that is reversed, Deleuze claims, in 'modern cinema' (post-War European, Japanese, and American independent film), which presents time directly in the image itself.

Deleuze's idiosyncratic construal of Bergson's metaphysics has the ultimate aim of undoing the opposition between 'image' and 'object', a move which Deleuze performs by positing an 'equivalence' between image and movement, matter and light (1986: 58–60). We should note that Bergson uses the term 'image' very broadly in his metaphysics, the equivalent of what other philosophers might call 'appearances' (1986: 58). This Bergsonian concept of the movement-image implies that cinematic images capture the movement *immanent* (inherent) to things in the world, the matter-light in perpetual motion that defines the Bergsonian 'fluxus' vision of the universe. Without going into the details of Bergson's process-metaphysics, we can provide a brief summary of the key varieties of movement-image that Deleuze derives from his Bergsonian analytic of cinema.

Once an image is related to a 'static' and selective point of view — what Bergson calls a 'centre of indetermination' in the image nexus — we have a *perception-image*, which can take 'objective' and 'subjective' forms (the establishing shots that open many films, or the shot-countershot format depicting dialogue). Perception, however, is linked to action, both in the sensory-motor schema of human cognition and in the image nexus composing narrative film. Once an image is related to a perception-image and to an encompassing milieu, we have the *action-image*; the familiar mid-shots, for example, of characters expressing their perception of a situation through action aimed at changing it in some way (like the Mexican standoff scene in Tarantino's *Reservoir Dogs* (1992)).

The link between perception and action, however, is a *complex* rather than reflex movement; the 'gap' or 'interval' between perception and action — whether in cognition or in narrative film — is filled by *affect* or *affection* (the ways in which our bodies are affected by movement). This yields the *affection-image*, which expresses bodily affect or emotion but also qualities and powers in an 'ontological' sense (as pure singularities). Affection-images are most familiar as the close-up of the face or of affectively charged objects, which serve to elicit affect but also express qualities in a sensuously heightened manner (the 'dancing bag' sequence in Mendes' *American Beauty* (1999), or the leaking pool of Lester Burnham's [Kevin Spacey's] blood that so fascinates Ricky Fitts [Wes Bentley] in the same film). Affection-images gain intensity, moreover, when the perception-action nexus is interrupted, thereby opening up an affective space for the expression of pure qualitative states or 'non-subjective' affects. For Deleuze, we should note, affects are not simply the expression of a subjective feeling or sensation on the part of a human subject; rather, they express 'pure qualities' manifested between subjects, in relation to objects, or even by places and landscapes.

Again following Bergson, Deleuze takes this perception-affection-action circuit to articulate the basic mechanism of action-driven narrative film. The latter is governed by what Deleuze calls the 'sensory-motor action schema' (1986: 155 ff): the linking of perception-, affection- and action-images depicting character-driven action within an encompassing milieu. The action-image is typically associated with *realism*, which Deleuze defines via the relationship between a milieu and behaviour: a milieu that actualizes various qualities and powers, and modes of behaviour expressing individuated responses to this milieu (1986: 141). Realist action-image cinema, in turn, is defined by two major forms: the 'large form' (1986: 142 ff), typically found in genres such as the documentary, the Western, psycho-social drama, *film noir*, and the historical drama, in which an initial situation (S) leads to action (A) that then modifies the situation (SAS_1); and the 'small form' (1986: 160 ff), in which action (A) discloses a partially obscure situation (S), which then leads to new action (ASA_1), typically found in genres such as melodrama and comedy.

CRISIS OF THE ACTION-IMAGE

The sensory-motor action schema, for Deleuze, provides the framework for the major traditions of narrative film (not only

Hollywood but Soviet, French, German, Japanese, and so on). Drawing on a historical account of film indebted to various French film theorists (Burch, Ropars, Schefer), Deleuze claims that the ascendancy of the sensory-motor action schema undergoes a crisis in the post-War period: a rupturing of the sensory-motor link, a loosening of plot, a dispersion of space, and self-consciousness concerning clichés, all of which herald the emergence of a new type of image — the *time-image*. (1986: 205–15; 1989: 1–13). The latter inverts the primacy of movement over time, interrupting the link to sensory-motor action in order to open up the dimension of time for its own sake. Such images are no longer sensory-motor in orientation but reveal instead 'pure optical and sound situations', a cinematic innovation that first appears, according to Deleuze, with Ozu (1989: 13). These are pure audiovisual descriptions that are no longer extended into action, that express a new way of depicting the world, opening up the intensive dimensions of time, affect and thought. A new cinema of 'the seer' replaces the old cinema of the agent (Deleuze 1989: 2). With this shift from sensory-motor action to pure optical and sound situations, and the subsequent development of a new cinema of the time-image, the transition to cinematic 'modernity' is achieved (Deleuze 1989: 5). Film thus realizes its 'essence' — its vocation expressing time, affect and thought — in the post-War historical transition from movement- to time-image cinema.

Not that classical cinema was unaware, we should note, of the expressive possibilities afforded by slackening action and opening up time. Some of the great Westerns — John Ford's *The Searchers* (1956), for example, or Huston's *The Misfits* (1961) — included disruptions of sensory-motor action narrative that would not be out of place in post-War European cinema. Deleuze's chronology, however, becomes somewhat confusing here: Ozu is credited with having invented pure optical and sound situations during the 1930s (before he came to sound film in 1936) (1989: 13–18), Welles' *Citizen Kane* (1941) is acknowledged as having introduced time-images through the use of deep focus (1989: 105–12), while the Italian neo-realists (Rossellini, De Sica, Visconti) are praised for having inaugurated time-image cinema immediately after WWII (1986: 211–13; 1989: 2–9). Deleuze admits that anticipations of pure optical and sound situations and time-image narrative are to be found in various periods and styles of filmmaking, but nonetheless holds that the crisis of the action-image emerged as a distinctive phenomenon in the post-War period, beginning with Italian neo-realism (from 1948), the French *nouvelle vague* (from 1958), New German cinema (from 1968), and American independent film during the 1970s (1986: 211).[4]

So what does Deleuze mean by the 'crisis of the action-image'? The simplest way of describing it is as a breakdown in the sensory-motor action schema, affecting both large (SAS) and small (ASA) forms of action-image narrative. In a surprising shift of theoretical register, Deleuze cites as a major cause of this apparent shift the collective loss of belief in historical agency. Thus in post-War European cinema, Deleuze claims, there was no longer a 'globalizing situation' that could be disclosed or transformed by 'decisive action'; rather, there were only disconnected actions or meandering plots that loosely comprised 'a dispersive set, in an open totality' (1986: 205). The ASA structure, too, was subjected to a similar critique: history was no longer determining, the consequences of action were no longer predictable, film was no longer concerned to 'transcribe events which had already happened', but aimed rather at 'reaching the event in the course of happening,' capturing actuality in an improvisatory manner or by invoking a narrative situation *in situ* (as in Italian neo-realist films) (Deleuze 1986: 206).

This crisis of the action-image, moreover, was driven by a *historical* dynamic, above all the traumatic effects of the experience of WWII, and a related scepticism towards overarching cultural-political ideologies (revolutionary Socialism, the American vision of a democracy of equals). Indeed, Deleuze identifies a plurality of historical factors as responsible for this crisis and the emergence of time-image cinema: shared cultural crises in meaning, new social movements, the shift towards an image-centred culture, the crossover with modernist literature, and the crisis in traditional Hollywood genres (1986: 206).

Pride of place, however, is given to Italian neo-realism — the first post-War style of cinema responding to a historical milieu in which characters confront situations they no longer fully comprehend. The distinctiveness of neo-realism lies in the way in which it disrupts the sensory-motor action schema by blocking the link between perception and action. The resulting images no longer refer to an encompassing or determinate situation, but rather to a reality that has become elliptical and dispersive (Deleuze 1986: 207). The conventional sensory-motor action schema is replaced by a meandering 'trip' narrative, which Deleuze calls 'the stroll' or urban voyage and return journey (1986: 208). The latter consist of loosely connected episodes with multiple characters occurring in generic urban spaces, the 'any-space-whatever' (like the rubble-strewn urban landscapes in Rossellini's *Rome, Open City* (1945)).

This disconnected and dispersed world is no longer sustained by any shared conception of history, vision of the future, or sense of communal belonging. Rather, the only things that sustain it are optical, auditory and psychic *clichés*, by which Deleuze means 'sensory-motor images of a thing': floating, anonymous images that are supposed to substitute for a disconnected reality in which we no longer really believe. The crisis in the action-image — encompassing the dispersive situation, deliberately weak narrative links, the voyage form, the consciousness of clichés and condemnation of plot — is also, however, an expression of a broader crisis, namely that of the 'American Dream' (the vision of individual liberty and fulfilment of historical destiny within a diverse community of equals) (Deleuze 1986: 210). Post-War cinema thus begins with a critical reflection on the dominant model of narrative film (Hollywood), but also questions the shared belief in the power of individual action to transform (historically meaningful) situations. The historical experience of the horrors of war, Deleuze suggests, produces the crisis in the action-image, which expresses a deeper historical crisis of meaning in post-War Europe, America and beyond.

'TWO AGES' OF CINEMA?

An attentive reader of the *Cinema* books will have noticed that Deleuze's historical narrative contrasts the creative inventiveness of Italian neo-realism and the French *nouvelle vague* with the pessimistic romanticism and empty clichés of American independent cinema. Altman's *Nashville* (1975) and Scorsese's *Taxi Driver* (1976), for example, are cited as instances of the stroll or voyage narrative, but also criticized for their romantic pessimism, their nihilistic and empty parody of clichés (Deleuze 1986: 208–10). Godard, Truffaut and Rivette, on the other hand, are praised for their inventiveness and creativity in experimenting with new kinds of image, character and narrative styles (Deleuze 1986: 213–14). It is hard to see, however, why the impetus for the creative exploration of time-image cinema need be exclusively attributed to European *auteurs* (such as Rossellini, Bresson or Godard) when there are many instances of post-War Hollywood cinema that would serve equally well as examples of the new time-image cinema.[5] Closer scrutiny reveals a much more complicated historical picture than Deleuze's neat separation of pre-War movement-image cinema and post-War action image cinema would suggest (see R. Smith 2001).

As a number of critics have noted, there seems to be a tension between Deleuze's conceptual taxonomy of image types and his recourse to a historical account of the shift to time-image narrative.[6] Jacques Rancière (2006: 107–23), for example, argues that Deleuze's attempt to contrast 'two ages' of the cinema — a classical movement-image cinema, and a 'modern' time-image cinema — is untenable, for it posits a 'fictive' distinction between movement-images and time-images, and relies on questionable 'allegorical' interpretations of selected film examples to support these historical-ontological claims. For Rancière, there are two key questions for Deleuze's analysis: (1) how to explain the relationship between 'a break in the art of images and the ruptures that affect history in general?' (2006: 108); and (2) how to recognize, in actual films, the evidence of this break or shift between these two image-regimes, as well as the distinction between the movement-image and the time-image in specific cases? Rancière's critical response is twofold: to question Deleuze's reliance on a historical account to explain a shift of a conceptual order, and to argue that the distinction between movement-images and time-images collapses once we submit it to critical scrutiny.

To take the latter point first, the distinction between movement-image and time-image begins to blur within the course of Deleuze's analysis. The affection-image, for example, already expresses pure qualities that articulate a virtual power of the image independent of sensory-motor narrative (Dreyer's silent masterpiece, *The Passion of Joan of Arc* (1928), is hardly 'sensory-motor' action cinema, being one of the finest examples of affection-image/time-image film). Moreover, this blurring of the distinction between movement- and time-images appears in the very examples that Deleuze adduces in order to show the differences between them. Bresson, for example, is praised for his use of the affection-image to construct any-spaces-whatever (Deleuze 1986: 108–11), an account of Bresson that is more or less repeated in *Cinema II* in relation to the theme of 'thought and cinema' (Rancière 2006: 112). The same film examples (say Dreyer or Bresson) can be used either to illustrate the role of affection-images, or to exemplify the breaking of the sensory-motor link that defines time-image cinema (Rancière 2006: 112). This equivocation renders doubtful Deleuze's firm distinction between movement-images and time-images, and his corresponding claims for the historical break with sensory-motor action narrative and transition to post-War time-image cinema.

Moreover, Deleuze supports his claims concerning the shift from sensory-motor action to time-image cinema by adducing film examples that function *allegorically*: films whose *narrative content* provides the 'evidence' demonstrating the crisis of the action-image. Rancière cites a number of pertinent examples here: Hitchcock's *Rear Window* (1954), with its immobilized photographer-protagonist 'Jeff' Jeffries [James Stewart], and *Vertigo* (1958), with its famous shot of Scotty [Stewart] hanging by his fingertips over the abyss; Bresson's *Au hasard Balthazar* (1966), with its linking of hands caring for, working and exploiting the eponymous donkey; or *Pickpocket* (1959), whose thieves caress, rather than seize, their booty; and Tod Browning's silent film *The Unknown* (1927), with its circus performer who fakes having his arms amputated until being forced to do so in reality (2006: 114–19). The immobilized observer, obsessive detective, caressing thief and self-amputating performer all serve as allegorical figures for the general 'crisis in the action-image'.

Rancière thus questions the validity of Deleuze's allegorical examples — whose narrative content is supposed to illustrate a generalized 'paralysis of action' — as evidence justifying the claims made concerning the transition to a distinctively 'modern' time-image cinema (2006: 116–17). For Rancière, this ambiguity between image-type and narrative content suggests that the distinction between movement-images and time-images is artificial — a 'fictive rupture' (2006: 119) that cannot be sustained in the face of cinema's complex dialectic between intentional and automatic elements, narrative and spectacle, representational form and aesthetic experimentation. Indeed, what Deleuze presents is less a shift from one discrete image regime to another than a 'dual perspective' model in which the same images/films can be analyzed either from the perspective of movement-image or from that of time-image cinema (Rancière 2006: 114).

Echoing, from a different perspective, Carroll and other critics of 'medium essentialism', Rancière too argues that cinema has no medium-specific 'essence' that could be read off a metaphysically grounded ontology of images or teleological historical narrative culminating in the 'modern' cinema of time (2006). The (Deleuzian) story of film, Rancière concludes, is thus a thwarted one, much like the 'film fables' defining cinema, forever divided between narrative content and visual spectacle that undo each other continuously (2006: 1–18). Deleuze's 'fictive' opposition between the 'two ages of cinema' (classical and modern) does not do justice to the hybrid character of film, and rests, moreover, upon an 'essentializing' 'ontology of the cinema argued for with bits and pieces gleaned from the entire *corpus* of the cinematographic art' (2006: 5).[7]

Paola Marratti (2008) has responded to Rancière's critique of Deleuze by dismissing the claim that there is a genuine contradiction between a conceptual taxonomy, or 'natural history', of images (1986: xiv) and a historical account of the emergence of time-image cinema in the post-War context. Indeed, the tension between these two positions is 'so obvious', Marrati observes, 'that it would be hard, even for Deleuze, not to notice it' (2008: 64). Marrati argues, however, that the appearance of contradiction is dissolved once we see that the *Cinema* books articulate Deleuze's *political* philosophy (Marrati 2008: x): an analysis of the relationship between '*forms of action and agency*' (2008: x), and a response to the 'problem of the broken link between humans and the world' following the collapse of revolutionary political hopes (whether American or European) (2008: 5). Deleuze's account of the crisis of the action-image is at the same time an analysis of the crisis of History. Hence any clash between the conceptual taxonomy of images and the historical 'two ages of cinema' is merely apparent. Deleuze's ethico-political thought, Marrati argues, is concerned rather with cinema as an artform giving us 'reasons to believe in this world'; restoring our belief in the latter through an 'immanent conversion of faith' (Marrati 2008: 85–7). From this philosophical point of view, the *Cinema* books are treatises on the problem of *nihilism*: the loss of *belief in the world* defining our contemporary cultural-historical malaise. Here we find unexpected common ground with Cavell, who approaches film in a similar spirit, namely as an artistic response to the problem of *scepticism*.

Marrati's 'allegorical' reading of Deleuze's *Cinema* books as works in political philosophy is ingenious. However, even if we accept Marrati's reading (which places a heavy load on the few passages where Deleuze gestures towards history and politics), the problems identified by Rancière remain: how to explain the link between the aesthetics of cinematic images and this historical crisis in agency; and what to make of the 'allegorical' readings of films Deleuze adduces to support this link between aesthetics, history and politics (especially given Deleuze's rejection of 'representationalist' accounts of cinema). Marrati's defence of Deleuze's project does not address Rancière's basic criticism, namely that Deleuze's Bergsonian ontology of images attempts to secure, in one stroke, an 'essence' of cinema that would allow the philosopher to conceptualize image-regimes, narrate the end of cinema, and rescue philosophy's vocation in relation to history, art and politics. We can add to this critique a contemporary observation: the appearance of hybrid forms of narrative cinema in which sensory-motor action and pure optical time-image narrative become 'indiscernible'.[8] Deleuze's historicist thesis looks doubtful given the flourishing of cinema that affirms the play of *mythos* (narrative) and *opsis* (spectacle), classical action-narrative and 'modern' optical and sound situations, in culturally diverse and aesthetically hybrid forms. Contemporary cinema is a happily thwarted fable indeed.[9]

VIEWING WORLDS: CAVELL

The shared *problématique* that nonetheless emerges between Deleuze and Cavell involves the question of the *relationship* between film and philosophy. For both thinkers, philosophy and film engage with problems — in particular, *scepticism* and *nihilism* — that cut across cultural, aesthetic and ethico-political domains. Both thinkers also argue that philosophy cannot merely be 'applied' to film as its object; rather, film and philosophy enter into a *transformative* relationship that opens up new ways of thinking. As Rodowick observes, Deleuze's work on cinema (like that of Cavell, I would add) is concerned with a single question: 'how does a sustained meditation on film and film theory illuminate the relation between image and thought?' (Rodowick 1997: 5) From this perspective, we might regard Deleuze and Cavell as exemplifying two distinctive paths for the film-philosophy relationship to pursue: conceptual-izing cinema in response to the historico-philosophical problem of a 'loss of belief in the world' (Deleuze); and overcoming scepticism via the engagement between film and philosophy, elaborating how film and philosophy think together in ways yet to be explored (Cavell).

WHY DOES FILM MATTER?

First published in 1971, Cavell's *The World Viewed* (1979) is a landmark work in Anglophone philosophy of cinema, being one of the first philosophical studies dedicated to the question of film ontology. Why is this encounter between film and philosophy so important? Cavell's answer is simple: the experience of film affords us a way of contending with *scepticism* — arguably, *the* problem of modern thought — thereby helping restore meaning in a culture that still struggles with philosophy's disenfranchisement of the ordinary. With the scientific revolution, transition to secularism, and Enlightenment emphasis on rational autonomy, the ancient problem of scepticism takes on a renewed urgency in the modern age. It also mutates into the broader cultural-philosophical problem of *nihilism* so important for Deleuze. Modern scepticism — the view that we can have no certain knowledge of the world; that we remain metaphysically isolated from reality/Being — has troubled philosophy since at least Descartes. Modern philosophy has, of course, tried to vanquish scepticism by showing that objective knowledge *is* possible (mathematics, logic, science); that we can attain *certainty* about ourselves and the world in some respects, but that such claims always remain open to sceptical doubt. Despite the success of modern rationalism in conquering epistemic scepticism, the knowledge that really matters to us — about the self, morality, or our relations with others — remains frustratingly uncertain.[10]

What do these ruminations on scepticism and metaphysics have to do with cinema? Film, for Cavell, literally (cinematically) stages this 'sceptical' concern. The mystery of film is how it can present a visual world of movement and time that captures aspects of our experience of reality but which also remains intriguingly distinct and separate from it; a world that is present to me, that I perceive and experience, but from which I am absent or disconnected. Film shows or displays, moreover, the interplay of presence and absence in the image; making present objects, figures and events that are absent, yet which enjoy a ghostly presence in the image-world. It also shows, however, that this image-world — what Cavell calls 'the world viewed' — is nonetheless *meaningful*; a restoring of the sundered link with the world that has been lost in modernity. From this film-philosophical point of view, Cavell argues, film can be viewed as 'a moving image of skepticism' (1979: 188). Echoing Bazin, for Cavell the cinema — whatever other enjoyments it affords — is motivated by our desire for metaphysical connection with the world, 'the wish for selfhood', like all art (1979: 22); yet it shows us that we can find this retrieval of meaning only in ordinary experience, however ambiguous or uncertain it may be, and however much the spectre of scepticism still haunts it.

Following the tradition of classical film theory, *The World Viewed* commences with an inquiry into the ontology of the cinematic image. Unlike traditional studies, however, Cavell opens with an autobiographical reflection on his motivation for writing the book: to account for the shift from his lived experience of the movies to his philosophical interest in their nature (1979: 3–15). The movies matter to us, perhaps more than any other artform; yet philosophy has hitherto ignored them, regarding them as trivial entertainments (suggesting that philosophy has not yet been properly struck by the provocation to thought that movies enact!). Hinting that movies have changed since the 1960s, Cavell situates his own meditations as an attempt to marry philosophical reflection with aesthetic experience. He thus offers a way of thinking about how film, like other arts, now exists 'in the condition of philosophy' (1979: 14), having entered into a condition of *modernism*. The latter, for Cavell, refers to the way that film seeks to renew itself by relating to its own past; the way films seek 'to invite and bear comparison' with past achievements of cinematic history (1979: 216).

So what is film? Inspired by Panofsky (1977 [1934]) and Bazin (1967), who claimed that the medium of movies refers to 'physical reality as such', or that it 'communicates by way of what is real' (Bazin 1967: 110), Cavell turns to the relationship between photography and film. What Panofsky and Bazin mean, Cavell explains, is that the medium of film has a *photographic* basis, and that photographs are *of* a world (1979: 16). When applied to film, their question becomes: 'What happens to reality when it is projected and screened?' (1979: 16) This question is linked with the question of how we experience reality more generally, not only how we perceive it but how we interpret, remember, or imagine it. As any filmgoer will attest, we recollect films as well (or as poorly) as we do events in our past, or even our dreams. We can be haunted by images from films seen many years past; some images, scenes, or characters can become more familiar and significant to us than other people or even one's own memories. So what are we experiencing when we watch a film?

Unlike painting, which 'represents' something in the world,

photography and film, for Cavell, do not represent so much as 'capture' things; they present us, 'we want to say, with the things themselves' (Cavell 1979: 17). We recognize here Cavell's version of what we earlier discussed as the 'transparency thesis': that cinematic images are not representations but presentations of what they depict, a view based on the claim that (pre-digital) photography is a realist medium that retains an ontological link between image and referent. Now, a photograph of a landscape is clearly not the same thing as a landscape painting. A portrait of me is a likeness or visual representation; but a photograph is *of* me (not just *like* me). I don't say, 'that's a good likeness of me in front of the Sydney Opera House'; I say, 'that's me in front of the Sydney Opera House' (likewise for the Opera House). Should we then say that photographs present us with 'the thing itself'? But a photo of the Opera House is no building. So what is the ontological link between a photograph and what it depicts? It is not a likeness nor is it like a replica, according to Cavell; it is something more ontologically mysterious: a trace of the past, of a presence that is no longer present for us. In a photograph, an image with its own aura or magic, we see things that are not present. What does this mean?

The photo is present to me; but what it depicts is not. Cavell draws a parallel with sound recordings: when I hear Maria Callas singing *Tosca*, am I hearing her voice, or merely the *sound* of her voice? The distinction might seem spurious. It does not matter whether I am attending a live performance or listening to a CD recording, you might reply, I would still be hearing the sound of Callas' voice. When I listen to a recording of Callas, I am listening to a transcription of her voice at the time when it was recorded; what I *hear*, however, is a trace of the past, a singular performance (Callas performing *Tosca* at La Scala), now reproduced in the present (as I listen with pleasure on my stereo). So there is no problem saying that audio recordings reproduce the sound of something that is no longer present (an instrument, a voice). Can we say the same of photographs? Cavell argues that photographs do not reproduce a 'sight' (or 'look') of something no longer present; rather, they present something that is hard to name, for which a word appears lacking in our language (1979: 19). Objects do not have 'sights' in a way that would account for their likeness in an image (though Plato may disagree). Nor can we say, as some philosophers might, that photos reproduce 'sense-data' (my visual sensation of something), for in that case we could no longer distinguish between the photo and the thing photographed. Is a photograph, as Bazin suggests, therefore like a 'visual mould' of an object? Not really, because the original, Cavell observes, remains *present* in the image. Photographic images, to be sure, are manufactured or 'constructed' images of the world; but what they capture, mechanically and automatically, is the world itself, not a mere likeness of it. It is this mechanism or *automatism* in photography's capturing and reproduction of images that finally satisfies, as Bazin put it, 'our obsession with realism' (quoted in 1979: 20).

Against contemporary philosophers of film, whose concerns (alas!) are primarily epistemic and ontological rather than aesthetic or cultural, Cavell, like Bazin, points to the existential human need that motivates our creation of images (whether in painting, photography or film). Photography, Cavell remarks, satisfied a wish, growing in the West since the Reformation, 'to escape subjectivity and metaphysical isolation — a wish for the power to reach this world, having for so long tried, at last hopelessly, to manifest fidelity to another' (1979: 21). After the advent of nihilism or what Nietzsche called 'the death of God', painting and photography (and later, film) aimed to re-establish our sense of connection with the world. These were arts that aimed a sense of *presentness*; not just of the world's presence to us, but, more pressingly, a sense of our presence to it (Cavell 1979: 22). During the course of Western modernity, despite — or perhaps due to — the rise of science and technology, consciousness becomes increasingly estranged from reality, interposing 'subjectivity between us and our presentness to the world' (Cavell 1979: 22). When subjectivity became what is most properly present to us, individuality became metaphysical isolation. Hence the route taken to connect with the world was via *subjectivity*. This is the path of *romanticism*, whether in art/literature (Blake, Wordsworth) or in philosophy (Kant, Hegel, Heidegger, Wittgenstein); a movement that Cavell sums up as 'the natural struggle between representation and the acknowledgment of our subjectivity' (1979: 22).

Here Cavell shows his allegiance with the romanticist response to scepticism or nihilism. Visual art, for Cavell, is precisely a response to scepticism, a human expression of selfhood against metaphysical isolation, and thus a way of revivifying our sundered sense of connection with the world. Photography overcomes subjectivity in a manner unavailable to painting, namely through *automatism*, which is to say, 'by removing the human agent from the task of reproduction' (Cavell 1979: 23). It maintains the *presentness* of the world by removing us from it; the reality of a photo is present to me whereas I remain absent from it. Photos depict a world that I can know and see but to which I am not present; and such a world is a 'world past', a past world (Cavell 1979: 23). Film or the art of moving images inherits and projects this world — a *screened world* or 'world viewed' that is present to us but for which we *are not*. With this insight into the modern condition — the age of the 'world-image' (as Heidegger puts it) or 'the world viewed' (as Cavell does) — we have an answer to the question as to why movies matter philosophically.

Cavell develops further this contrast between film and photography, moreover, by considering the different relationships that painting and photography bear to reality. It makes no sense to ask what lies behind an object in a painting, whereas one can always do so with a photograph. A painting, in this regard, *encloses* or *delimits* a world; the limits of the painting (its frame) are the limits of its world (to paraphrase Wittgenstein). Photographs, on the other hand, *do* depict an aspect of the world; we can always ask what lies beyond the limits of the image, beyond its frame, since the cropping of the image by the camera cuts out aspects of the world that could nonetheless have been photographed (Cavell 1979: 24). A painting *is* a world (Turner's ocean); a photograph is *of* the world (Ansel Adams' landscape) (Cavell 1979: 24). Photographs imply the existence of a world beyond the image, whereas paintings depict a world within the image-frame.[11]

Moving pictures, moreover, screen photographic images of the world — a world that is *screened*, supporting nothing but a projection of light, which Cavell takes in at least two senses. The silver screen both 'screens' me from that world (I am not present to it); and it 'screens' the world from me (removes its physical existence) (Cavell 1979: 24). Unlike a photographic frame, the screened world has no frame or border. Rather, from a phenomenological point of view, the film-world has indefinitely extendible and flexible boundaries, thus allowing filmmakers to avail themselves of all the devices of 'variable framing' (indexing, bracketing and scaling) (Carroll 2008: 124 ff). The camera, for Cavell, can extend the 'frame' of the film in many ways; it can focus on some aspects or objects, calling attention to salient aspects of objects, events or characters within the film-world, or it can just 'let the world happen' (1979: 25). As far as defining the medium is concerned, Cavell proposes the descriptive definition of film as 'a succession of automatic world-projections' (1979: 73): film captures movement (and time) in the world, within the image, and between images composing a film ('succession'), and it does so 'automatically', without direct human intervention, thanks to its photographic character. Film captures the ontological reality of a 'world', even a fictional one, by presenting it to us, who remain absent to it, photographically. And it does so via a 'projection' on screen, projecting human figures in a world from which we remain forever absent, thus creating a phenomenological and aesthetic rupture, as well as continuity, with experience (Cavell 1979: 73).

AUDIENCE, ACTOR, STAR

As Panofsky noted back in 1934, cinema introduces important differences not only in theatrical versus cinematic performance but also between theatre and cinema audiences (1977). In the theatre, we are not present to the actors but they are present to us; actors are, of course, aware of the audience but must, by convention, ignore their existence in order to maintain the theatrical illusion (unless breaking 'the fourth wall'). In the cinema, however, we are 'mechanically absent' to the film actors (1979: 25), thanks to the manner in which cinematic performance is captured on film. I am present, not to something happening (on the stage), but to something that has happened, which I can now absorb (like a memory or a dream) (Cavell 1979: 26).

All the same, film actors can still address the camera; direct address is not uncommon, whether in modernist or in comic film (Bergman's *Summer with Monica* (1953); Godard's *Vivre sa vie* (1962); The Marx Brothers in *Duck Soup* (1933)). In these cases, however, we still remain 'mechanically absent' from the world of the film, even if the screen performer appears to address us 'directly' (it is 'any-viewer-whomsoever' being addressed, rather than me specifically). Is this just because theatre viewing involves 'live' performance, in the presence of real actors, rather than a cinematic performance of actors recorded on film? Although Bazin claimed that we *are* in the presence of actors on screen, as though seeing him or her via a relay of mirrors, for Cavell the situation is more subtle and complex (live television is probably closer to Bazin's 'prosthetic image' or 'relayed mirrors' scenario). Cinematic images, to be sure, depict human figures, but what does this mean? Projected images of human beings — of 'a human *something*, … unlike anything else we know' (1979: 26) — raise ticklish (ontological) questions specific to the medium of film.

Take Bette Davis as Margo Channing in Mankiewicz's *All About Eve* (1950). She is clearly, even vividly, present to us on screen; but we are not present to her, for ontological and mechanical reasons. So *what* (or rather, *who*) is thus present to us? Is it Margo Channing or Bette Davis? 'Both', one wants to say. This mysterious coalescence of character and actor in cinematic performance is, however, far from obvious. Carroll claims that moving images depict actors performing characters, which characters are projections (cinematic, aesthetic and dramatic, we might say) based on the actor's performance. We see Bette Davis on screen and at the same time behold Margo Channing warning us about the bumpy night ahead. But are things so clear-cut? The paradox of cinematic performance, if you will, is *how* actor and character can be co-present within a cinematic performance: how can I be engaged by Margo Channing, yet also be perceiving Bette Davis, which together would appear to strain my immersive involvement in the fictional world? On the other hand, if actors were merely living visual props for viewers to imagine characters for themselves, as Walton (1990) and others have argued, then we would not identify screen actors and characters as closely as we do. Imagine, for example, Joan Crawford playing Margo Channing; would it still be 'Margo Channing' that we are imagining? (Given that what we know of 'Margo Channing', of course, depends on what we experience in watching *All About Eve*). *That* Margo Channing (one wants to say '*the* Margo Channing') is indissociably linked with Bette Davis's stunning performance (as 'Mildred Pierce' is indissociably linked with Joan Crawford). Joan Crawford as 'Margo Channing' would not just be a different actress, hence a different performance; she would be another embodiment of 'Margo Channing', a different character than the one we currently know.[12]

Cavell argues that stage actors work themselves into a role and eventually 'yield' to the character; the actor 'incarnates' the character, playing a role that is analogous to a position on a chessboard or in a sporting game (1979: 27–8). The film actor, by contrast, 'takes on' a character, drawing on his or her temperament, skills, endowments and previous acting roles, but only accepting 'what fits' for the purposes of a particular cinematic performance (1979: 28). The screen performance is the projection of a character 'study' in which the actor's presence continues to 'show through' his or her performance. The character is not fully 'incarnated' but subordinated to the actor's screen presence. As much as I enjoy Margo Channing's antics, I am always conscious of Bette Davis' performance, and her cinematic presence is what charges Margo's character with such dramatic brio. Cinematic performance involves a complex aesthetic interplay between actor and character (and the actor's previous cinematic roles), which is why a film actor's physiognomy and gestures, his or her capacity for expressive cinematic 'projection', is far more important than traditional stage-acting craft.

SCREEN 'TYPES' AND FILM GENRES

The film 'star' thus differs from the stage performer in a number of ways. We follow successive incarnations of the screen actor (rather than his or her characters) from film to film (not repeated performances of a dramatic character, as on the stage). As Cavell observes, after *The Maltese Falcon*, 'Bogart' means 'the figure created in a given set of films' (such as *The Maltese Falcon* (1941), *Casablanca* (1942), or *The Big Sleep* (1946)); had those films not been made, Bogart as we know him would not exist (even if he had made other films), and the name 'Bogart' would not mean what it does (1979: 28). Film stars, unlike stage actors, exist essentially for the camera, hence for our appreciation of them on screen; the creation of a (screen) performer, moreover, is also the creation of a recognisable character 'type': the vamp, the hard-boiled detective, the criminal mastermind, the action hero, the romantic heroine, the alienated anti-hero, and so on. Screen acting is thus inseparable from the great cycles of screen narrative that we call *genres* (Cavell 1979: 29 ff). Of all the possible aesthetic paths it might have taken, why did film develop into conventional narrative cycles (genres)? We cannot explain this by simply referring to the *technical* or *material* properties of the medium (as Bazin falsely argued). Nor is it a matter of a cultural or ideological determinism that dictated the hegemonic rise of Hollywood-style narrative; after all, the 'Hollywood style' has been transplanted, hybridized and transformed in the most multifarious ways (Bollywood, for example). Rather, the medium, Cavell maintains, has to be created or invented *artistically* by making various possibilities of the medium *significant*; that is, by discovering new ways of making meaning via the inheritance and transformation of cinematic traditions (1979: 68 ff).

From this point of view, the medium of film comes into its own when the possibilities of screen acting in conventional narrative become explicitly articulated. Indeed, screen actors embody an individuated *type*: an *individuality* that is distinctive from, but also representative of, the ordinary individual with his or her dominant social role; and an individuated expression of the 'myth of singularity' — the narrative fantasy of an individuality that could withstand fate, social circumstance, the materiality of the world itself (1979: 35–6). Such types feature in, and support, the enactment and propagation of cinematic genres; secular expressions of mythic narrative cycles, genres constituted a founding artistic discovery, which is to say invention, of the medium of movies.[13]

Indeed, the emergence of narrative cycles as genres populated by types is an expression of the *democratizing* tendency of film, its inherent egalitarianism (Cavell 1979: 34–5): the visual equivalence between human figures, objects and settings appearing on the screen (see also Rancière 2006: 8–11). The invention of the medium of film means developing genres expressing types that exploit the various affordances or 'automatisms' of film in artistically satisfying ways. Does Cavell fall foul here of Carroll's rigid ban on 'medium essentialism'? Not quite; there *is* a relationship between the medium of film and its artistic possibilities, but this is a relationship of *creative invention*, of 'finding as founding' in an Emersonian spirit, rather than any specious ontological determinism or rigid aesthetic teleology.

Cavell cites, as illuminating examples here, two classic cinematic comic types (Charlie Chaplin and Buster Keaton) whose cinematic artistry relies on two essential features of the cinematic medium that together comprise 'the world viewed': (a) the *projection of the human image* upon the screen (the screening of the actor as type or individuality rather than as a particular character); and (b) the *ontological equivalence of the human figure* in relation to its physical environment (that is, in relation to the world of inanimate objects, of nature, and of larger social forces). Both features of the medium are what make visual comedy possible on screen. Chaplin uses the *'projected visibility'* of the human image to fine aesthetic effect, his comic tics and gestures expressing 'the sublime comprehensibility of his natural choreography'; and he uses the *ontological equality* between people and objects to great comic effect, a levelling that permits 'his Proustian or Jamesian relationship with Murphy beds and flights of stairs and with cases on runners on tables on rollers' — a Nietzschean heroism of survival, of tightrope walking across the abyss (Cavell 1979: 37). Keaton, too, artfully exploits this projected visibility and ontological equality in his daring comic escapades; his predicaments imbue his melancholy countenance with a 'philosophical mood' while also expressing the 'Olympian resourcefulness of his body', qualities that together render Keaton perhaps 'the only constantly beautiful and continuously hilarious man ever seen' (Cavell 1979: 37).[14]

CINEMATIC MYTHMAKING AND THE 'END OF THE MYTHS'

Unlike contemporary philosophers of film, for whom science holds the key to understanding cinema, Cavell readily acknowledges its 'mythic' quality — its enduring fascination with the creation of images of human beings, and its role as the modern, secular expression of a cultural desire for mythmaking.[15] Despite their disagreements over the medium, Cavell accepts Bazin's account of the 'myth of total cinema' (1987: 17–28). This myth expresses the 'idea of and wish for the world re-created in its own image' (Cavell 1979: 39), which film achieves 'automatically' through the *automatisms* of the moving image (the artistic realisation of the various possibilities afforded by the medium). Film fulfils the mythic dream — evident in Plato's Ring of Gyges as much as in Freud's voyeur — of invisible visibility (being able to see all, but not being seen in turn). It satisfies this wish or desire, moreover, without any involvement on our part; I do not have to *do* anything, yet my wish is automatically satisfied, by *magic*, as it were (Cavell 1979: 39). Cinema grants us a power of seeing all while absolving us of responsibility for this power. This magical-technical realisation of the myth of invisible visibility, film's ironic inversion of modern scepticism, thereby becomes 'an expression of modern privacy or anonymity' (Cavell 1979: 40). The 'world's projection' through movies thus parallels, but also questions, our modern sceptical orientation; our 'inability to know' ourselves, others, or the world (Cavell 1979: 40–1). Film 'screens' the fact that we experience ourselves as 'displaced' from the world, 'naturalizing' this condition of existential displacement from our environment, rendering it meaningful, even pleasurable.

As is well known, Cavell has written two books on 'classical'

Hollywood of the 1930s and 1940s, the first on the genre of 'remarriage comedy' (1986) and the second on the 'melodrama of the
unknown woman' (1991).[16] His numerous shorter pieces on film,
video and television, moreover, have been collected in another
volume edited by William Rothman (2005). Already in *The World
Viewed*, however, one finds reflections on the end and future of
Hollywood — reflections that resonate strikingly with those of
Deleuze on the difference between pre- and post-War cinema. Cavell
too notes the shift in cinematic practice since WWII, commenting on
the 'end of the myths' and 'loss of conviction' that sustained classical
Hollywood narrative and genres:

> I assume it is sufficiently obvious that these ways of giving
> significance to the possibilities of film — the media of movies
> exemplified by familiar Hollywood cycles and plots that justify
> the projection of types — are drawing to an end. And this means
> ... that they no longer naturally establish conviction in our
> presentness to the world. (Cavell 1979: 60)

Like Deleuze, the crisis signalled by the exhaustion of genres and
'end of the myths' is also a crisis of belief — the loss of a sense
of connection with the world. Deleuze describes this phenomenon
as a 'loss of belief in the world'; Cavell as a loss of 'conviction in
our presentness to the world'. They amount to the same cultural-
cinematic diagnosis, which we can express as an acknowledgement
of the effects of *nihilism* or *scepticism*. For both thinkers, moreover,
this is not a cause for despair so much as an occasion for thought: to
understand the source and significance of this crisis in narrative and
genre, and to explore the possibilities that contemporary cinema has
begun to realize in its various attempts to question the nature and
prospects of the (mutating) medium of film.

Narrative film since the 1960s and 70s, according to Cavell, has
moved away from the traditional Hollywood emphasis on genres
and types — that is to say, from the expression of generic types
or culturally resonant individualities. Indeed, Cavell comments on
the recycling of traditional narratives, the hyperbolic inflation of
received techniques, and the seeming 'interchangeability' of film
actors, characters and plots (1979: 69–72). It is as though film
had lost conviction in its own aesthetic and mythmaking power;
as though it were estranged from its own history and thus from

113

its future — Cavell's version of Deleuze's complaint against the ubiquity of cinematic, psychic and cultural *clichés*. Again, for both Deleuze and Cavell, the future of the art of film turns on *belief*; belief in the possibilities of the medium, in inheriting and renewing its own traditions, in having something meaningful to offer to a cultural milieu afflicted by a diffuse and inarticulate scepticism.[17]

Like Deleuze, but from an American perspective, Cavell also identifies a post-War break with the belief in individual and collective agency. Following the traumatic historical experience and moral disorientation brought about by WWII, the Cold War and Vietnam, many of the myths of cinema — as of history, politics and morality — have been shattered:

> These beliefs flowered last in our films about the imminence and the experience of the Second World War, then began withering in its aftermath — in the knowledge, and refusal of knowledge, that while we had rescued our European allies, we could not preserve them; that our enemies have prospered; that we are obsessed with the ally who prospered and prepared to enter any pact so long as it is against him; that the stain of atomic blood will not wash and that its fallout is nauseating us beyond medicine, aging us very rapidly. (Cavell 1979: 63)

Films such as Robert Aldrich's *Kiss Me Deadly* (1955) and Kubrick's *Dr Strangelove* (1964) readily come to mind. Some of this historical loss of belief, however, is also due to a more positive shift in social mores and cultural sensibilities: we no longer believe, for example, in chauvinist depictions of women, which opposed beauty and intelligence, intimacy and demonstrativeness (1979: 63–4); nor in the demand for the bullish machismo of men who must be strong, silent and brooding, or else upstanding, outspoken and heroic (Cavell 1979: 67). The possibilities of the body, again anticipating Deleuze, now provide possibilities for new expressions of selfhood that promise a renewal and reinvention of types — both male and female — involving the cinematic 'myth of youth', the 'vanity of personal freedom', and the democratic athleticism of the body (Cavell 1979: 68). Despite these signs of renewal, the degeneration of film's erstwhile conviction in its own aesthetic possibilities, in its capacity to discover and deploy the 'automatisms' of the medium, signals its belated and uncertain entry into the condition of *modernism*.

Here one might ask whether such signs of modernist cinematic self-reflection are really so recent. Arguably, film has always been 'modern', concerned to reflect on its own history ('movies come from other movies', as Cavell observes), and thus able to renew itself in relation to its own historical traditions. Film has always been modern and pre-modern at once, synthesizing traditional narratives with reflections on genre, the history of film, and cultural mythologies. Indeed, cinema, we can say, is an expression of the modern *aesthetic regime* of the arts, which combines elements of an ethical concern with the socio-cultural use of images, an emphasis on representational narrative, and an egalitarian aesthetic of experimentation across all possible genres, styles and subject-matters (Rancière 2004; 2006: 7–11). Whatever the case historically and culturally, contemporary film, in its troubled self-consciousnesss, cannot avoid asking the inescapably philosophical question, "What is film?", or better, "What becomes of film in a sceptical age?". It must retrieve and reinvent the possibilities of its still-evolving medium, now turned digital, and in so doing will be 'asking exactly whether, and under what conditions, it can survive' (Cavell 1979: 72).

FORKING PATHS

Both Cavell and Deleuze ground their respective paths of film-philosophy in the cultural-philosophical crises in meaning that go by the names of scepticism or nihilism. Both thinkers see cinema as offering creative responses to this shared problem, whether through the invention of new images and styles of narrative film, or film styles and genres in which scepticism is both enacted and overcome. Both also point to the shift in film during the course of the previous century, from a classical to a post-classical phase in which film 'exists in the condition of philosophy'; a modernism in which film 'has lost its natural relation to its history' (Cavell 1979: 72), and thus strives to invent new cinematic myths, narrative styles and artistic uses of the medium. Where both thinkers differ is in their particular presentation of the film-philosophy relationship: Deleuze's taxonomy of images draws on a plurality of film-examples to instantiate a conceptual framework articulating the shift from movement- to time-image cinema.[18] Cavell's philosophical readings of particular films perform singular forms of philosophical film criticism that show, rather than tell us, what the relationship between film-philosophy might become,

115

in the light of film's vocation to project and overcome scepticism at once. This fork in the paths opened by Cavell and Deleuze thus leaves us with a tantalizing question: can films 'do philosophy' in a distinctively cinematic way?

CHAPTER SIX

SCENES FROM A MARRIAGE: ON THE IDEA OF FILM AS PHILOSOPHY

One of the more original contributions to contemporary aesthetics is the idea that film can engage in its own distinctive kind of thinking: the idea of film *as* philosophy. Defenders of the 'film as philosophy' thesis have argued that certain kinds of film are capable of screening philosophical thought-experiments (Wartenberg 2007); that film can philosophize on a variety of topics, including reflection on its own status, in ways comparable to philosophy (Mulhall 2002, 2008); or that film has its own affective ways of thinking that alter the manner in which philosophy can be experienced (Frampton 2006). Critics of the film-as-philosophy idea, by contrast, have argued that such claims are merely metaphorical: for these critics, film, as a visual narrative art, does not give reasons, make arguments, or draw conclusions, hence it cannot be understood as 'philosophical' in the proper sense (Baggini 2003; Russell 2006); or, given the ambiguity of film narrative, if there *are* philosophical aspects to a film, these are usually subordinate to its artistic and rhetorical ends (Smith 2006). Alternatively, critics argue that any philosophy to be gleaned from a film is either due to the philosophical acumen of the interpreter, or else is confined to the expression of an explicit aesthetic intention on the part of its maker/s (Livingston 2006, 2009b). The difficulty with such contentions, however, is that they often assume a too-narrow or reductive conception of what counts as philosophy, or else fail to reflect on the variety of ways in which film and philosophy — or indeed philosophy and art — can be related. My suggestion is that the most productive way of exploring the idea of film as philosophy is as an invitation to rethink the hierarchical relationship between philosophy and art. The encounter between film and philosophy invites us to explore novel ways in which our conventional under-standing of philosophy — and aesthetic receptivity to new kinds of experience — might be renewed and transformed.

SCENES FROM A MARRIAGE: MARIANNE AND JOHAN

Ingmar Bergman's *Scenes From a Marriage* [*Scener ur ett äktenskap*] (1973) opens with a comfortable bourgeois couple, Marianne [Liv Ullman] and Johan [Erland Josephson], posing with their daughters for a family portrait. The photographer's assistant cheerfully directs them for the camera, an enviably successful couple whose mutual differences have been reconciled over time, Johan's confident ration-alism tempered by Marianne's compassionate sensitivity. As they pose for the camera, they present an image of domestic bliss, belied by the evident discomfort in Marianne's nervous gestures and Johan's pompous irony. In a brilliant piece of narrative scene-setting, the assistant shifts imperceptibly from portrait photographer to the 'directorial' role of documentary interviewer, asking them to describe themselves and their relationship. Johan, a noted professor of what we would today call cognitive psychology, half-ironically lists his abundant virtues (high intelligence, social conscience, pillar of society, devoted father, excellent lover), whereas Marianne, a family law practitioner, finds herself at a loss for words, describing herself blankly, almost anonymously, as being married to Johan and mother to two daughters.[1] As they begin to relax into the rather artificial situation of being scrutinized by the camera (the off-screen, diegetic one as well as the self-reflexive, cinematic one), they narrate the story of the modest beginnings of their romance. Theirs is a marriage of mutual consolation between two disappointed lovers who find solace in each other's company, but whose relationship can never quite shake off the sense of contingency that haunts their image of personal success. The only dissonant note is sounded at the end of their interview, on the topic of mutual disagreements. Johan suddenly releases Marianne's hand and declares his endorsement of a cynical individualism and world-weary realism, whereas Marianne quietly reiterates her belief in moral compassion and emotional sensitivity. Her gentle retort is pointedly apt: 'If we were raised as children to care more about one another,' she remarks, 'the world would be a very different place.'

This opening sequence from *Scenes From a Marriage* is a striking instance of what Mulhall calls 'film as philosophising' (2008: 3–10). In addition to Johan and Marianne's discussion of cynical individualism versus moral compassion, there is a focus on the spectators' pleasure in discovering who this couple is, what the particular tensions within their relationship might be, and a provocation concerning the unreliability of the characters' self-analysis, their performances of sincerity or authenticity, and our own investment in this cinematic 'interview' scenario. It is also a remarkable instance of 'film in the condition of philosophy': it is a framing moment in which the film questions the possibility of its own project, that of presenting a 'portrait of a marriage'; it draws attention to the self-referential paradoxes that arise by entering into the photographer's/interviewer's/director's predicament of eliciting performances for the camera that at once reveal and conceal the truth of its subjects. Precisely because of its status as film in the condition of philosophy, it also offers a suggestive way of thinking about the recent nuptials between philosophy and film. From being erstwhile foes and then indifferent strangers, philosophy and film have recently joined hands, unlikely partners providing solace to one another in a sometimes felicitous, sometimes fractious, marriage of convenience.

Recently separated from the psychoanalytic-semiotic framework of 1970s screen theory, film studies has found a new theoretical vigour and intellectual respectability in analytic philosophy and cognitivist psychology. Philosophy, facing what we might call a muted midlife crisis, mulling over its cultural relevance, has found in film an enlivening pedagogical resource, and in film studies a rejuvenating site of theoretical confusion. For distracted philosophers, here was an area of study thrillingly 'corrupted' by 'bad theory', hence badly in need of disciplinary re-education. A spirited Eliza Doolittle — think Audrey Hepburn in Cukor's *My Fair Lady* (1964) — awaiting elocution lessons and deportment training from a pompous Professor Higgins [Rex Harrison]: here was a pedagogical challenge bound to rouse the philosopher's flagging spirits! The troubling 'other' in this marriage of convenience, we might say, is the spurned paradigm of 'Grand Theory'. While dismissed by both film studies and philosophy alike, it remains a disturbing presence constantly threatening to undo the possibility of a rapprochement between these estranged partners (like Johan's jealous mistress Paula, in *Scenes From a Marriage*, who hates conflict yet cannot abide allowing Johan to visit Marianne or his children). Despite their traumatic parting and divorce, Marianne and Johan manage to maintain a fitful, yet rewarding relationship, discovering an unconventional intimacy in their occasional trysts maintained over many years.

Can the same be said of the nuptials between film and philosophy? Taking my lead from this question, I analyze the recent interest in the 'film as philosophy' thesis: the idea that film does not simply reflect philosophical themes but can engage in philosophizing, broadly construed, in an independent manner. This could be a true marriage, provided both parties are acknowledged as equals whose union preserves their particular differences. Like any marriage, it works best when film is acknowledged as equal yet different, rather than as unruly pupil or intellectual subordinate.

THE IDEA OF FILM AS PHILOSOPHY

The field of philosophical aesthetics is long accustomed to the argumentative use of exemplary works of art to illustrate a theoretical point, clarify an argument, or support an inquiry. Much work in recent philosophy of film bears out this observation, with philosophers typically adducing aptly chosen films in the course of discussing philosophically relevant topics. Indeed, philosophers have long accepted the idea that films, like other artforms, can contribute to philosophical reflection, whether by illustrating philosophical ideas, exploring situations and problems of general philosophical interest, or eliciting sophisticated criticism and analysis by suitably engaged theorists.

In recent decades, however, a bolder thesis has been advanced by a number of philosophical film theorists: the idea that film not only provides handy pedagogical illustrations or a lively stimulus to philosophical reflection, but can engage in philosophy in a manner comparable to, although differing from, philosophy itself. The best-known exponents of this view — the 'film as philosophy' thesis — would include Stanley Cavell (1979, 1981, 1996), Gilles Deleuze (1986, 1989), Stephen Mulhall (2002, 2008), Daniel Frampton (2006) and Thomas Wartenberg (2007), although each of these film-philosophers offers a distinctive version of the 'film as philosophy' thesis, whether more or less bold, moderate, or, for some, 'bogus'.

The work of Cavell and Deleuze, arguably diverse originators of a distinctive film-philosophy approach, has been continued by a host of philosophical successors. Stephen Mulhall, one of the premier Cavellians, has developed his own bold version of the 'film as philosophy' thesis (2002, 2008). For Mulhall, films can philosophize and make 'real contributions' to contemporary philosophical debates, for example, on the relation of human identity to embodiment (for which the *Aliens* quartet, the subject of Mulhall's book *On Film* (2002) is praised). To quote the best-known statement crystallizing Mulhall's 'strong' claim:

> I do not look to these films as handy or popular illustrations of views and arguments properly developed by philosophers; I see them rather as themselves reflecting on and evaluating such views and arguments, as thinking seriously and systematically about them in just the ways that philosophers do. Such films are not philosophy's raw material, nor a source for its ornamentation; they are philosophical exercises, philosophy in action — film as philosophizing. (Mulhall 2002: 2)

This claim has provoked a storm of debate and disputation, some philosophers applauding Mulhall's championing of an "open border" between philosophy and art, notably literature, drama and film, others denouncing this claim as a sophistical attempt to elevate artistically dubious popular entertainment to the lofty heights of 'professional' philosophy (see Baggini 2003; Russell 2006). As we shall see, it is the claim that Paisley Livingston (2006) attacks directly in his deflationary critique of the very idea of film as philosophy. For the moment, however, I note that Mulhall, inspired by Cavell, is urging us to consider the merits of popular films and film genres as vehicles for philosophical reflection, engagement, even argumentation, broadly construed. Thus Mulhall analyzes at length how the *Alien* quartet — Ridley Scott's original (1979), James Cameron's *Aliens* (1986), David Fincher's *Alien³* (1992), and Jean-Pierre Jeunet's *Alien Resurrection* (1997) — not only make philosophically noteworthy contributions to our understanding of human identity, embodiment, horror, sexuality, gender, technology, nature and mortality, but also engage in complex and sophisticated self-reflection on their status as cinematic fictions, the relationship between original and sequel, the question of artistic inheritance, and the significance of the 'star' in film narrative and audience reception (2002).

In the second edition of *On Film* (2008), Mulhall develops and extends this line of film-philosophical inquiry by offering a reading of Spielberg's *Minority Report* (2002) as a meditation on the question of moral agency. The film, for Mulhall, is a complex science fiction/crime thriller response to the hypothetical challenge of a scientific/spiritual concept of predetermination versus our faith in human openness towards the future. At the same time, the film is a metafilmic reflection on the future of cinema as a 'memory of the future' (not to mention an intriguing commentary on Tom Cruise's ambivalent status as popular star, and the varieties of cinematic 'punishment' to which his narcissistic screen persona is frequently subjected). Mulhall also analyzes at length the three *Mission: Impossible* films (directed by Brian de Palma (1996), John Woo (2000) and J. J. Abrams (2006) respectively), exploring the complex shifts in identity undergone by Tom Cruise's character in relation to screen persona, visual physiognomy, bodily performance, and the translation of televisual into cinematic worlds. Whether this trilogy of stylistically impressive, kinetically charged and generically sophisticated films bears the weight of Mulhall's brilliant critical ruminations is left for the reader, or dedicated viewer of the *Mission: Impossible* franchise, to decide.

In any event, for Mulhall, the film and philosophy relationship can take at least three forms, all of which may be present in philosophically sophisticated films: (1) films can reflect upon, question, even contribute to our understanding of significant philosophical questions or problems ('films as philosophizing'); (2) films can question or explore the nature of the cinematic medium in a manner comparable to philosophy ('philosophy of film'); and (3) films can reflect upon their own conditions of possibility or their own status as cinematic fictions — for example, as comprising a series of sequels within an inherited genre ('films in the condition of philosophy') (2002, 2008: 1–11). We should note that these are not hard and fast distinctions, and that films counting as 'philosophical' often engage in all three forms of philosophical reflection. Crucial to Mulhall's Cavellian-inspired film-philosophy is that such claims are not to be defended by general arguments over the 'film as philosophy' thesis, but by detailed analyses and critical interpretations of the films themselves. For Mulhall, as for Cavell, this is the only way to debate, argue, or defend the claims made for their philosophical significance (for example, whether they can reflect on the 'dialectic of originality and inheritance' inherent to the composition of cinematic sequels).

This point, as Mulhall complains, has been rather lost on his philosophical critics, who persist in identifying his film-philosophical approach as the application of a stand-alone methodology or independent theoretical argument. Such is the case, for example, with Paisley Livingston (2006), who avoids any detailed engagement with Mulhall's readings of the *Alien* quartet, opting instead to refute Mulhall's claims through general arguments or theoretical criticisms (as I shall address shortly). From Mulhall's perspective, however, it is the 'priority of the particular' (2008: 129 ff) that matters in aesthetics and in philosophy of film more specifically, assuming that we wish to do justice to the aesthetic complexities of film, and to entertain the possibility that films can philosophize. To do so, however, also demands that we remain open to the kind of self-questioning that philosophy generally demands of other disciplines, and indeed should demand of itself. Such self-questioning, in which philosophy is put into question via its encounter with film, is not what we find in critics of Muhall's approach to film-philosophy. To be sure, the more conventional 'philosophy of film' certainly depends upon critical arguments and theoretical claims aiming at the highest level of generality. Cavellian or Mulhallian film-philosophy, on the other hand, prioritizes the particular, responds aesthetically to the singularities of the work, and develops its argumentative claims on the basis of philosophically informed film criticism (as I shall attempt to do in Part III of this book).

THE FILM AS PHILOSOPHY THESIS: BOLD, MODERATE, OR BOGUS?

An oft-recited criticism of some approaches to the film-philosophy relationship, reiterated by Mulhall (2002: 2; 2008: 4), is that they take films as 'mere illustrations' of philosophical ideas, and so cannot be counted as instances of film-as-philosophy in the proper sense. Thomas Wartenberg (2007: 32–54), however, has argued persuasively against the presumption that illustration cannot be a valid philosophical role for film to play. On the contrary, Wartenberg argues, there are many ways in which films can be philosophical. They can serve as critical illustrations of a complex philosophical thesis (Chaplin's *Modern Times* (1936) as an illustration of Marx's theory of alienation and exploitation within capitalist society) (Wartenberg 2007: 44–54). They can articulate complex philosophical thought experiments (the Wachowski Brothers' *The Matrix* (1999) as an experiment — for characters and viewers — in Cartesian radical scepticism) (Wartenberg 2007: 57–75). They can argue against a philosophical thesis by presenting a filmic counterexample (Gondry/Kaufman's *Eternal Sunshine of the Spotless Mind* (2004) as a counterexample to utilitarian moral philosophy) (Wartenberg 2007: 76–93). They can both illustrate a philosophical theory and present a cinematic thought experiment (Carol Reed's *The Third Man* (1949) as an exploration of our moral intelligence and critical response to Aristotle's theory of friendship) (Wartenberg 2007: 94–116). And they can also perform varieties of self-reflection on the nature of the cinematic medium (structural avant-garde films such as Warhol's *Empire* (1964) and Tony Conrad's *The Flicker* (1965) as foregrounding the background that ordinarily remains unremarked in our experience of film (Wartenberg 2007: 117–132)). Wartenberg adopts a pragmatist, local rather than global approach, arguing that the link between film and philosophy should be demonstrated in a variety of particular cases, showing the various ways in which they can be philosophically significant, the diverse ways in which philosophy can be screened. Nonetheless, Wartenberg argues, we should reject the 'extreme' version of the 'film as philosophy' thesis presented by Mulhall (that films philosophize in 'just the ways philosophers do'), and defend instead the more modest claim that they can engage in a variety of philosophical explorations of film — via suggestive illustration, thought experiment, counterexample and self-reflection — in ways that contribute to enhancing our understanding of both film and philosophy.

Not all philosophers of film, however, are convinced that film can be philosophical in the ways that Mulhall and Wartenberg claim. Paisley Livingston (2006), for example, has articulated a powerful critique of the idea of film as philosophy, targeting in particular the 'bold thesis', as he puts it, that 'films make creative contributions to philosophical knowledge, and this by means exclusive to the cinematic medium' (2006: 11). Having undertaken a critique of this bold thesis, either for positing an ineffable cinematic contribution that cannot be articulated discursively, or for having a philosophical content that is fundamentally dependent on pre-existing philosophical ideas, Livingston advocates a modest version of the claim that films, nonetheless, can contribute to philosophy; namely, either as helpful pedagogical illustrations, or as stimulating examples for the hard work of philosophical analysis (2006, 2008). We should note here Livingston's emphasis on 'philosophical knowledge', the *epistemic* aspect of the bold thesis, as well as his requirement that this contribution be *exclusive* to the cinematic medium (the 'exclusivity thesis') (2006: 11–12). The bold (epistemic) thesis includes, furthermore, two key constituents: (1) an account of which *exclusive capacities* of film are capable of making a special contribution to philosophy; and (2) an insistence on the *significance* and *independence* of this epistemic contribution, where this contribution does more than reflect general philosophical themes or ideas. Indeed, a bona fide case of film-as-philosophy, for Livingston, would be one that realizes a historically innovative contribution to recognized philosophical debate on a given topic, and does so in an independent manner; that is, where the communication of the film's philosophical contribution 'would not be dependent on a subsequent paraphrase' (2006: 11).

The point here is that, in order to fulfil the bold thesis, a film cannot be just a skilful rehearsal or novel illustration of familiar philosophical themes. That a film might explore well-known philosophical ideas — to do with morality, existence, love, or metaphysics — would not suffice for the film to count as independently philosophical. It would have to make independent philosophical points or claims in a distinctively cinematic manner, and articulate such points or claims in a way that goes beyond 'mere illustration', pedagogical instruction or theoretical platitude (as some critics argue is the case with the *Matrix* trilogy or with the *Alien* quartet).[2]

Like Wartenberg, Livingston will defend a moderate version of the 'film as philosophy' thesis, but insists on a much stronger degree of philosophical intention on the part of the filmmakers. He insists, furthermore, on the way that this independent contribution must use specifically cinematic means in order to achieve its philosophical aspirations. This constraint is underlined in order to rule out cases where a philosopher might be filmed delivering a philosophical lecture; such a film recording (as we might find on YouTube, for example) might well communicate philosophical content, but not by means exclusive to the cinematic medium (it could equally be delivered verbally, in audio recording, or as a written text). Livingston summarises the bold thesis on film-as-philosophy thus: it refers to 'the idea that films do make historically innovative and independent contributions to philosophy by means exclusive to the cinematic medium or art form' (2006: 12).

Having outlined the 'bold thesis', however, Livingston argues that it falls foul of 'an insoluble problem of paraphrase' that takes the form of a 'fatal dilemma' (2006: 12). Either the philosophical content of a film cannot be paraphrased, hence remains ineffable or incommunicable, which means that doubts can be raised about its existence or its intelligibility (since communicability and rationality are required for a thought or idea to count as philosophical), or the film's philosophical significance can be so paraphrased, in which case it is not exclusive to film or has no necessary connection with film as an artistic medium (and might indeed be better expressed philosophically, which is to say, linguistically). Even if we moderate the requirement of exclusivity (that the philosophical contribution of film must be expressible in a manner exclusively bound up with the medium of film), this nonetheless leads to a *reductio* or trivialisation of the 'film as philosophy' thesis, for in this case any filmic recording of a philosopher presenting a philosophical paper or engaging in a philosophical discussion (French philosopher Alain Badiou being interviewed on the BBC TV current affairs programme *Hard Talk*, for example) would count as an instance of 'film as philosophy'.[3] Here, however, the philosophical content seems in no way dependent upon its delivery via the medium of film, since a sound recording or verbatim transcription would presumably convey the same content equally well.

If one were to reject this approach, however, and to argue instead that the 'properly cinematic' philosophical contribution of the film resists paraphrase (that it can be referred to but not stated in words), then doubts arise, Livingston argues, as to the validity of the philosophical insights purportedly being expressed by the film. Appeals to a cinematic *je ne sais quoi* (Livingston 2006: 13) that a philosophically inclined viewer claims to have experienced will remain doubtful if it cannot be further explicated with reference to reasons or arguments to justify the claims being made. Such esoteric philosophical insight thus remains either stubbornly subjective or untenably dogmatic; hence it cannot be adduced as plausible evidence supporting the 'bold epistemic thesis', namely that it 'has significantly advanced philosophical knowledge' (Livingston 2006: 13) in a manner exclusively dependent upon the medium of film.

One might nonetheless want to argue that such cinematic insights *can* be paraphrased, where a 'paraphrase' is 'the result of an attempt to provide an interpretative statement or thinking through of that item's meanings' (Livingston 2006: 13). In this case, however, we would be admitting that the relationship between film and philosophy is one in which film is dispensable; that is, we need not refer to the film itself but could simply rely on the paraphrase in order to reveal the film's philosophical content. Film, on this view, would be shown to depend upon language in order to communicate its philosophical insights; but philosophy has no need of film in order to do the same. The result is that philosophy maintains its position of epistemic superiority. Thus, for Livingston, philosophy can happily regard film as providing 'pedagogically useful illustrations or evocations of previously published philosophical reasonings' (2006: 13), but it cannot regard film as capable of philosophizing in its own right. A film that attempted to explore, in an artistically sophisticated manner, philosophical ideas or the life and work of a particular philosopher — say, Derek Jarman's *Wittgenstein* (1993) — would still depend, Livingston avers, upon 'linguistically articulated background thoughts that are mobilized in both the creation and interpretation of the film's philosophical significance' (2006: 13). In these cases, films remain parasitically dependent upon philosophy, whereas philosophy can exist and assert itself independently of film (or any other artform). The sceptical lesson to be drawn from this fatal problem of paraphrase, Livingston concludes, is that 'the cinematic display's contribution *to philosophy* can be neither independent nor historically innovative — as the bold thesis would have it' (2006: 14).

Does this mean that Plato was right to demand the banishment of the poets (or filmmakers) from the rationally governed city? Not quite. In his recent study of the films of Ingmar Bergman, Livingston argues, rather, that we need only drop the bold thesis; that is, reject any exclusivity requirements concerning film's philosophical contribution and any strict epistemic constraints concerning its capacity to advance philosophical knowledge. The right alternative, Livingston contends, is a more moderate 'film as philosophy' thesis, according to which we reject the haughty dismissal of film as 'merely illustrative', but also avoid the bold claims that films can philosophize in their own right. Instead, we should embrace the more modest view that film can be a welcome helpmeet to philosophy, providing lively examples conducive to pedagogical instruction, or stimulating source material for the conceptual work of analysis and argument. This rather deflationary conclusion is a good example of what we might call the *philosophical disenfranchisement* of film: philosophy's inveterate tendency to subordinate art as an inferior way of knowing, one that is theoretically completed by philosophy proper (see Sinnerbrink 2010, 2011). In the difficult marriage between philosophy and film, philosophy 'wears the trousers' (to use J. L. Austin's rather off-colour phrase), deciding the terms of engagement and judging the worthiness of its cinematic partner in the mirror of philosophy's own standards.

In order to forestall charges of philosophical disenfranchisement, however, Livingston has recently conceded the possibility that films might make a modest philosophical contribution of their own in special cases. Adapting what he describes as a 'moderate' (though actually very strong) 'intentionalist' thesis on art (namely that the meaning of an artwork depends upon grasping the artist's demonstrable intentions), he argues (2009b) that films *can* be regarded as philosophizing, provided we can show — using verifiable textual or biographical evidence external to the film itself — that the author/director intended to explore identifiable philosophical ideas in an artistically serious way.

Livingston's case study here is the cinema of Ingmar Bergman, long regarded as one of the most philosophical of modernist European directors. Indeed Bergman has traditionally been interpreted as exploring existentialist themes in a distinctively cinematic style, and has often been aligned with the thought of Kierkegaard and Nietzsche, not to mention the dramas of Ibsen and Strindberg. If there were ever an uncontroversial candidate for the title of 'cinematic philosopher' — to quote the title of Irving Singer's recent philosophical study (2007) — it is surely Ingmar Bergman.

Livingston's novel contribution to Bergman criticism, however, is to argue that there is little evidence to link Bergman's films or concerns as an artist with Kierkegaard, for example, or post-war French existentialism (Sartre and Camus). Despite some minor biographical evidence of familiarity, Bergman apparently did not engage much with Kierkegaard's link to 'Danish Hegelianism', as Livingston remarks, and only ever staged one Camus play (*Caligula*) in his youth (and that as an anti-establishment provocation) (2009a: 560–1). Given the paucity of demonstrable biographical or external evidence in their favour, the standard 'existentialist' interpretations of Bergman, or even Christian-Lutheran ones, remain little more, Livingston claims, than speculative surmises or vague interpretative conjectures.

Be that as it may, there is a thinker who Bergman himself claims as a major influence: the little-known Finnish positivist and psychologist, Eino Kaila.[4] Since we have here, according to Livingston, a demonstrable case where an artist was influenced by a philosopher's work, and intentionally sought to realize these ideas, we can confidently assert that this is a bona fide case of film-as-philosophy. Confirmation of this claim, for Livingston, can be found in the way that Bergman's films evince a sophisticated engagement with Kaila's ideas on the irrational sources of desire and action, and on the ineluctable conflict attending most human relationships. On Livingston's view, Bergman's *The Seventh Seal* (1957) or *Scenes From a Marriage*, for that matter, are 'philosophical' only insofar as they are intentional efforts to express, or even go beyond, philosophical ideas that Bergman derived from his study of Kaila (2009b).

There are a number of objections that we can raise concerning Livingston's 'modest proposal'. The first concerns the overly demanding 'intentionalist' account of art at work in his argument. Artistic (and philosophical) meaning, for Livingston, is anchored exclusively within the author's explicit intentions; but this ignores the contextual and cultural-historical dimensions of the work's production, as well as the active role of audiences, viewers or critics in interpreting the work. The second is Livingston's dismissal of the possibility that intentionality can be displayed *within the work itself*; that we can impute an artistic or, for that matter, philosophical intention to a work in order to make sense of its cinematic, narrative or thematic structure or elements. We can do this (and often have no other choice if we are to interpret the work) regardless of whether we can demonstrate that the filmmaker (or screenwriter) *explicitly* intended to make a philosophical point or realize a philosophical idea. Thirdly, Livingston assumes, furthermore, that novelists, dramatists or filmmakers can only adopt, translate or apply philosophical ideas that are derived from their reading of an accepted philosopher's works. This assumption, however, begs the question of whether film can be philosophical. For the question at issue is whether there are *independent* ways in which films can 'screen philosophy'. Livingston, however, claims that the only way to do so is by construing film as *dependent* on a philosophical author's ideas, which the filmmaker then attempts to portray; but this is to prejudge the ways in which it might be possible for film to be, or be regarded as, independently philosophical, and therefore cuts dead the film-as-philosophy 'debate' before it has even begun.

These objections raise a more general concern about how we should approach the film-philosophy relationship. We might ask on what grounds we should accept that the philosophical contribution of a film (or any other work of art) depends on locating a philosophical source that the filmmaker intended to realize in making the film. Why assume that films can be philosophical only if a critical interpretation can be anchored in an already recognized philosophical position? Would Bergman's films be any less philosophical if we acknowledged that Ibsen and Strindberg were equally important dramatic and philosophical sources for his films? On Livingston's view, Bergman is philosophical because of Kaila's influence *as a philosopher*, and because of Bergman's elaboration of Kaila's theoretical views. There are, of course, more obvious cases of direct philosophical influence on a filmmaker's work: Eisenstein's Hegelian-Marxist dialectics, Godard's Brechtian-Marxism, Hitchcock's Catholic-Freudianism, the Wachowski Brothers' allusions to Jean Baudrillard in *The Matrix* (see Constable 2009), and so on. On Livingston's view, however, very few filmmakers would qualify as cinematic philosophers, since it is rare to find philosophical sources being explicitly cited or deliberately portrayed in movies.

On the other hand, it is not impossible. Some philosophers, for example, have maintained that the films of Terrence Malick — a former student of Stanley Cavell's, translator of Martin Heidegger, and inheritor of American transcendentalist thought — can also be regarded as philosophical because of their realisation of phenomenological, existentialist and transcendentalist themes (see Clewis 2003; Davies 2009b; Furstenau and MacEvoy 2007; Silverman 2003). Showing that Bergman was impressed by Kaila's philosophy, or that Malick's films evoke Heideggerian themes, however, does not mean that these philosophical sources therefore determine the meaning — or philosophical contribution — of these filmmakers' superlative works. Rather, it is in the artist's creative appropriation and reworking of inherited cultural sources that we find and acknowledge the work's aesthetic and philosophical achievements. The point is less about the *origin* of the philosophical influence than the *originality* of the film's treatment of culturally inherited ideas.

It is not in the critical detection of artistic intention, but in the *aesthetic transformation* of these intentions, that we find the film's original and independent philosophical contribution.

Bergman's *Persona* (1966) can be interpreted as 'existentialist', I would suggest, not simply because Bergman read and was impressed by Kaila but because of the cinematic originality of Bergman's aesthetic treatment of existentialist themes — and this applies whether or not the filmmaker expresses any such philosophical intention (as many filmmakers refuse to do), or where such philosophical sources are absent, questionable or obscure (as is typically the case in the interpretation of artists' intentions). Livingston's attempt to anchor the philosophical contribution of the film in the intentions of its author is philosophical film criticism masquerading as theoretical argument. Ironically, this is one of the theoretical sins for which the much-maligned 'Grand Theory' was so roundly castigated.

MARITAL CRISIS: SAVING THE FILM AS PHILOSOPHY THESIS

There have been a number of ingenious responses to Livingston's critique of the idea of film as philosophy. Accepting the basic terms of Livingston's argument, Aaron Smuts has defended a modified version of the 'bold thesis' concerning film as philosophy (2009a), arguing that Livingston's 'insoluble problem' of paraphrase *can* be resolved, provided we accept a more generous conception of what counts as a philosophically significant contribution (namely that films can provide 'reasons to believe' a philosophical argument, and do so by specifically cinematic means, rather than Livingston's more theoretically onerous 'historically innovative contribution to philosophical knowledge'). Smuts agrees with Wartenberg (2007) that films can make significant contributions to our understanding of philosophical problems and arguments through their creative use and innovative staging of complex thought experiments. The latter enable us to test our intuitions, discover inconsistencies in our assumptions or convictions, and can provide counterexamples to theoretical claims or arguments. According to Smuts, however, the 'film as thought experiment' position is still open to the objection that it is not the film so much as the *interpreter* who is doing the philosophizing (for example, providing the relevant interpretation of *The Matrix* showing how the fictional scenario presented in the film might be used in a philosophical argument concerning scepticism).[5]

Defending a version of the 'bold thesis', Smuts argues that we can show how (some) films are capable of producing arguments, provided we accept a generous enough definition of them, and suggests that an argument be taken as an articulated train of thought providing reasons in support of a conclusion (2009a: 413). Smuts' showcase counterexample of a film 'doing' philosophy is the 'God and Country' sequence in Sergei Eisenstein's *October* (1922), a sequence that presents, through Eisenstein's famous use of dialectical-intellectual montage, an analogical argument concerning the vacuity of religious idols across different cultures, and hence provides reasons supporting the sequence's intended atheist-materialist conclusion (2009a: 414–17).[6] Although Smuts provides a persuasive counterexample to Livingston's claim that films cannot 'do' philosophy, he accepts uncritically the terms of Livingston's account of the 'problem of paraphrase', in particular the claim that films are philosophical only if they can be paraphrased into suitably philosophical terms. Smuts shows that it does not follow from Livingston's argument that films cannot make a philosophical contribution by cinematic means, but he neglects to consider whether the account of philosophical paraphrase on which Livingston's argument relies is plausible.

PHILOSOPHICAL PARAPHRASE: PROBLEM OR HERESY?

Here I would like to question Livingston's account of the problem of paraphrase (an inversion of Cleanth Brooks' 'heresy of paraphrase'), as well as the conception of the film-philosophy relationship that his position assumes.[7] One of the problems with Livingston's argument lies in its assumption that the relationship between film and philosophy is essentially *epistemic*; namely, whether films can make medium-specific and linguistically independent contributions to 'philosophical knowledge' (2006: 15) concerning well-established issues such as 'personal identity, freedom, meta-ethics, moral dilemmas, or epistemology' (2006: 13). As Murray Smith, Wartenberg and Smuts remark, Livingston sets the standard for film making a philosophical contribution implausibly high (as though a film would count as philosophical only if its content were deemed publishable by a top international journal!). Why assume that a film's contribution to philosophy only concerns epistemic claims or furthering philosophical knowledge? As Stephen Mulhall and other philosophers have suggested, the philosophical contribution film can make is more akin to *showing* rather than saying: to questioning, reflecting, or disclosing through vivid redescription salient aspects of a situation, problem or experience, typically through the artful use of narrative, performance or cinematic presentation (montage, performance, visual style or metafilmic reflection). Film contributes to questioning or rendering problematic the background assumptions that we draw upon in framing specific arguments or making philosophical claims, whether on generally recognized themes or on what we might understand film to be.

The issue of paraphrase, however, merits further reflection. Livingston defines 'paraphrase' as providing an interpretation of the film's (philosophical) meaning (2006: 13). A film can be philosophical, indeed contribute to philosophy, insofar as we can paraphrase its content into a suitably philosophical interpretation. If we admit this possibility, however, then we are in conflict with the 'exclusivity thesis' — the view that the philosophical contribution at issue be communicated by exclusively cinematic means. Livingston's fallback position, as we have seen, is to admit that *some* films can be said to philosophize, provided we can demonstrate the filmmaker's intention to realize a recognized philosophical idea (such as Bergman with Kaila).

Let us consider some relevant examples of philosophical paraphrase: Livingston claims that 'Bergman's films are replete with characterizations informed by the perspective on human irrationality and conflict that Kaila codified in his treatise on philosophical psychology' (2009a: 566–7). Andras Balint Kovács claims that Tarkovsky's films express the tradition of Russian Christian personalist philosophy (notably the work of Nikolai Berdyaev): the cinema, for Tarkovsky, was 'a particularly vivid and powerful tool to represent the struggle of the spiritual person to prevail in a world where everything from politics to science and consumer culture denies its existence' (Kovács 2009: 590). Or consider Lars von Trier's *The Five Obstructions* (2003): a maverick filmmaker/character called 'Lars von Trier' (played by von Trier) challenges his filmmaker-mentor 'Jørgen Leth' (played by Leth) to remake one of Leth's early experimental films (*The Perfect Human* 1967), under increasingly demanding rules, or 'obstructions', imposed by the von Trier character, with 'von Trier' making the fifth and final 'Jørgen Leth' film himself. Mette Hjort paraphrases *The Five Obstructions* as thus providing 'a demonstration of the philosophical thesis that creativity finds a condition of possibility in constraint' (Hjort 2009: 637).

In each case, we have a philosophical paraphrase of a cinematic work, one that 'translates' its philosophical significance or contribution into a recognizable philosophical discourse or thesis. What Livingston calls 'paraphrase', then, is another way of saying philosophical *interpretation*; one that stakes a claim to capturing and translating the philosophical 'essence' of the film in question. How is the validity of such philosophical paraphrasing to be decided?

Here I would like to make a more general argument concerning the problem of paraphrase in cases where we are concerned with the idea of 'film as philosophy'. It is neither obvious nor uncontestable to claim that such paraphrases can readily capture a film's philosophical contribution. This is so whether we then take such paraphrases as violating the so-called 'exclusivity thesis' (as Livingston argues), or as confirming the film's philosophical contribution (as Smuts argues). For we are not dealing here with an argumentative claim so much as an *interpretative proposal*: a 'philosophical paraphrase' is not a theoretical claim about a film's philosophical content, but an interpretive claim or instance of philosophical film criticism. Such philosophical interpretations, however, are open to challenge and contestation; there are many ways in which a film might be paraphrased or interpreted, and it is not obvious by what criteria we decide between competing philosophical interpretations. This implies that the question of a film's philosophical contribution, indeed the very idea of film as philosophy, depends upon the philosophical interpretations of the films in question. We can only 'demonstrate' whether a film makes a philosophical contribution by offering aesthetically receptive, hermeneutically defensible and philosophically original interpretations of the films in question.[8] The 'film as philosophy' thesis is less a matter of theoretical argument (concerning, for example, the paradoxes of philosophical paraphrase) than of critical reflection and debate concerning competing interpretations of relevant films.

In sum, the only way to justify that a film has philosophized, or illustrated a philosophical idea, or exists in the condition of philosophy, is by way of a contestable philosophical interpretation of that film. Hence the validation of the 'film as philosophy' thesis depends upon our accepting that interpretation, or engaging in philosophical criticism concerning the merits of competing interpretations; and to do this, moreover, we will have to engage with aesthetic, hermeneutic and other relevant criteria that fall outside the domain of philosophical argumentation, narrowly construed. In sum, we can only defend the 'film as philosophy' thesis by inter-disciplinary means; that is, by offering contestable philosophical interpretations rather than relying solely on general arguments. This is essentially a restatement and defence of Mulhall's claims for the 'priority of the particular' in performing film-philosophy.

The idea of film as philosophy thus raises the question of what counts as 'philosophy'. It prompts us to consider the ways in which the encounter between film and philosophy might help us overturn the traditional Platonic prejudice against art. Many critics of the film-as-philosophy idea, however, miss this opportunity to deal with the marital discord in their midst. Like Johan and Marianne, the marriage between philosophy and film remains calm, orderly and secure, provided that one partner dominates the epistemic agenda or sets the terms of (interpretive) engagement for the other. Hardly a recipe for marital bliss! Yet the film-philosophy encounter also points to another possibility: reinventing this relationship, overturning the hierarchy between philosophy and art, emancipating both partners through a genuine meeting of minds. How this more felicitous encounter between film and philosophy might work is the subject of Part III of this book.[9]

PART III: CINEMATIC THINKING

Having examined the analytic-cognitivist turn (Part I), and new approaches defining contemporary philosophies of film (Part II), Part III of this book attempts to put into practice the film-philosophy approach explored in the preceding two chapters. Film-philosophy emphasizes the importance of aesthetic responsiveness to particular films, defending whatever theoretical claims one might make with reference to the kind of film-philosophical readings that one offers. I take as my guide here, as argued in Chapter 6, Mulhall's idea of 'the priority of the particular' (2008: 129 ff): the idea that the claims made in film-philosophy cannot be decided purely on theoretical grounds but require, as Cavell also argues, recourse to philosophical film criticism (1981: 1–42; 1996: 3–45); the testing of one's aesthetic engagement with particular films against philosophical reflection. I also draw on Deleuze's claim that cinema can enact a 'shock to thought' (1989: 189–224): that it performs a cinematic thinking in images that both challenges and resists philosophy, provoking us to think in response to what film enables us to experience, without, however, reducing cinema to a mere reflection of a philosophical thesis or framework. Taken together, these ideas present the most promising guides to performing what I am calling (romantic) film-philosophy.

Although Cavell and Mulhall (as well as Peretz 2008) have chosen popular genres and films for their philosophical readings, I have chosen more obviously art cinema/crossover (or generically hybrid) films: David Lynch's *INLAND EMPIRE* (2006), Lars von Trier's *Antichrist* (2009), and Terrence Malick's *The New World* (2005). One can imagine a straightforward criticism of this approach. By deliberately choosing 'art films', a critic might object, you are skewing the film-philosophy relationship in favour of 'philosophy' by avoiding, in typically 'elitist' fashion, the need to deal with popular genres and films. Such 'elitism', our critic might continue, simply reproduces the kind of philosophical disenfranchisement of film that you claim is overturned by the film-philosophy approach. Even if you were able to show that some films can 'do' philosophy, our critic might continue, say art films that may or may not have such philosophical pretensions, this would not show that 'film in general' can be philosophical, which is presumably what philosophical readings of popular genres and films intend to show.[1]

Mulhall (2008), for example, defends his choice of films belonging to popular genres by arguing that, if one can show that films such as *Mission: Impossible* can be taken seriously as philosophy, then the same can be said, *a fortiori,* for films and auteurs belonging to the 'philosophical canon' (say Bergman, Godard, Tarkovsky, Antonioni, Malick, *Rashomon, The Thin Red Line, Memento, Being John Malkovich,* and so on). While I take Mulhall's point, there is no reason therefore to avoid responding to such films, especially when they are among the most challenging and rewarding instances of 'philosophical' cinema, and there is no reason to assume that the 'film as philosophy' thesis must be made a fully general claim. Indeed, it may be that there are only singular instances of filmmaking that elicit suitably 'philosophical' forms of criticism. Like aesthetic value, philosophical value may be an evaluative, rather than 'objective', property of individual works; more a matter of acknowledging and appreciating than detecting and determining.

In any event, I would admit that there is a degree of 'elitism' (more a moralising accusation than a philosophical objection) in choosing certain films rather than others — exercising one's aesthetic or philosophical tastes cannot help but be so. This is an 'elitism', however, that is plural and open-ended; an 'elitism' of aesthetic, artistic and philosophical achievement, rather than pernicious ideological exclusion. Excellence in cinematic art can be achieved in many ways, in many styles, and in many genres (in popular romance as much as experimental film, in horror as much as documentary, in self-reflective art film as much as action or science fiction genres). Moreover, as Cavell remarks (1979: 219), films that take the condition of film as their subject enjoy an inherent philosophical advantage or greater degree of self-understanding than other less self-aware or self-questioning works. It is only fitting that films inviting the viewer to think, to feel, and to question, should have their invitations accepted.

I would add that there is also an *ethical* decision at stake in devoting time and thought to films that deliberately take the path less chosen, that question established conventions, and that experiment with evoking news ways of thinking and feeling. In a global cultural and economic marketplace dominated by certain types of stories or ideological points of view, there is ethical purpose in devoting attention to the more marginal, more questioning, more aesthetically and intellectually demanding films that one encounters.[2]

Why choose these three particular films for more extended reflection? There are three main reasons: (1) these are films in which the filmmakers explore non-mainstream narrative, while engaging, more or less critically, with the Hollywood tradition; (2) these films are generic hybrids (blending genres in novel, aesthetically challenging ways), which also explore a variety of issues or themes of philosophical interest, including their own status as cinematic works; finally, (3) these are films that display a striking 'resistance to theory', which makes them challenging test cases to explore the hypothesis of *cinematic thinking* — a non-conceptual or affective thinking in images that resists cognitive closure or theoretical subsumption. Generically hybrid films such as these — spanning art film, cinematic metafiction, Hollywood noir, psychological horror, historico-mythic epic, and romance genres — provide an excellent occasion for the exploration of cinematic thinking by way of detailed film-philosophical criticism.

CHAPTER SEVEN

HOLLYWOOD IN TROUBLE: DAVID LYNCH'S *INLAND EMPIRE*

Can films philosophize? This question has exercised many philosophical film theorists (Frampton 2006: 183–203; Wartenberg 2007,
Mulhall 2008: 3–11, 129 ff), with most critical debates centring on
the philosophical status of narrative film (as illustration of ideas,
as thought-experiment, as cinematic self-reflection on the medium,
and so on). Few philosophers, however, have questioned whether
the way philosophy is understood might be transformed through
its encounter with film. From the perspective of film-philosophy,
however, this is one of the decisive questions raised by this encounter.
From this point of view, works of cinematic art do not generally
make abstract universal claims in theoretical or argumentative terms.
Rather, they aesthetically (that is to say, cinematically) disclose novel
aspects of experience, question given elements of our practices or
normative frameworks, challenge established ways of seeing, and
open up new paths for thinking. The philosophical dimensions of
film, on this view, are enacted or performed rather than posited or
proven, which implies, as I argued in Chapter 6, that the question
of 'film as philosophy' cannot be decided by theoretical argument
alone. Rather, the only way to establish reliably, and contestably, that
particular films can be philosophical is by translating the kind of
experience they afford into aesthetically receptive and theoretically
inflected film criticism.

Instead of arguing, however, that bringing philosophical reflection
to popular film genres shows how such films can be philosophical,
I would like to explore the reverse scenario: responding to films —
such as Lynch's *INLAND EMPIRE* (2006) — that both provoke and
resist philosophical reflection. Such films, of varying provenance,

genre, style and commercial popularity, have aesthetic and cinematic qualities that prompt an experience conducive to thought; films that provoke, incite, or force us to think, even if we remain uncertain as to what kind of thinking (or writing) might be adequate to such an experience. These are films that 'resist theory', evoking an experience that is aesthetic and reflective, yet where the former cannot be reduced to, or even overwhelms, the latter. Such films communicate an experience of thinking that resists philosophical translation or paraphrase; thus they are films where we encounter what I am calling *cinematic thinking* in its most intensive and dramatic forms.

'A WOMAN IN TROUBLE'

One such film is David Lynch's *INLAND EMPIRE* (2006), Lynch's first feature since his critically acclaimed *Mulholland Drive* (2001). Recalling the experimental character of his debut feature, *Eraserhead* (1976), *INLAND EMPIRE* is notable for a number of reasons. It announces Lynch's farewell to film, being entirely shot on digital video (a low-tech Sony PD-150) and then transferred to 35mm film (see Lynch 2006: 149, 153). It was filmed without a finished script, using an intuitive, improvisatory approach (the original idea came from a fourteen-page monologue written by Lynch and performed by Laura Dern in two long takes over seventy minutes). It combined fragmentary elements from various short experimental videos that Lynch had recently made (using digital video) and posted on his website (for example, the *Rabbits* vignettes) (see McTaggart 2010: 141–5). It eschewed the lush cinematic quality of *Mulholland Drive*, embracing instead a 'primitive' video aesthetic — amateurish, televisual, disorienting but also experimental (the striking use of lens flare, blinding light, and images of facial distortion from the subtle to the grotesque). The film explicitly draws on Lynch's decades-long practice of transcendental meditation (TM), interest in Eastern thought and religion (particularly the *Upanishads*) and recent cultural activism (setting up the David Lynch Foundation with the aim of introducing TM practices to troubled schools). Like *Mulholland Drive* and other classic metafictions (Wilder's *Sunset Boulevard* and Godard's *Contempt* [*Le Mépris*]), it extends Lynch's critical reflections on the corruption of the grand Hollywood tradition and offers a plea for the renewal of Hollywood's complex relationship with European art film traditions. Like the other filmmakers I shall discuss (von

Trier and Malick), Lynch has maintained a critical relationship with Hollywood throughout his career, working both with and against the Hollywood system, exploring an alternative path of cinematic art that remains in critical dialogue with Hollywood narrative. From this point of view, *INLAND EMPIRE* could be described, in Cavell's apt phrase (referring to Makavejev's appropriation of Bergman), as an act of 'criticism by images': a film that makes the significance — indeed the *question* — of film its subject (2005: 17). We might call this *cinematic criticism* or film-*as*-criticism; a sophisticated version of film-as-philosophy (what Mulhall calls 'film in the condition of philosophy'); namely, film reflecting upon its own nature, possibility and prospects in a distinctively cinematic manner.

Finally, *INLAND EMPIRE* represents the apogee of Lynch's fascination with feminine performance. I mention here the sequence of performances linking Patricia Arquette's melancholy *femme fatale* double-act in *Lost Highway* (1997); Naomi Watts' uncanny doubling of Hollywood starlet and Babylon victim in *Mulholland Drive*; and Laura Dern's traumatic dissociation into multiple intersecting characters, from successful but fading Hollywood star (Nikki Grace), brittle Southerner (Susan Blue), to traumatised survivor undergoing a psychic breakdown (the Battered Woman). Nikki Grace/Susan Blue/the Battered Woman coalesce in the film's most traumatic sequence, Laura Dern as a disoriented actress/whore, stabbed and slowly dying on Hollywood Boulevard. The latter sequence — the culmination of the film-within-a-film *On High in Blue Tomorrows* [*OHiBT*] — is a powerful enactment of the death of Hollywood and its cinematic rebirth; a criticism in images of a Hollywood that has become corrupted, hence in need of spiritual and artistic renewal.

'THERE'S AN UNPAID BILL THAT NEEDS PAYING'

A bright shaft of light cuts across the darkness and briefly illuminates forbidding metallic letters: INLAND EMPIRE. What does it mean? Lynch's most recent feature films have all been set in the Los Angeles/Hollywood Hills area, a locale that suggests the coexistence of film worlds within American culture, but which Lynch also submits to a variety of subtle displacements. This is notable, for example, in the contrast between corrupted Hollywood and creatively transfigured Los Angeles in *Mulholland Drive* (the

Club Silencio sequence featuring Rebekka Del Rio's stunning Spanish (and mimed) rendition of Roy Orbison's song, 'Crying'); or in *INLAND EMPIRE*'s comparable shift from corrupted (and haunted) Hollywood studios to 'the Valley' (the San Bernardino Valley/Riverside county areas) known as 'Inland Empire' — a dual locale that is then further displaced, in time and space, onto 1930s Europe (the 'Baltic region' scenes shot in Łódź, Poland).

Clearly, however, there is more than geography or history at play here. To borrow a term from Guy Debord, we are dealing, rather, with something like *psychogeography*. Debord used this term to describe the interplay between geography, affectivity and action, particularly in situations of urban *dérive*, aimless wandering or estrangement from a familiar urban environment.[1] With Lynch, however, the landscape is as much psychic as urban, cinematic as psychological. We could equally call this a 'psychotopology'[2] — a topology of cinematic spaces that enfolds disparate but related diegetic worlds, diverging narrative lines, cultural-historical locales, aesthetic sensibilities, and cinematic media.

INLAND EMPIRE (capitalized, so expressing an 'idea') is a meditation on the crisis of Hollywood film crystallized through the traumatic experiences of actress Nikki Grace and her character Susan Blue [both played by Laura Dern], 'a woman in trouble', according to Lynch's one-line summary of the film. It is film about film in crisis, about Hollywood in trouble, where this crisis afflicting Hollywood — the 'Inland Empire' of cinema — also holds open the possibility of rebirth and transformation: (1) through the power of cinematic performance, in particular that of the feminine screen actress; (2) by reconnecting Hollywood with the tradition of European cinema, reanimating the sundered relationship that still haunts Hollywood, 'an unpaid bill that needs paying'; and (3) overcoming the limits of traditional Hollywood filmmaking practice by embracing the experimental possibilities and creative independence afforded by digital video technology, which promises new ways of telling stories, even a re-democratizing of the medium. This is an act of performative criticism in the grand style, replete with what Lynch enigmatically calls cinematic 'ideas' and narrative 'abstractions' (2006: 23, 25, 29, 83–85).[3]

THE MARKETPLACE AND THE ALLEYWAY

The film's remarkable opening sequence — what we might call its Prologue — crystallizes all of these elements through the use of beautifully ambiguous abstractions. By this I mean pure sound and image sequences that disrupt representational conventions and narrative cues, thereby opening up an affectively charged space (and time) of intensive aesthetic responsiveness. The film opens with a black-and-white image of an antique gramophone needle scratchily playing, the hissing underscore accompanied by disorienting beams of light.[4] A male voice recounts: 'Axxon N.: the longest-running radio play in history, tonight ... continuing in the Baltic region.' The image's circular motion, eternal repetition and ghostly recording of experience all point to the film's fascination with the role of recording technology. Gramophone needles, movie cameras, DV cameras, even the strange *camera obscura* using cigarette and silk screen that we see later in the film; all of these devices make possible this haunting capture of an absent presence, this ghostly presence of the past. The tale to be told in the film is the oldest in the world; a mythic cycle of love, betrayal and revenge. Only here it is a tale haunted by something unspeakable, a nameless and faceless dread, mediated by audiovisual technologies capable of recording, capturing and transforming experience.

The story begins in 'an old hotel room on a grey winter's day'. A corridor appears, one of the many domestic interiors, thresholds and portals that punctuate the film. A man and a woman, speaking Polish, their faces obscured, enter a room. It becomes evident that she is a prostitute; her intimidating client orders her to undress and then asks whether she 'knows what whores do'. She does. Her bondage and fear, transmuted through faceless images of sexualized movement, hint at the questions of identity, of becoming lost, of being haunted by the past, and of returning to oneself. This disorienting dissolution of identity is multiplied in the sequences that follow. Accompanied by Chrysta Bell's haunting rendition of Lynch's poignant song, 'Polish poem', we see, now in colour, the same young woman, the anonymous prostitute, trapped and traumatized, sitting half-dressed on the bed of a hotel room, tears streaming down her cheeks. The Lost Girl [Karolina Gruszak], as she is called, watches a tiny television screen, on which we see sped-up images of the very film we are about to watch (the Visitor #1 [Grace Zabriskie]

145

sequence that will follow shortly). After the screen loses its image, the film cuts to the notorious Rabbits sequence (taken from Lynch's website), which features a trio of humanoid rabbits, one male and two female, acting out disconnected fragments of a surreal TV sitcom drama. These impassive animal ciphers repeat mantra-like, nonsensical phrases that will recur throughout the film, but which all vaguely suggest the theme of adultery, or of a mystery to be revealed (while also recalling *Mulholland Drive*).[5] They also mark, allegorically, the stereotypical versions of the 'old story' of love, betrayal and revenge — the married couple and adulterous, disrupting 'third' — that will figure in various permutations throughout the rest of the film.

The room is connected, via one of the many portals within the film (its 'psychotopology'), to a baroque drawing room featuring two Polish characters. The one, an impassive Mr Roque-like figure, listens to the urgent, belligerent request of the other [Krzysztof Majchrzak], who will turn out to be a character known as the Phantom: 'I seek an opening, do you understand? I seek an opening!' We do not know what opening this is, what world this character seeks to enter, nor what his menacing purpose there might be. The viewer too, no doubt, would welcome an opening at this point, as the image of the Phantom fades from view, followed by that of the male Rabbit framed by the portal/doorway. This nesting of multiple narrative layers will continue over the following sequences, which cut abruptly between what seem like distinct narrative lines or between seemingly disparate cinematic worlds.

The sequence that follows is Visitor #1's [Grace Zabriskie's] surreal neighbourly chat with actress Nikki Grace [Laura Dern], one of those unnerving sequences in Lynch's films where a 'messenger' conveys a warning or portent from 'another place'. Who is she? Though her identity is left unexplained, Visitor #1 reappears at the very end of the film, which is bookended by her uncanny meeting with Nikki Grace about the cursed film in which she is fated to perform. Lynch's deliberately 'amateurish' use of DV is striking here, with a disorienting mobility the camera, strangely flat interior shots, uneven use of 'raw' sound, unsettling long takes, and uncomfortably wide shots of characters talking at a distance, which are then contrasted with disturbingly distorted close-ups, exaggerating Grace Zabriskie's unnerving gaze and witchy intonations. We might call this Lynch's belated 'Dogme' moment: the whole sequence defamiliarizes conventional cinematic space and narrative dialogue, evoking a mood of uncanniness, temporal disorientation and visceral dread.

Visitor #1 asks about Nikki Grace's upcoming movie, about the part that Nikki is unsure whether she will get. The Visitor insists that she will; she asks, with increasing aggression, whether the film is about marriage, and whether her husband is involved, which only perplexes Nikki all the more. The Visitor then relates two enigmatic parables, upon which Nikki is supposed to meditate:

A little boy went out to play. When he opened the door he saw the world. As he passed through the doorway he caused a reflection. Evil was born. Evil was born and followed the boy.

And now the variation: A little girl went out to play, as if half born; lost in the marketplace. Then — not through the market-place, you see that, don't you — but through the alley behind. This is the way to the palace. But it isn't something you remember.

As Anna K. Schaffner points out, these two parables articulate the narrative trajectory followed by the main male and female characters, despite their various doublings throughout the film (2009: 285). The male characters — Nikki's husband Piotrek Krol/Sue Blue's husband Smithy [Peter J. Lucas], Devon Berk/Billy Side [Justin Theroux], and the Phantom/Crimp [Krzysztof Majchrzak] — remain haunted by their reflections, their uncanny *Doppelgängers*, what Lynch calls the 'evil that men do'. The women characters, however, notably Nikki Grace/Susan Blue/the Battered Woman [Laura Dern], but also the Polish 'Lost Girl' [Karolina Gruszak], become 'lost in the market-place'; an ambiguous phrase that could refer to Hollywood as much as to spiritual desolation. Yet they will also find themselves again 'through the alley behind', becoming 'fully born', eventually finding the spiritual, psychological and artistic path to 'the palace'. This mythic-cinematic truth has been forgotten, whether figured 'karmi-cally' as action and reaction begetting a cycle of reincarnation, or cinematically as repaying the unpaid debt to alternative traditions of art cinema. But this is not something we remember.

The Visitor has come to remind Nikki of the debt she owes, of the Evil men do, and of the risk that she might become another 'Lost Girl' in the marketplace. A mysterious cinematic world is opened up — Hollywood, now distorted and disturbed, a site of corruption and lostness — in which a formerly famous actress vying for a part will find herself in trouble. The Visitor then asks whether there is a murder in this movie. Nikki denies this, but the Visitor violently insists ('brutal fucking murder!'). With the Visitor's bizarre conclusion, temporal frameworks begin to fray, narrative warning merges with metaphysical speculation, cinematic worlds collide:

I can't seem to remember if it's today, two days from now, or yesterday. I suppose if it was 9.45, I'd think it was after midnight. For instance, if today was tomorrow, you wouldn't even remember that you owed on an unpaid bill. Actions do have consequences. And yet, there is the magic!

In a disorienting moment of cinematic *mise-en-abyme*, the Visitor alludes to the framing narratives that we have encountered thus far, but also to the mystery that is to unfold throughout the rest of the film (the 'original crime' committed on a street 'in the Baltic region' between 9.45 and midnight, some time back in the 1930s). Like a perverse film director, she leads Nikki through the performance she is going to make, the curse she is going to reincarnate, while sounding a warning about the ineluctability of fate that follows wrong actions. 'If it was tomorrow,' she observes, 'you would be sitting over there', pointing towards an empty sofa. 'Do you see?' As Nikki looks across, her face aghast, she sees herself and two girlfriends talking; she receives a call telling her she has the longed-for part, crying jubilantly as her husband watches intently from the stairs above. The warning has been given, the prediction announced, the debt has been called in; the corrupted cinematic myth has been set in motion once again, a debt that needs paying in order to be discharged.

A 'CRITICISM IN IMAGES'

These seemingly disparate visual sequences and narrative strands are presented sequentially in a manner that both provokes and defies interpretive coherence; yet they co-exist, linking up multiple, nested narrative lines, within the cinematic multiverse that is *INLAND EMPIRE*. In Lynch's films, cinematic psychogeography is an aesthetic modality in which place and sensibility, locale and subjectivity, transhistorical moods and multiple temporalities interconnect and communicate. These elements are then enfolded, in 'topological' fashion, creating portals of communication between disparate cinematic and psychic worlds. The 'other place' (and time) enfolded within *INLAND EMPIRE* is the 'Baltic region' (or rather, the city of Łódź, Poland), which also communicates with an alternative film-world (the aborted Polish-German art film *47* [*Vier-Sieben*]), sequences from which we glimpse later in the film (scenes that reveal the nature of the crime of passion committed on a Polish street in the 1930s, marked by a scratchy, hiss-ridden underscore).

The psychogeography of *INLAND EMPIRE* immediately directs us to consciousness, the 'psychic' dimension of the film, in all senses of the term. *INLAND EMPIRE* as a whole could be described, quite literally, as a 'filmind', to adapt Daniel Frampton's neologism,[6] or more concretely, following Deleuze, as an instance of 'cinema of the brain' (1989: 204–15). Expanded consciousness encompassing conscious and non-conscious, cognitive and intuitive modes of experience — 'diving within', as Lynch says of transcendental meditation — is the most elementary sense of the title/idea of *INLAND EMPIRE*. As mentioned above, this is evident in the traumatized consciousness of Nikki Grace [Laura Dern], who plays another character, Susan Blue, in a cloying but disturbing Hollywood romantic melodrama, *On High in Blue Tomorrows* (*OHiBT*). The latter film-within-a-film appears at first to be an anachronistic Minnelli-Sirk-style melodrama that soon degenerates into soap opera, and then later into something like psychological horror. *OHiBT* is directed by a comically Lynchian parody of a director, Kingsley Stewart [Jeremy Irons], who is at once enthusiastic and creatively bankrupt (the theme of 'debt' — creative, cultural, cinematic, even 'karmic' — looms large in the film). As Visitor #1 warns Nikki Grace, she and the rest of the crew making *OHiBT* owe on an unpaid bill.

As it turns out, *OHiBT* is a film that harbours a dark secret. Director Kingsley Stewart confesses to his leading actors that *OHiBT* is actually a remake, based on a Polish gypsy folktale, of an unfinished 1930s film called *47* [*Vier-Sieben*], which was abandoned after its leading actors were murdered. The accursed film has now been resurrected by the studio, without the filmmakers' knowledge, as a Hollywood remake of the unfinished European original. As soon becomes clear, these two films will mirror and inversely reflect each other, disrupting any boundaries between actor and character, past and future, filmic and non-filmic worlds. As in the original, Nikki Grace and Devon Berk begin an adulterous affair while making *OHiBT*, thus mirroring that of their characters Susan Blue and Billy Side. Again echoing *47*, and as prophesied by Visitor #1, *OHiBT* has to do with marriage and culminates in a brutal murder (Nikki Grace/ Susan Blue/the Battered Woman, stabbed with a screwdriver and dying slowly on Hollywood Boulevard). The creative bankruptcy of Hollywood, its sterile repetition of 'cursed' stories, its unacknowledged debt to the past, needs to be overcome; but Nikki Grace/Sue Blue, avatar of a corrupted Hollywood tradition, will have to die symbolically in order for this debt to be acknowledged, for the curse to be lifted, and for a new way of telling stories to be possible.

It is worth noting that the 'end' of *OHiBT* only occurs in the concluding half-hour of *INLAND EMPIRE*, after the dramatic on-screen death of Sue Blue, suggesting that much of what we see in the film is the disintegration of Nikki Grace/Sue Blue's consciousness as part of, or unfolding within, the degradation/transformation of *OHiBT* into the genre of psychological horror. The performance here of a distinctively *cinematic* form of criticism (Cavell's 'criticism by images') is hard to miss, with its equation of Hollywood corruption, prostitution and underworld violence. Hollywood's Dream Factory has become an all-encompassing cinematic-mythic nightmare.

AXXON N.

Both films-within-the-film (*OHiBT* and *47*) appear to be cinematic incarnations of a more mythic version of the tale, with the perplexing but neurologically resonant name of 'Axxon N.', 'the longest running radio play in history', a circular, recurring myth of action and reaction, transgression and retribution, love, betrayal and revenge. What is meant by 'Axxon N.'? All we see in the film is a scrawled name and white line/arrow on various doors. These doors mark portals or 'openings' into the topologically connected film studio/ cinema theatre/filmind labyrinth within which Nikki Grace/Susan Blue/the Battered Woman gets lost, only to confront herself in one of the film's most remarkable moments of self-referential narrative looping.

While making love in an unsettlingly blue-lit room (which will turn out to be the bedroom of Smithy's house), Nikki/Sue tells Devon/Billy about a nightmarish experience she had during filming the previous day. Walking down an alleyway after shopping, she spies strange markings on a metal door: Axxon N. Following the line/arrow through a doorway, she enters a strange labyrinthine set/theatre/world in which she, becoming increasingly panicked, stumbles upon 'Smithy's house' (the film set to be used for the filming of *OHiBT*), while being watched malevolently by her husband in a bright green suit. To her horror, she discovers (as do we) that she is now trapped inside the cinematic world of *OHiBT*. Nikki/Sue is now split and doubled: into actor and character, performer and adulterer, actress on set having an affair with her co-star, and character trapped within a film in which she is destined to do the same.

These topologically communicating filmworlds now set the stage for the film's own vertiginous doubling; its nesting of interconnected cinematic worlds, multiple narrative lines, and blurring character identities. The psychotopology of *INLAND EMPIRE* not only challenges Nikki/Sue and Devon/Billy but our own capacities to make sense of what we see and hear, to navigate the paradoxically intersecting 'parallel worlds' comprising Lynch's film (see Orr 2009). Although linked visually to the image of eternal return, of circular mythmaking, and to recording technology, we could also suggest that 'Axxon N.' is a figure suggesting the (cinematic) mind/brain (see Frampton 2006: 73 ff; Deleuze 1989: 204–15). While some critics have proposed that it violates all sense, referring, paradoxically, to an 'axiom of unintelligibility' (Critchley and Webster 2010), one can more fruitfully approach the resonances of 'Axxon N.' as a cinematic 'axon' or brain/nerve cell linking multiple layers of consciousness: it is a complex Lynchian film idea that Deleuze has suggested is an important strand of contemporary cinematic art.[7] 'Axxon N.' is cinematic thinking in action: a topologically linked series of nested narrative filmworlds; a rhizomatic 'filmind' or 'Inland Empire'; the self-consciousness of a corrupted Hollywood tradition, now undergoing its own sceptical crisis of belief.

THE LOST GIRL

This dissociation of consciousness within the film — actress Nikki Grace's disintegration in playing Susan Blue, becoming another character, the Battered Woman, who persists throughout *OHiBT* and on to the end of *INLAND EMPIRE* — arguably mirrors that of the viewer. We do not comprehend so much as intuit the fragmented, nested, mysteriously connected strands that link the ambiguous narrative 'abstractions' (or 'big fish' ideas) composing the film (see Lynch 2006: 139 ff). Our surrogate on screen, witness to the 'curse' corrupting Hollywood (and its consequences), is the young Polish woman, the Lost Girl [Karolina Gruszak], whose framing story both opens and closes the film. *INLAND EMPIRE* shows what becomes of a woman, this particular actress, with all her multiple personae, when projected on screen, when our shared cinematic, psychic and cultural worlds collide.

I have suggested, in a fragmentary way, that there are three related senses of the idea of *INLAND EMPIRE*: cinema understood as (Lynchian) psychogeography; consciousness in an expanded sense, embracing aesthetic forms of awareness as well as film under-stood as a cinematic mind/brain (Axxon N.); and the topologically communicating filmworlds of Hollywood and European art cinema (the Hollywood remake of *47*). Moreover, *INLAND EMPIRE* is a cinematic criticism of the contemporary crisis of film that Lynch diagnoses as a 'putrefaction' (to use his term) of Hollywood; a failure to acknowledge or renew its creative relationship with the tradition of European cinema to which Lynch, like other Hollywood auteurs, owes a profound debt.[8] Forgetfulness, it happens to us all.

Lynch's irony here does not involve the clichéd trope of 'postmodern pastiche', but is rather a transcendental or romantic irony (see Wilson 2007) evoking an impossible, fractured whole. *INLAND EMPIRE* encompasses Hollywood and its difficult relationship with the European tradition; a whole that can be evoked only in fragments, through self-referential play, acknowledging its own (and our own) cinematic and interpretive limits. To say this, however, is just to say that the film engages in its own distinctive kind of cinematic thinking; an intuitive, affective, aesthetic reflection on the possibilities of cinema today, one that both invites and resists trans-lation — or paraphrase — into philosophical film theory.

PUZZLE-FILM OR CINEMATIC THINKING?

Here I would like to distinguish the exploratory, fragmentary approach I have taken from the more theoretical temptation to classify the film generically. Indeed, it is not difficult to see *INLAND EMPIRE* as an example of what Buckland and Elsaesser have recently called the 'puzzle film' (Buckland 2009: 1–12) or 'mind-game film' (Elsaesser, 2009: 13–41). Buckland and Elsaesser are referring to the recent crop of crossover arthouse and genre films (*Being John Malkovich, Eternal Sunshine of the Spotless Mind, Memento, Lost Highway, Adaptation, Mulholland Drive, Caché*, and so on) that deliberately disrupt conventional narrative structures, withhold information, leave ambiguous clues calling for indeterminate interpretation, dissolve the boundary between diegetic reality and fantasy, and so on. As Elsaesser observes, we can typically identify two dimensions at play in the mind-game film: games are being played with the character or characters within the film, who may not understand the situation they find themselves in, or are being tormented by external forces they do not fully comprehend (for example, director Adam Kesher in *Mulholland Drive*, Fred Madison and his wife Renée in *Lost Highway*, or the (European) variation, Georges and Anne Laurent in Michael Haneke's *Caché*);[9] and games are being played with the film-viewer, who is presented with a discontinuous or fragmentary narrative, strewn with ambiguous clues, unresolved narrative threads, and disturbing, fascinating, or shocking images that do not serve any immediate narrative purpose. (*INLAND EMPIRE* certainly has its share of such images, such as the remarkable slow-motion night shot of Laura Dern, illuminated by a spotlight and rushing towards the camera, her face contorting in a demonic yell.)

The 'mind' aspect in mind-games films typically involves complex explorations of characters' states of consciousness, the disintegration of their subjectivity, often in relation to the experience of psychic trauma, the blurring of fantasy and reality, or uncanny encounters with characters who turn out to be fantasized or even supernatural (the Fred Madison/Pete Dayton transformation in *Lost Highway*, along with bizarre 'messenger' figures such as *Lost Highway*'s The Mystery Man [Robert Blake] or even Visitor #1 from *INLAND EMPIRE*). It would be tempting, therefore, to show that *INLAND EMPIRE* revels in the kind narrative, cinematic, psychological and philosophical game-playing — a 'mind-game, played with movies', as Lars von Trier says — defining the 'mind-game' genre.

Such a generic analysis, however helpful, is nonetheless too intellectualist in its account of why these films fascinate or how they might enact a kind of cinematic thinking (as we shall see in the next chapter, it recalls Noël Carroll's (1990) cognitivist account of horror in which it is the pleasure of solving various intellectual puzzles that overrides any affective displeasure we might experience). Haneke's *Funny Games* (1997/2007) as well as Lynch's *INLAND EMPIRE*, would both qualify as 'puzzle films' on this account. Yet this classification would fail to capture the aesthetic and traumatic dimensions of these films, the kind of shock to thought that they provoke; an experience that remains at odds with the disengaged, intellectually curious, puzzle-solving attitude of the cognitivist film viewer. Such a generic analysis would also overlook the profound *metacinematic* dimensions in films like *Mulholland Drive* and *INLAND EMPIRE*, their performance of cinematic criticism or a 'criticism in images'. Far more than a fragmented 'puzzle plot', *INLAND EMPIRE* is a cinematic metafiction meditating on the glorious history, corrupted present and fragile future of Hollywood in its fractured relationship with the European tradition. It is an audacious act of cinematic criticism — an act of cinematic thinking — that gestures towards the liberation of post-Hollywood independent (DV) filmmaking around the globe.

'DO YOU WANT TO SEE?'

Lynch often describes cinema as an artform with the aesthetic power to tell stories with beautiful 'abstractions'. As in *Mulholland Drive*, these are abundantly evident in *INLAND EMPIRE* (such as the two dance sequences in the film: the 'Locomotion' in Smithy's house performed by the vanishing whore chorus; the other, 'Sinnerman', in Nikki Grace's mansion, watched serenely by Nikki/Laura Dern). There are, moreover, striking parallels between the two films: both centre on the splitting of Hollywood/Los Angeles (Hollywood versus the Hispanic world of LA in *Mulholland Drive*; Hollywood versus the Inland Empire region in *INLAND EMPIRE*); both centre on the making of a Hollywood film (*The Sylvia North Story* and *On High in Blue Tomorrows*); both have narratives that contrast the corruption of contemporary Hollywood and the promise of a new kind of cinematic storytelling; both centre on the power of feminine performance, Hollywood's reliance on and destruction of great screen actresses (Naomi Watts as Betty/Diane, Laura Dern as Nikki/Sue); both feature a splitting of the female lead, an actress whose character dissociates into multiple personae (Diane as Betty, Nikki as Sue/the Battered Woman); both involve a murder mystery that remains enigmatic and unresolved (the mysterious corpse in 'Rita's' apartment, the two lead actors murdered in the film-within-a-film, *47*). Both films also end with the central actress/woman in trouble character engaging in a (symbolic) suicide or act of self-destruction in order to be reborn as a new identity (Betty/Diane's concluding 'suicide' by gunshot in her bedroom; Nikki/Sue/the Battered Woman's shooting of the Phantom/Crimp outside the Rabbits' room). Finally, both films feature a mysterious theatre space, with red curtains and blue symbolic touches: an oneiric figure for the coalescence of cinema and consciousness (the woman with blue hair who utters the final word, 'Silencio!', in *Mulholland Drive*, and the blue kimono that Nikki/Sue/the Battered Woman leaves on plush red theatre seats in *INLAND EMPIRE*).[10] It is within this uncanny theatre (Club Silencio in *Mulholland Drive*, the 'Axxon N.' theatre in *INLAND EMPIRE*) that both actresses (Betty/Diane and Nikki/Sue/the Battered Woman) confront their cinematic alter egos and experience the mystery of cinematic performance: 'Actions do have consequences. And yet, there is the magic!'

In a striking sequence, Sue Blue is instructed by a ghostly vision of the Lost Girl, whose face hovers uncannily against black-and-white images of the phonograph needle. She explains what Sue has to do if she, too, 'wants to see'. She is told that she must be wearing 'the watch' ('it had something to do with the telling of time'), light a cigarette, burn a hole in a silk slip and peer through it, thereby entering a (cinematic) portal to multiple, overlapping temporal and cinematic worlds.[11] This 'hole' or makeshift *camera obscura* allows access between worlds and reappears in a number of arresting images (the silk slips, the Rabbits' room with an animated burning hole in the corner of the wall).[12] Apart from having hypnotic, hallucinatory powers, the cinematic apparatus, for Lynch, is also a ghostly haunting machine; an uncanny apparatus for recording ideas, dreams and desires, for transcribing the magic of performance and communicating abstractions, thoughts and moods that resist linguistic expression. The 'murderous gaze' of the 35mm Panavision camera used to film the film-within-the-film, instrument of the curse linking *47* and *OHiBT*, is contrasted with the clairvoyant vision of Sue Blue (and her chorus of whore/sisters) burning a hole in the (silk) screen with a cigarette. This 'home-made' synaptic opening allows us access to the 'other side'; the unconscious source of ideas within these enfolded cinematic mind-worlds. Like *Mulholland Drive*,

INLAND EMPIRE performs an extraordinary self-reflection on the hybrid history of Hollywood; it broaches the idea of a cinema newly liberated (like the Lost Girl) thanks to the creative conjunction of DV technology and imaginative consciousness.

'THIS IS THE WAY TO THE PALACE'

Where the two films differ most notably, however, is in their concluding sequences. In *Mulholland Drive* the final 'Silencio!', uttered by the mysterious Blue-Haired Lady, remains an enigmatic dead-end, a concluding note to the tragic self-destruction of Diane/ Betty. *INLAND EMPIRE*, by contrast, concludes with a gesture of liberation, a joyous adieu to Lynch's idiosyncratic film-worlds. As *Mulholland Drive*'s 'Rita' [Laura Elena Harring] blows a knowing kiss, an amateurish dance troupe begins an exuberant routine, miming to Nina Simone's 'Sinnerman'. This final sequence captures the extraordinary coalescence of cinematic worlds comprising *INLAND EMPIRE*. Nikki Grace/Laura Dern, now watching rather than performing, sits peacefully in a room hosting various characters from the film (the one-legged sister of Smithy, Niko with her pet monkey and chic blond wig, reminiscent of Alice in *Lost Highway*), and is replete with playful references to other Lynch films (*Blue Velvet* (1984), *Twin Peaks* (1990–91) and *Mulholland Drive*).

What to say about this joyously enigmatic conclusion? *INLAND EMPIRE* is Lynch's elegy for film; a film after the 'end of film', yet one that intimates the possibility of cinema's rebirth in a digital, egalitarian age. It is a powerful instance of cinematic criticism, a work of cinema 'in the condition of philosophy' (Mulhall 2002, 2008). In communicating with the ghosts of Hollywood's past and hypnotizing us with a dark vision of its future, Lynch has made a film that is at once a self-critique and transformation of (digital) cinematic art. The framing and concluding tale, the Lost Girl's story, which repeats that of her cinematic sisters (Nikki/Sue/the Battered Woman), is about a woman in trouble, and an allegory of a corrupted Hollywood in need of cinematic and spiritual renewal. The film's hopeful conclusion, Nikki/Laura seated peacefully in blue, her traumatic performance redeemed, now watching others perform, hints at the aesthetic possibilities of a liberated cinematic thinking.

CHAPTER EIGHT

'CHAOS REIGNS': ANTI-COGNITIVISM IN LARS VON TRIER'S *ANTICHRIST*

THE FALL

Sensuous black-and-white images of a couple showering together, shot in slow motion, are accompanied by a poignant aria, ('Lascia ch'io pianga' [Let me weep]), from Handel's opera *Rinaldo* (1711). In an adjacent room, we see a desk with three figurines, and a window, mysteriously opening, curtains blowing against the night sky, with snow slowly falling outside. The couple begin to make love, in the conventional cinematic manner, which is interrupted by an explicit shot of penetration, in rhythm with the aria. In the child's room, we see a teddy bear, tied to a balloon, floating mysteriously above the child's cot. A shot of the three figurines on the desk reveals their identity: Grief, Pain, and Despair. As the couple make love, falling as they do, a baby monitor comes into focus, the parents oblivious to the child's cries. The child climbs out of his cot, teddy bear in hand, feet falling gracefully to the floor. He brings the bear to the window, pretending to show him the view. As the couple continue their lovemaking, the child opens a childproof gate; he stands before a doorway, witnessing his parents' coupling, and turns away, glancing enigmatically towards the camera. The open window beckons; snowflakes blow gently across the desk. His parents continue their lovemaking, oblivious to the tragedy about to unfold. The boy climbs onto the desk and sweeps away the figurines; clutching his teddy bear, he steps through the open window and out on to the snow-covered ledge. As the couple's lovemaking reaches its peak, the boy's feet slip on the powdery snow, and he falls, slowly and gracefully, on to the snow-covered pavement below. As he falls, one of many images of falling punctuating this sequence, images of his parents' faces are intercut, expressing both pain and pleasure, as the poignant aria draws to its end. A close-up of his teddy bear striking the snow-covered ground is followed by a close-up of the woman, eyes shut and mouth open, crying out in pleasure. The aria, along with the whirling washing machine, comes to a graceful close.

PHILOSOPHIES OF HORROR

The paradoxical pleasure we can derive from tragic art has occupied philosophers from Aristotle and Hume to Hegel and Nietzsche. Why do we enjoy tragic art when it induces negative emotional responses? Aristotle, in the *Poetics* (1996), famously addressed the puzzle posed by tragic art: tragedies depict terrible events, irreconcilable, unavoidable conflict, undeserved misfortune, and innocent suffering, thus eliciting in spectators the contrasting emotional responses of fear and sympathy/pity. Tragedies thereby generate the effect of *catharsis* on the audience; both a therapeutic purging and psychological purification of negative or destructive affects. The irreconcilable and inevitable nature of the dramatic conflict enables us to understand the limits of human knowledge and action; it also allows us to appreciate more acutely how an excess of virtue as much as of vice, an overreaching beyond the natural bounds of our allotment, can lead to catastrophe and ruin.

The philosophical problem of tragedy has been a central pre-occupation of 'Continental' aesthetics, from Hegel's account of the ineluctable conflict between equally valid yet irreconcilable cultural-normative principles, to Nietzsche's speculations on the affirmative artistic interplay between Apollonian and Dionysian impulses (the will to form versus the will to formlessness). Yet tragic art, as has often been observed, flourished historically only in particular contexts and for brief periods of time (ancient Greece, Renaissance Europe). Within the Anglophone philosophical tradition, it is Hume who offers the paradigmatic account of tragedy, one that has been revived in recent debates within analytic-cognitivist philosophies of film. According to Hume's 'On Tragedy' (1965 [1757]), the negative affects induced by tragic art are converted into positive ones, either through aesthetic appreciation of the narrative, or by the satisfaction of our intellectual curiosity concerning the source of our displeasure. In *The Birth of Tragedy* (1967 [1872]), Nietzsche rejected Humean 'conversionist' or Aristotelian 'reconciliationist' solutions to the so-called paradox of tragedy. Rather, tragic art, he argued, expresses a tragic conception of existence: knowledge is not necessarily tied to virtue; Good does not always triumph over Evil; pleasure can be found in destruction; existence remains opaque to the moral and intellectual demands of reason.

It is against this background of philosophical reflection on tragedy that we encounter contemporary theories of horror, wayward offspring of tragedy (the other being melodrama). Inspired by Hume, Noël Carroll's landmark book, *The Philosophy of Horror* (1990), catalyzed the continuing wave of philosophical interest in horror film. Drawing on an Aristotelian approach to categorizing and analyzing narrative genres, Carroll offers a broadly analytic-cognitivist answer to the 'paradox of horror': why it is that we seek out and expose ourselves to fictions that provoke negative, displeasurable responses we ordinarily strive to avoid. Contra Aristotle, Nietzsche or Freud, Carroll's (Humean) answer refers to the aesthetic and intellectual pleasures afforded by contemplating a well-wrought plot or by satisfying our narrative curiosity concerning the film's monstrous source of horror.[1] The cognitive pleasure in mastering this horror allows the viewer to overcome the negative affective experience of such films, with their visceral shocks, traumatic scenarios and involuntary 'startle' effects.

Carroll's analysis is noteworthy for being the first serious philosophical engagement with the horror genre, which had hitherto been mostly ignored or else treated as a source of colourful case studies in psychoanalytic or critical theory. Thanks to Carroll's intervention, Horror is now one of the favourite genres of philosophical film theorists (see Carroll (1990); Freeland (2002); Shaw (1997, 2001); Smuts (2003, 2007)). In a modest homage to Aristotle (and Hume), Carroll distinguishes and categorizes horror as a genre, describing its distinctive and most typical narrative plots and features and offering a broadly cognitivist response to the paradox of horror. While emphasizing horror's generic features, Carroll also foregrounds the subjective response that it engenders; he defines 'art-horror', for example, as a particular combination of fear, disgust and physical agitation in response to a biologically hybrid or 'interstitial' monster that threatens the physical and emotional integrity of the characters (1990: 27–35).[2] According to Carroll, we do not experience pleasure as such in a horror film. Rather, we *tolerate* horror in order to enjoy the compensatory cognitive pleasures afforded by contemplating pleasing aesthetic form or satisfying our powers of reasoning, reflection and inference. All these cognitive powers come into play in resolving the narrative enigmas posed by 'the monster':

> Experiencing the emotion of art-horror is not our primary aim in consuming horror fictions ... Rather, art-horror is the price we are willing to pay for the revelation of that which is impossible and unknown, of that which violates our conceptual schema. (Carroll 1990: 186)

For Carroll, it is our cognitive curiosity that explains the fascination of horror; we endure fear and disgust as incidental by-products of this narrative and cognitive quest. Horror is no exploration of the irrational or expression of repressed desires; rather, it shares the scientist's quest to understand the unknown and overcome our fear and disgust through cognitive comprehension. Carroll's detailed analyses of various horror plots add weight to his thesis that the paradoxical pleasure in horror is more aesthetic and cognitive than masochistic or irrational (1990: 97–128). As many critics have pointed out, however, Carroll's generically grounded theory seems to exclude important films and even subgenres that would ordinarily be included in any comprehensive account of horror (see Shaw 1997). A notable case here is Hitchcock's *Psycho*, whose unnerving protagonist, Norman Bates [Anthony Perkins], is hardly a biological monstrosity; there is also the subgenre of psychological horror, where supernaturalist elements may be present without any biologically heterogeneous 'monster'.

In a related vein, for Carl Plantinga (2009a) the answer to the paradox of horror lies in a cognitive 'reconceptualization' or (non-Freudian) 'working through' of the negative affective experiences that such films elicit. Despite their unpleasant, even traumatic character, the horror viewer's cognitive conversion of negative into positive emotions reframes the former's negativity in such a way, Plantinga argues, that 'their overall impact is both cognitively and emotionally satisfying, comforting, and pleasurable' (2009a: 179). The discomfiting nature of horror is not so much the price we pay for cognitive satisfaction as the source material for an affective conversion; instead of compensating us for our affective discomfiture, horror converts this affective negativity into surplus cognitive and psychological satisfaction. Like Carroll, Plantinga follows Hume in arguing that the negative affects of horror and anxiety can be converted, in a well-wrought horror film, into dominant affects like the natural pleasure we take in mimesis or imitation. Plantinga, however, extends Hume's 'two-stage' account of this process of cognitive conversion: we can take aesthetic pleasure in the artful presentation of the disturbing content of a tragic narrative; and in contemplating a tragedy we can 'convert whatever negative emotional responses are elicited into pleasurable emotions and feelings' (such as aesthetic pleasure in beauty and eloquence of language) (2009a: 175). Plantinga thus foregrounds the role of *affective conversion* through *cognitive and aesthetic appreciation*. For both Carroll and Plantinga, then, we enjoy horror films as a kind of cognitive, affective and aesthetic tonic, rather than for any vicarious experience of repressed desires or ideological anxieties (Wood 1986), fascination with the power of evil (Freeland 2002), confrontation between, or identification with, the destructive power of the monster (Shaw 1997, 2001), or for the perverse enjoyment of 'recreational terror' that they might afford (see Shaw 2008, 35 ff).

Both Carroll and Plantinga, moreover, reject the Freudian 'return of the repressed' thesis that hitherto dominated theoretical discussion of horror films (Wood 1986; Clover 1992). According to this view, horror allows us to sublimate the traumatic dimensions of our fascination with death, sexuality, violence and abjection by entertaining otherwise repressed fantasies, anxieties and social taboos. Psychoanalytic film theory also added an ideological-critical dimension to this analysis by arguing that horror films, with their uncanny aliens, monstrous others and threatening sexuality, also served as allegories of ideological and socio-political anxieties that could otherwise not find cultural expression (Wood 1986). Until recent years, psychoanalytic film theory thus offered a way of explaining our continuing fascination with horror films and their persistent preoccupation with sexuality, death, violence and abjection. What has changed in the last two decades, however, is not so much the nature of horror as the theoretical paradigm in which horror is comprehended: the analytic-cognitivist turn from psychoanalytic to cognitivist theory, from Continental aesthetics and critical theory to analytic aesthetics and moral-cognitive psychology.

Horror, in this regard, serves as a veritable battleground for the confrontation between rationalist and romanticist conceptions of human being: will reason triumph over the forces of darkness, or will the autonomy of reason be undermined by the forces of irrationality? Psychoanalysis holds that our rational autonomy is always subject to the vicissitudes of repressed desire and the forces of the unconscious; cognitivism rejects such speculative postulates, arguing that all the phenomena psychoanalysis has claimed as its own can be better explained by cognitive processes, naturalistic motivations and rational desires. Analytic-cognitivist philosophies of horror have therefore tended to drop the unconscious, suppress the significance of sexuality, and downplay the ascription of ideological dimensions to horror.[3] Instead they offer updated cognitivist versions of the Freudian 'sublimation' thesis (*sans* the unconscious), arguing that it is the pleasure of cognitive mastery and aesthetic appreciation that trumps the negative affects elicited by horror films. In the uncanny battle between reason and its other, it is cognitive mastery and psychological satisfaction that win out against the irrational or irreconcilable in human experience.

But what of films that resist such accounts of horror as cognitive puzzle-solving, aesthetic contemplation, or affective conversion? Here I shall consider the case of Lars von Trier's *Antichrist* (2009), a film that resists the kind of intellectualist theories of emotional response that are prevalent in philosophical film theory. Even more, the film subtly suggests that psychoanalytic accounts of horror cannot be entirely dismissed (another case of the 'return of the repressed'?), despite the barrage of attacks that Freud has endured at the hands of cognitivist theory and recent philosophies of horror ('Dreams are of no interest to modern psychology', as Charlotte Gainsbourg's character observes. 'Freud is dead, isn't he?').

Although *Antichrist* remains resistant to any ready theoretical comprehension, it nonetheless recalls a more Nietzschean account of tragic art: enacting an aesthetic critique of Enlightenment optimism while also eliciting a (quasi-religious) sense of awe or sublimity in response to the nihilism of modern rationalism. As Aaron Smuts observes, psychoanalytic theories at least attempted to account for our ambivalent experience of horror, allowing for the possibility that pleasure in cognitive mastery could not account for all of horror's disturbing psychological effects (2009b: 513).[4] The recurring cultural preoccupation with horror — predicated on what contemporary science cannot fully explain, yet persisting as a source of fascination, fear and disgust — suggests that there are broader cultural, psychological and ideological dimensions at stake in such films.

If we *can* take pleasure in destruction, violence, sexuality and abjection, the question would be how and why horror allows us to experience vicariously these forms of cognitive disorientation and affective intoxication. It is difficult to respond to a film like *Antichrist* as simply satisfying our desire for cognitive mastery (since that is refused by the film), or aesthetic contemplation (since this is both elicited, then rendered traumatic as the film unfolds), or to say that it provides a serious metacinematic commentary on violence, sexuality, misogyny, or other cultural anxieties and myths (because of the deeply ambiguous character of the film's treatment of such themes). From this point of view, *Antichrist* can be described as von Trier's anti-cognitivist *trauma* film (since trauma is what resists the kind of conversion, mastery or sublimation to which horror is supposed to be subject). Precisely because of its traumatic character, *Antichrist* offers a cinematic counter-example to prevailing cognitivist theories of horror. As such, it is a violent provocation to thought; a traumatic case of *cinematic thinking*.

GRIEF

The remarkable opening sequence or prologue of *Antichrist* gives way to a different visual style in the film's first chapter, 'Grief', which assumes a more Dogme-esque realism (hand-held camera, rapid movements, obvious zooms, absence of music, and so on), albeit with a cool palette of greens, blues and greys, and rather polished visual sheen. 'Grief' is one of four chapters composing the film, the other three being 'Pain (Chaos Reigns)', 'Despair (Gynocide)', and 'The Three Beggars'. The film concludes with an epilogue in which Handel's *Rinaldo* aria reappears, mirroring the prologue's black-and-white visual style and slow-motion imagery, but presenting a very different perspective, sensibility and meaning.

The attentive viewer of the prologue will have been struck by its extraordinary stylization; von Trier's blatant violation of the self-imposed constraints of the Dogme-95 manifesto (the use of slow-motion black-and-white imagery, non-diegetic music and digital post-production special effects (for the talking fox), rather than the profilmic 'analogue' effects deployed in von Trier's earlier films such as *Element of Crime* (1984) and *Europa* (1991)). Some critics have compared the film with von Trier's most pure Dogme effort, *The Idiots* (1998). It is more apt, however, to relate it to his earlier foray into the horror genre, *The Kingdom* (*Riget*) I and II (1994 and 1997), as well as his earlier telemovie, *Medea* (1988), which was based on an unfilmed Carl Dreyer script (based on Euripides' play) that von Trier completed as an original interpretation of Dreyer. Comparisons between *Antichrist* and *The Kingdom* (or *Medea*) are instructive, less for the generic parallels or thematic concerns they suggest than for the striking differences, variations and contrasts they reveal.

The Kingdom [*Riget*] is a recognizably generic treatment of horror, crossbred with the hospital soap opera and melodrama. It uses and abuses these generic conventions, lacing the supernaturalist elements of haunting (of the Kingdom hospital by the ghost of a dead girl), parapsychology (hilariously depicted by the indefatigable Frau Drusser [Kirsten Rolffes]) and abject monstrosity, with an exploration of institutional violence, incest and sexual abuse, the conspiratorial subculture of institutional secret societies, and the covering-up of medical malpractice. It also heightens the art-horror-soap-opera drama with a streak of satirical Scandinavian humour (marvellously carried by the late Swedish actor Ernst-Hugo Jaregard, playing the neurotic neurosurgeon Stig Helmer). With its suppressed murder, haunting of the hospital, sepia-tinted tones, Down's Syndrome chorus, and ironic commentary by von Trier himself,[5] *The Kingdom* plays with horror, soap opera and crime thriller conventions in a manner consonant with the kind of Carroll-Plantinga accounts of horror that emphasize the role of cognitive mastery, aesthetic pleasure, or affective conversion.

Medea (1988), by contrast, is more suggestive than *The Kingdom* of the direction *Antichrist* takes in its treatment of trauma or in attempting a cinematic form of tragedy. Shot on grainy, colour-drained video, *Medea* exploits the latter's visual possibilities in order to evoke the Dreyeresque tradition of silent (or near-silent) film, with the use of gothic intertitles, minimal dialogue, unearthly images of sea, sand and field, firelit interiors of castle corridors and obscure caverns to create the visual and aural dislocation necessary to evoke a mythic time and place. Von Trier uses the flatness of video to maximum effect, draining the colour from the image to a startling degree, and allowing characters to merge into shadowy or evocative backgrounds in ways that underline the film's status as an anachronistic, necromantic evocation of the spirit of ancient tragedy. Indeed, *Medea*'s aim is to present a modern cinematic rendering of the trauma of Euripides' tragedy. Inspired by Dreyer's script, von Trier's version does not ameliorate or soften the traumatic dimensions of Medea's infamous revenge upon Jason for his betrayal of her (by marrying Creon's daughter, Glauce). Harrowing in the extreme is the sequence depicting *Medea*'s methodical murdering of her two sons. She hangs the younger, crying and wailing, from the branch of a desolate tree on a windswept rise; then assists the older, witness to the first killing, as he places a makeshift noose around his own neck. Jason's fury as he gallops towards this tragic scene is breathtaking, shot from above as horse and rider whistle through windswept grassy plains and the sandy littoral zone. His pain and anguish, upon finding his dead sons, are unbearable; it is a moment of unmitigated tragedy rare in cinematic art. *Medea*'s visual inventiveness, traumatic subject-matter and reflexive attempt to render tragedy in a cinematic idiom are thus important, if neglected, precedents for von Trier's aesthetic project in *Antichrist.*

The prologue of *Antichrist* defies Dogme-convention through its obvious use of extra-diegetic music (recalling the opening of *Dogville* with its use of Pergolesi's *Stabat Mater*). Handel's aria, which featured in Corbiau's entertaining musical-sexual-historical romp, *Farinelli* (1994), tells of Almeria's pain and suffering, her thwarted love for the noble but forbidden Knight Rinaldo:

Leave me to weep
over my cruel fate
and let me sigh for liberty.
May sorrow break
the bonds of my anguish,
if only for pity's sake.

The effect of the musical accompaniment in *Antichrist*'s prologue, however, is not simply to set the mood of pain and loss, but to cast doubt on the veracity of the tragic event being depicted. One cannot but be struck by the highly stylized presentation of the child's death and of his parents' apparent obliviousness to his fate. What we see is less an exposition of the background plot than a fantasmatic version of events distinctively coloured by the characters' subsequent experiences of trauma. This leaves the sequence highly ambiguous and open to conflicting interpretations. A number of clues, for example, suggest that the parents did not see or hear, and so could not know, what was happening with their son. Later in the film, however, a different version of events is suggested, equally stylized (shot in black and white), with the mother seemingly aware of her son's imminent fall to his death. All the same, certain images provoke irresistible questions. Why was the boy's teddy tied tantalizingly to a floating balloon? What of his chunky boots, which we see arranged the wrong way round (anticipating a crucial scene later in the film)? Was the baby alarm inaudible or simply ignored? Whatever the case, the abrupt transition from the traumatic event — the fantasmatic framing of the child's death — to the aftermath of that event — the wife's profound grief, her husband's imposition of cognitive therapy — suggests that the truth of this traumatic event will remain tantalizingly out of reach. It remains an intractable source of grief, pain and despair that cannot be entirely overcome, whether through cognitive clarification, narrative mastery, or aesthetic sublimation.

The story shown in *Antichrist* is gothic in its uncanny effects, yet mythic in its psychological density and cultural-religious resonances. A child dies while a couple is making love. Eschewing conventional medical treatment, the shattered couple leave their home, the scene of the tragic death, and head for their remote forest cabin (with the evocative name of 'Eden'), where the wife [Charlotte Gainsbourg] is supposed to overcome her grief and anxiety by undertaking cognitive exposure therapy under the guidance of her husband/ therapist [Willem Dafoe]. Instead of catharsis or conversion, however, what ensues is a nightmarish, supernaturally tinged, life-and-death struggle, at once psychological and sexual. The suppressed guilt over their child's death returns to haunt both husband and wife — identified simply as 'He' and 'She' in the credits — in diametrically opposed ways. Assuming the burden of guilt for her child's death, She also brutally punishes her husband, sexually and physically, as both accomplice and tormentor, before finally mutilating, even 'castrating', herself. Displacing this guilt on to her, He thereby allays his own anxiety and fear, perhaps even his misogyny, by strangling her to death, before burning her, witch-like, on a pyre. He then leaves Eden, alone, his cognitive therapy having led to him murdering, rather than curing, his wife. Before returning to civilisation, however, he has a final series of visions, in which he sees the forest strewn with the corpses of other women who have been sacrificed in the past. In the final ambiguous image, he beholds, accompanied again by Handel's aria, a vast throng of faceless women emerging from the forest, silently overtaking him as he attempts to flee the scene of his wife's immolation.

A MARITAL TRAUMA FILM

The basic plot, visual style and mythic resonances of *Antichrist* suggest a number of other films belonging to what we might call the marital/familial trauma variant of psychological horror. Here we could mention, among others, Polanski's *Rosemary's Baby* (1968), Nicolas Roeg's *Don't Look Now* (1973), Friedkin's *The Exorcist* (1973), Lynch's *Eraserhead* (1977), Kubrick's *The Shining* (1980), Georges Sluizer's *The Vanishing* (1988), Hideo Nakata's *Ring* (1998) and *Dark Water* (2002), and so on. In all of these films, there is a central couple, husband and wife, usually with a child, a background of sexual or marital conflict or breakdown, a child (or spouse) who either disappears or dies. The couple is subjected to inexplicable trauma, whether natural or supernatural; attempts to heal their relationship and to overcome their trauma, thus re-establishing the couple, if not the family, usually end badly, with violent conse-quences. It is as though the couple, or nuclear family unit, is subjected to the most extreme forms of trauma in order to see how much they can withstand. Alternatively, the couple itself is shown to be constituted via various forms of repressed conflict, antagonism or trauma that eventually manifest in hyperbolic form (hallucinations, visitations, possessions, visions, supernatural forces, monstrosities of nature, inexplicable violence, and so on).

A suggestive example pertinent to *Antichrist* is Bergman's only psychological horror film. *Hour of the Wolf* (1968) is narrated by a woman [Liv Ullman], whose artist-husband [Max von Sydow] has disappeared on a desolate island where they have come for him to pursue his painting. Although she regards this as an opportunity to rekindle their troubled marriage, it is clear, from an early scene where she is silently rebuffed, that all is not well between them. After an uncanny encounter with a mysterious and elegant old woman, who seems to know all about the artist's secret passions and private escapades, the wife reads his diary and learns of his artistic torments and demonic visions, his sexual humiliation and self-destructive paranoia. During the 'Hour of the Wolf' — the dark night of the soul before dawn, when most people die and malevolent spirits roam — he tells her of his nightmares, visions and obsessions, many of which form the subject-matter of his sketches, drawings and paintings. Attempting to make contact with the outside world, he and his wife suffer a series of psychological humiliations at the hands of a band of sophisticated but unnerving local aristocrats, who invite them to dinner at their 'Castle' before taunting the artist's 'freedom' with the promise of a fantasmatic sexual encounter with one of his former lover/muses (Veronica Vogler). Suffice to say, the realisation of his desire ends in violence and transgression, the aristocrats mutating into demonic figures and the artist fleeing into a darkened forest with threatening trees, tormented by a monstrous raven. His wife is left alone on the island to narrate to us the strange tale of her husband's disappearance, leaving us only with questions without answers. Bergman's film, it is worth noting, was made after his nervous breakdown, while von Trier's *Antichrist* emerged out of his well-publicized depression. A work of therapy, von Trier called it, channelling Strindberg, Poe and Bergman.[6] In both cases, a couple in trouble retreat to an isolated location, one that evokes the sublimity of nature but also imbues it with supernaturalistic overtones. In both films, a written text plays a crucial role, opening up or exposing the psyche of one protagonist to his or her spouse: the artist's diary and sketches in *Hour of the Wolf;* the woman's illustrated thesis/journal 'Gynocide' (on the history of medieval witch-hunts) in *Antichrist.* Both films end with the death of one of the couple (the artist/husband in Bergman's film; Her/the wife in von Trier's). Both also feature a mysterious raven as harbinger of death, exploring the sublimity of nature — the forest or 'the woods' — as a figure for the breakdown of the characters' psychic integrity.

Another striking instance of the marital-familial trauma film, as well as an obvious reference for *Antichrist*, is Nicolas Roeg's psychological thriller, *Don't Look Now* (1973) (see White and Power 2009). As with *Antichrist*, Roeg's film also opens with the tragic accidental death of a child; a young girl in a red coat who drowns in a pond outside her family home (the sequence also accompanied by a poignant musical score). Her art-curator father [Donald Sutherland] has intimations of the tragic event, signalled by a mysterious figure in red and an uncanny streak of blood spreading across a photograph of a church stained-glass window he is studying just moments before the girl drowns. To deal with their grief and heal their marriage, the couple travel to Venice, where the husband has been contracted to restore a Byzantine Church. While there, his wife befriends two peculiar English psychics who claim to be in contact with her dead daughter. The husband, for his part, becomes convinced that he has glimpsed his daughter's figure, in her distinctive red coat, wandering through the dark lanes and alleyways of Venice, and becomes increasingly obsessed with finding her — only to encounter an eruption of real violence as the 'child' whom he finally confronts (a dwarf-like serial killer at large in Venice) turns on him and slits his throat.

In both *Antichrist* and *Don't Look Now*, we find the same irresolution of the marital and sexual discord that follows the traumatic death of a child. The grief, pain and despair the couple experience cannot be successfully converted into more positive affective or cognitive dispositions; even fleeing the domestic scene of tragedy, whether to a mountain cabin (*Antichrist*) or streets of Venice (*Don't Look Now*), leaves intact the traumatic kernel of the event. Recalling the literary traditions of gothic horror and the fantastic (Poe and E. T. A. Hoffman), in both films the fantasmatic overlays the traumatic, sexual passion intersects with deathly violence, and the traumatic experience of guilt, pain and despair returns to haunt the couple in the form of psychic breakdown and destructive trauma.

In von Trier's film, the couple ('He' and 'She') deal with grief and anxiety by returning to 'Eden', their forest cabin (a return to the prelapsarian Garden of Innocence, presumably, in which the couple, He and She, will rediscover the nature of Good and Evil). They have retreated from the scene of their domestic trauma in order for the woman to confront the source of her fear and anxiety, which she can only obliquely identify as 'the woods'. This is already a psychologically unsettling dynamic, since the most fearful thing, for any parent, has already happened, and that within the intimate space of the familial home. The reality of marital-sexual discord, following the tragic death of their child, prompts a psychological flight into the 'supernaturalistic' space of Eden.[7] Indeed, the dramatic shift from fantasmatic prologue to traumatically real aftermath is signalled in the opening shots of 'Grief', which shows the child's stricken parents walking slowly behind the hearse carrying his coffin. The shot, now in colour, with intrusively realistic sound, is presented from within the hearse, from the dead child's point of view, as it were.[8] Through the hearse's rear window, we see the father weeping (his only expression of emotion until his concluding murderous rage), while his mother, ashen and stony-faced, collapses on the pavement in what is the start of a severe depression — an 'atypical grief pattern', as her doctor says — that will last over the coming months. The faces of the funeral procession are smudged or erased (as in the epilogue, which features a crowd of anonymous, faceless women leaving Eden). From the start, this tragic marital drama is principally psychic and fantasmatic; a cinematic enactment of trauma, yet one that resists psychological reductionism, aesthetic sublimation, or cognitive mastery.

THE THREE BEGGARS

Each of *Antichrist*'s first three chapters deals with a powerful negative emotion or affect (grief, pain, despair), with the fourth chapter, entitled 'The Three Beggars', combining these in bringing the narrative to its traumatic conclusion. It is tempting to assume that these sections of the film, in keeping with the more realist visual style, tell the 'real' story of the couple's traumatic attempts to deal with their grief and anxiety. Yet these chapters, if attentively viewed, also undermine the neat separation of the film into a fantasmatic prologue/epilogue and apparently 'realistic' narrative development. For these supposedly 'realist' chapters also include supernaturalist visions and apparently 'objective' correlates in nature (falling acorns, dying animals, falling trees) confirming the reality of evil manifesting itself to the traumatized couple in Eden.

In addition to the slow-motion, black-and-white images (accompanied by Handel) and the more realist, Dogme-style colour imagery of the four main chapters, we must add a third series, which we might call the stylized gothic/supernaturalist images of a sublime but malevolent nature. These are most evident in the remarkable hypnosis sequence as the couple are travelling by train towards their mountain retreat. The man induces the woman to enter a hypnotic state and to visualize her approach to the woods near Eden, guiding her to lie on the grass and merge into it. This shot, from above, of her body merging with the verdant grass, recalls similar shots in other von Trier films (Grace's merging into the apples in the back of Ben's truck in *Dogville;* or the shot of the distraught Jason, near the end of *Medea*, merging into the grass after having discovered his murdered sons). This third series of images is filmed again in slow motion and in colour, yet with a stylized, contrasting palette reminiscent of the paintings of Caspar David Friedrich (which feature lone figures in dark and forbidding landscapes, dying trees amidst desolate forest clearings, branches illuminated against the night sky and surrounding darkness, misty forests tinged by supernaturalist menace). The most striking image in this gothic/supernaturalist series is of the couple, seen from behind and prone on the ground, making love against an ancient, gnarled tree trunk, whose twisted roots are punctuated by emerging hands and arms poised in stylized agony. Interestingly, just before pulling back to reveal this stunning cinematic tableau, the camera pauses close by the back of his neck, suggesting that the tableau we then see is anchored to the husband's perception of their Wagnerian *Liebestod* embrace.[9]

Indeed, each chapter concludes with the male character experiencing a 'supernaturalist' vision that challenges the assumption that he is a stilted stereotype of dogmatic rationalism. He is madder than he appears, whereas She is more sane that He assumes. After being 'cured' of her crippling fear, He is unresponsive, as though She now no longer sustains his desire ('I never interested you until now,' She remarks, 'now that I am your patient'). Indeed, the film enacts a kind of psychological and dramatic chiasmus: She begins in grief, is supposed to confront her fear, but confronts guilt instead; He avoids his grief by adopting the mask of therapist, thereby suppressing his own pain and despair, which only reveals his own hidden fear and anxiety. In this sexual life-and-death struggle, his attempts to cure, indeed control, her grief, pain and despair only succeed in inciting her guilt; her attempts to enforce their traumatized marriage end with her violent physical and sexual revolt, her brutal attempts to punish him as well as herself. A marriage made in heaven, or rather in Eden, seems to end in hell.

Against the temptation to see the film as a misogynistic tract, we should note that all the 'supernaturalist' visions in the film are witnessed by He (the husband/therapist), rather than by She (the wife/patient). *Her* moment of vision is an ambiguous reimagining of the crucial moment of the child's accident, in which She (remembers? imagines? believes?) that she tacitly allowed her child to fall to his death. At no point does She have a 'vision' of the kind that He experiences in the forests of Eden ('You shouldn't underestimate Eden', she warns him, telling of her experience the previous summer of hearing an uncanny crying in the forest, a lost child wailing, as though the forest itself were in pain, a harbinger of the trauma to come). At the end of each chapter, by contrast, there is a supernaturalist vision expressive of *his* own psychic trauma: in Chapter One (Grief), it is the Deer in the forest with a dead fawn emerging from its womb; in Chapter Two (Pain), it is the self-lacerating Fox who utters the gnomic law, 'Chaos Reigns'; in Chapter Three (Despair (Gynocide)), it is the mysterious Raven lying buried beneath the ground that cannot be killed; and in Chapter Four it is the ghostlike vision of the 'Three Beggars' — Deer (Grief), Fox (Pain), and Raven (Despair) — as He attempts to leave the forests of Eden after strangling and burning his wife ('When the three beggars arrive, someone must die', she intones, ironically, for it is *She* who will die in the end).

In contrast, the female character (She) has an initial experience of recovery ('I'm well again; I'm cured!' she exclaims, at the end of Chapter Two, before accusing him of desiring her suffering, wanting her to remain as traumatized victim). After confronting her with photographic evidence that she repeatedly put their son Nic's boots on the wrong feet, thus causing a 'minor deformity', She becomes increasingly tormented by guilt and turns violently against her husband, frightened that he will abandon her to her guilt and grief. More inquisitor than interlocutor, He has been unable or unwilling to grieve, to experience pain and despair himself, until she literally *forces* him to do so (a perverse version of trauma therapy, perhaps).

Following her shocking, self-inflicted genital mutilation, presumably a punishment for the burden of (sexual-moral) guilt she has assumed, we see a repetition of a remarkable earlier sequence of images of anxiety (blurred vision, palpitations, nausea, tinnitus and trembling). This time, however, it is not *her* body we see manifesting this anxiety (as in the earlier sequence) but *his* eyes, ears, veins, fingers and flesh. It is *his* fear and anxiety that has been at issue all along; his fear of 'Me' (Herself) (as he notes in his little pyramid diagram depicting the psychological sources of her anxiety), which turns out to be a cryptic and ironic self-diagnosis. The cognitive therapy that He has imposed upon his wife/patient has been nothing but a symptom of his own grief, pain, and despair. It is He who ends up acting out the violent misogyny that was the subject of her abandoned thesis ('Gynocide') on the history of medieval witch-hunts. As She warns, He should not have underestimated Eden and its malevolent power.

FILM AS PHILOSOPHY AND/OR CINEMATIC THINKING

What is one to make of the film's allusions to the history of misogyny (in particular the persecution of witches), to mythology (both pagan and Christian), and to a portrait of nature imbued with a metaphysical (even supernatural) conception of evil? Here again, the film both invites and thwarts aesthetic reflection, philosophical interpretation and affective conversion. On the one hand, the 'nature' that prompts men and women to do evil is clearly symbolized by the 'Three Beggars' that appear throughout the film, whether in symbolic form (the statuettes) or in shamanistic animal manifestations (Grief, the Deer; Pain, the Fox; and Despair, the Raven). On the other hand, the status of this symbolism, as well as the references to mythology, history, Freudian as well as cognitivist therapy, remain deeply ambiguous, dubious, even undecideable. There is no comforting aesthetic, moral, or cognitive resolution to be achieved at the conclusion of the film. We are left with only the traumatic insight that it is Grief, Pain and Despair that are together responsible for the evil that men/reason do to women/nature.

This insight, however, such as it is, remains deeply ambiguous, even undermined by the film's ambivalent conclusion, which hints that the cognitive therapy that was supposed to cure the woman of depression was itself a kind of violence. The husband's misguided therapy unleashes a latent misogyny that leads him to act out yet another historical repetition of the cycle of persecution, conflict and violence that is the history of Western culture's (masculinist?) attempts to rationally master and control (internal and external) nature. At the same time, the perverse conclusion that She draws from her thesis research into Gynocide, trumped by her own mad experience of the malevolent force of nature, is both endorsed and questioned by the film. We are forced to endure the affective dissonance of violent psychological, sexual and physical trauma; but also the cognitive dissonance of attempting to reconcile clashing yet complementary worldviews that do not cohere in any rational whole. Indeed, the film's treatment of intractable trauma can only be confronted obliquely, through a cinematic performance of trauma, one that resonates in the darker reaches of our psyches.

'CHAOS REIGNS'

A number of commentators have noted that the film remains, despite its allusions to and engagement with horror, all but impossible to classify generically. Rather than a variation on the conventional psychological horror film, *Antichrist* is better understood as a marital/sexual/psychological *trauma* film. Trauma differs from horror in being resistant to the kind of cognitive mastery or affective conversion that, for Carroll and Plantinga, provides the 'metaphysical comfort' (as Nietzsche would say) we apparently procure from horror films. *Antichrist* nonetheless invites, even demands, such engagement, provoking the viewer or critic into philosophically directed interpretation, while at the same time thwarting attempts to achieve the cognitive or aesthetic comprehension that would ameliorate our negative affective response to the film.

For all that, one could still ask whether this film is simply a hyperbolic staging of misogyny artfully disguised in cinematic and metaphysical garb. Many critics have responded to *Antichrist* in this way, assuming that von Trier's misogynistic thesis is that nature really *is* the source of evil, that women's bodies are controlled by nature, hence the evil nature of women (the title 'Antichrist' incorporating the symbol of the female sex).[10] There are many snares and pitfalls, however, with this kind of 'literalist' reading of the film as a moral, metaphysical, or even misogynistic tract. For one thing, we are presented throughout with the male character's view of the female character, initially as depressive patient and finally as demonic force of nature. We witness *his* increasingly disturbing visions of malevolent evil manifesting in nature (her hypnotically induced images of approaching Eden belong to the third series of images, which are evocative, melancholy and hallucinatory, but devoid of supernaturalist elements). The dramatic caesura involves *his* confrontation of her as having been, perhaps unconsciously, responsible for the death of their child. That women are evil is the perverse conclusion that *He* draws from their 'therapeutic' experience in Eden. It is *She* who ends up both as manifestation, and sacrificial victim, of the logic of misogynistic violence, which concludes with the devoted husband and cognitive therapist burning his wife's corpse.

The epilogue, which revisits Handel's 'Lascia ch'io pianga' aria, presents us again with remarkable black-and-white, slow-motion images that lend an aura of fantasmatic intensity to the husband's uncanny vision. We see him emerging alone from the forest, eating berries, only to be struck dumb by the vision of myriad 'faceless' women emerging, indomitably, from the woods. What to make of this ambiguous ending? Although he may have killed her, fulfilling her prediction that visitations by the 'Three Beggars' (Grief, Pain and Despair) always end in death, he can never destroy what Woman/Nature/Eden stands for, whether in cultural history or in the masculine imaginary. On the other hand, his misogynistic vision may be yet another manifestation of nature's evil; the uncanny return of a repressed image of nature as demonic force that remains uncontrollable by (masculine) reason. The film provides no purchase on the matter, remaining ambiguous between these alternatives, ending on a note of irresolution that thwarts emotional catharsis as much as intellectual comprehension.

For these reasons, prevailing theories of horror cannot really do justice to *Antichrist*'s cinematic, psychological, metaphysical and cultural-theological dissonances. It resists the kind of intellectualist puzzle-solving or aesthetic sublimation that, for Carroll, explain our paradoxical pleasure in horror. It also resists the conversion of negative into positive affect that Plantinga claims is horror's defining feature. One could, to be sure, adopt Cynthia Freeland's argument (2002) that the way to resolve the paradoxical nature of horror, especially in a psychological trauma film such as *Antichrist*, is to interpret it as expressing our culturally enduring fascination with the power of evil. Yet the psychological, narrative and aesthetic manifestations of evil in *Antichrist* are radically ambiguous: part hallucination, part mystical vision, part objective correlate of psychic trauma, part sublime cinematic spectacle. The 'evil' haunting *Antichrist*, grasped in a Nietzschean rather than Christian sense, is the aesthetic means by which psychic and bodily trauma can be manifested or acknowledged. From this point of view, as Daniel Shaw suggests (2001, 2007, 40–41), our vicarious pleasure in horror is a Nietzschean form of affective alignment with the power of the monster or malevolent force as well as a correlated sympathy with the unfortunate victim of that force.

Antichrist, however, depicts a life-and-death struggle that disrupts any ready identification between perpetrator and victim; the malevolent force — nature within and without — is as much a manifestation of psychic trauma as it is a phenomenon permeating the gothic sublimity of nature. Instead of locating a mechanism of conversion, sublimation or rationalization, we are forced to remain within the unbearable phenomenology of traumatic horror, with its harrowing experience of cognitive disorientation and affective intoxication. Inspired by Euripides' *Medea* as mediated by Dreyer, *Antichrist* is von Trier's 'impossible' attempt to move beyond the horror genre and to stage a cinematic tragedy. The question is whether von Trier's cinema of cruelty can be both ambiguously cathartic and irreducibly traumatic: a 'therapeutic' shock to thought and a cinematic Shaman's trip.[11]

CHAPTER NINE

SONG OF THE EARTH: CINEMATIC ROMANTICISM IN TERRENCE MALICK'S *THE NEW WORLD*

BETWEEN WORLDS

Cinema has often been compared with myth. Can a film express the kind of mythology that might reorient a disoriented world? Or is this merely the dream of a naive romanticism, a cinematic romanticism? Terrence Malick is a filmmaker who has been both praised and criticized for the romanticism, even 'naivety', evident in his work. Consider the opening sequence of his recent historico-mythic epic, *The New World* (2005). The film opens with an image of quiet movement across the surface of water, as though we were in a canoe gliding across the water at dusk, accompanied by a mesmerizing voiceover, a young woman's voice, dreamily reciting lines from a poem or proem: 'Come, Spirit. Help us sing the story of our land. You are our mother, we your field of corn. We rise from out of the soul of you.'[1] Her voice recites this verse against the background sounds of birdsong, crickets and water. A cut to an image of a beautiful young woman, shot from below, arms raised heavenward, giving thanks to the sky. This sequence is followed by the credits proper, set against a background of animated maps of the Virginia region festooned with animals, birds and waterways, but also marked by ships, dwellings and battles.

Compare this with the opening sequence of *The Thin Red Line* (1998), which begins with images of a crocodile sliding under the water, vast jungle trees and treetops illuminated by sunlight, and a Southern male voiceover asking, 'What is this war in the heart of nature?'[2] *The Thin Red Line* similarly includes images of children swimming underwater illuminated against the water's surface reflecting the sky, set to Fauré's *Requiem*, followed by an image of Private Witt [Jim Caviezel] serenely paddling his canoe, greeting the local fishermen, children playing rhythmically with pebbles on the sand; a beautiful new world that serves as idyllic backdrop for the violent encounter between worlds that is soon to follow. Sub-aquatic images have featured regularly in Malick's films. Think, for example, of Bill's [Richard Gere's] extraordinary death scene in *Days of Heaven* (1978), which shows, again from below the water's surface, the reverse sequence, from life to death: Bill's/Gere's face crashing into the water after having been fatally shot in the back.[3] Crucial scenes from *The New World* will also feature water or a return to water, Pocahontas/Rebecca [Q'orianka Kilcher] praying to her Mother/Spirit, or at the end of the film, standing, fully clothed, smiling joyously after having been immersed in water at the moment her spirit is released in death, or the concluding images of water running over rocks, which gives way to the final sublime shot of treetops swaying in the wind.

The opening image of *The New World*, accompanied by gradually swelling horns announcing Wagner's famous *Rheingold* prelude, features naked figures swimming amidst fish and set against the sunlit surface of the water.[4] We momentarily glimpse a beautiful young woman, her face seen from beneath the water, her hand gently touching the water's surface. The extended cut of the film[5] dwells on the figure of young girls, one in particular, swimming gracefully beneath the surface, with a voiceover, possibly hers, that continues: 'Dear Mother, you fill the land with your beauty. You reach to the end of the world. How shall I seek you? You, the great river that never runs dry.' We cut to an image of strong young men, seen again from beneath the water's surface, pointing intently off into the distance. The next shot reveals three ships, imposing and grand, entering the harbour and announcing the central contrast of the film: between the New World, that is also a mythic world immersed in nature, and the Old World, that is a historical world of the colonial settlers who have come to establish the first permanent colony on these shores (an inter-title announces that we are about to enter (Western) history: *Virginia, 1607*).

The images of the ships' occupants, commanders, sailors, and the like, show a mixture of responses, from wariness and caution to amazement and wonder. A porthole image — a frame within the film frame — shows the ships sailing into harbour from yet another perspective beneath the surface of things. Here and throughout the film there are recurring images of framing, of the world viewed, subtly drawing attention to this cinematic framing of a mythic historical encounter. From a darkened background we see a handsome face emerge, a prisoner in chains peering out towards the world, then gazing skyward, hands outstretched, echoing the image of Pocahontas worshipping in the prologue. His purpose here, however, is not to worship but to catch the water dripping down on his face from the grill up on deck. The images of Pocahontas [Q'orianka Kilcher] and Smith [Colin Farrell], however, are already linked and twinned; the contrasts between freedom and constraint, community and exile, between New and Old Worlds, already deftly set in motion.

The film cuts back to the excited figures on shore, running from their village to a higher vantage-point from which they can see the strange apparition. Our attention is drawn to one character in particular, Pocahontas [Kilcher], whose perspective and response frames that of her people and of the film itself, gazing in amazement as the ships sail closer to shore. The film cuts back to the handsome prisoner on the ship, peering again through a porthole, an image that neatly frames another of longboats heading towards the shore, as he smiles in joyful anticipation. These two are destined to meet, their worlds to collide, their fates to entwine; yet this is an encounter whose outcome cannot, as yet, be anticipated, nor one in which our background knowledge of the legend or subsequent history of Pocahontas and John Smith is supposed to figure. It is a moment preparing for an encounter between worlds, between myth and history; an encounter that the film signals shall be presented in a manner that is naive, mythic and poetic, rather than documentary, historical or political. This will be an encounter between worlds that also raises the question of marriage; a question in a *romantic* key, as the Wagnerian prelude (the first of three renditions in the film) vividly suggests.

VIEWING WORLDS

The opening sequence of *The New World* lasts for a little over eight minutes. By the end of this prelude, we are thoroughly immersed in the strange liminal space and time between history and myth; a mythic history in which events and characters have not yet crystal-lized into historical personages or a retrospectively narrated and thus comprehended event (see Martin 2007a: 213). We are amidst a cinematic mythology and poetic thinking of the nascent, as yet undetermined, moment of encounter between Old and New Worlds. This is a film that is not only about time but which reveals time, provided we are open and receptive to the kind of temporal transfor-mation that it seeks to effect. Indeed, Malick is a filmmaker who is noted for taking his time: time to make films, time for us to become immersed in his unique cinematic worlds, time for us to appreciate the critical and aesthetic achievement of his work thus far.[6] Not every filmgoer or critic, however, takes this time over or with Malick's work. Despite widespread praise for his cinematic achievements, his reputation as an elusive, maverick genius working at the margins of Hollywood, the critical response to *The New World* has been, as Lloyd Michaels notes, 'generally disheartening' (Michaels 2009: 84). Instead of receptivity to cinematic mythology, or critical reflection on artistic achievement, we find mocking ridicule or hasty dismissal, as though the difficulty of a film, its resistance to superficial appro-priation, were markers of its artistic or intellectual failure.

As Adrian Martin observes, we should remember that all of Malick's films had mixed reviews when first released, even those now regarded as classics (2007a: 218). This tells us something important about practices of film criticism that refuse to take the time required for artistically — and philosophically — challenging works, and hence fail, in their haste to pass judgement and in their refusal of aesthetic reflection, 'to take the measure of Malick's achievement' (Martin 2007a: 218). Despite this critical hesitation or aesthetic uncertainty, or perhaps because of it, one of the most common ways to approach Malick has been from the viewpoint of philosophy. Indeed, Malick has recently been canonized as one of the few genuinely 'philosophical' filmmakers working today,[7] his works having attracted a variety of philosophical interpretations, from claims that his films are instances of Heideggerian cinema (Clewis 2003; Furstenau and MacEvoy 2007; Kaja Silverman 2003; Rhym 2010) to claims that they are better appreciated as cases of 'film as philosophy' (Critchley 2005; Sinnerbrink 2006).

The question that concerns us here is to consider what it means for a filmmaker's work to be philosophical, a case of film as philosophy, or indeed as cinematic thinking. In what follows, I shall approach

The New World as a work of cinematic thinking that attempts to transform the familiar Pocahontas legend by presenting the historical encounter between Old and New Worlds in the register of poetic myth. It is a 'song of the earth' in a romantic key, evoking not only Heidegger but Emerson, Nietzsche and Stanley Cavell. This is hardly surprising, given that Malick studied philosophy with Cavell at Harvard, was a Rhodes Scholar at Oxford, and translated an important Heidegger text, *The Essence of Reasons*, in 1969. As Cavell comments, with reference to Malick's *Days of Heaven*: 'I think the film does indeed contain a metaphysical vision of the world; but I think one feels one has never quite seen the scene of human existence — call it the arena between earth (or days) and heaven — quite realized this way on film before' (Cavell 1979: xiv, xvi) — a comment that could equally be directed at *The New World*.

At the same time, *The New World*, like Malick's other films, cannot be reduced to any specifically philosophical theme, idea or perspective. Rather, the film enacts a kind of cinematic thinking that invites philosophical and aesthetic responses, while articulating a kind of thinking that resists translation into a ready-made thesis, position or argument. It demands a way of thinking that is not entirely reducible to the philosophical, or which subtly transforms the ways in which we assume a traditional philosophical or theoretical response to the film might be expressed. Instead of applying a ready-made framework to the film, be it Nietzschean (Macdonald 2009), Humean (Cousins 2007), or Arendtian/post-Colonialist (Morrison 2007), cinematic thinking invites an exchange that allows the thinking immanent within the work to be translated between media of thought (between film and philosophy). In this sense, philosophy is not a hermeneutic master key so much as an accompaniment to the film (in the sense of a musical accompaniment); elaborating and translating the uniquely cinematic aesthetic experience into a register that opens up a transformative encounter with philosophical reflection.

ON ROMANTIC NAIVETY

How, then, to approach this enigmatic and untimely work? Celebrated and criticized at once as Hollywood's most elusive auteur, Malick's work has always attracted an ambivalent mixture of critical admiration and mixed box-office success (Flanagan 2007:

138–9). *The New World* is no exception, presenting a strikingly poetic evocation of one of America's founding myths, the story of Pocahontas and Captain John Smith. Following nineteenth-century tradition, Malick renders the latter as a romantic tale of thwarted love, misguided ambition and spiritual reconciliation; but unlike tradition, he lingers on the ambiguous dimensions of intercultural conflict, explores diverging attitudes towards nature between Old and New Worlds, and shifts the narrative focus towards the usually neglected marriage between Pocahontas/Rebecca and tobacco grower John Rolfe. Despite its apparent shift into the genre of historical epic, it resonates deeply with his other, generically idiosyncratic works — *Badlands* (1973), *Days of Heaven* (1978) and *The Thin Red Line* (1998) — by presenting a mesmerizing cinematic meditation on our relationship with nature, our experience of mortality, and the nature of love.[8]

The film's central romantic narrative — the love triangle between Pocahontas/Rebecca, John Smith and John Rolfe — has an important allegorical meaning in at least two registers: the possibility of a successful marriage or cultural exchange between Old and New Worlds, and the possibility of achieving a kind of reconciliation with nature — our own mortal nature as well as the nature upon which we depend — that would sustain any such intercultural reconciliation. At the same time, the film attempts to present an 'impossible' experience fusing mythic history, subjective reflection, and a metaphysical perspective in which nature itself speaks. This audacious undertaking has prompted some of the film's philosophical critics to disavow *The New World*'s romantic naivety. Far from being anachronistically naïve *The New World* recalls the kind of 'aesthetic mythology' called for by the early German romantics in response to the crisis of reason and meaning afflicting the modern world (see Critchley 1997: 99–114). From this point of view, *The New World* explores the potential for cinema to enact alternative forms of world-disclosure, aesthetically revealing, through cinematic art, new ways of being, of dwelling, within a world-context and relationship with nature that is under pressure from a destructive rationalism, reductive instrumentalism and imperialist violence.

Malick approaches this aesthetic mythology with romantic *naivety*: the innocence of mythic history for which the burdens of the past, and of the present, are magically transfigured. As Adrian Martin notes, the film presents characters as though they were not yet fully formed, depicting them 'in the uncertain, twilight, becoming state before such a congealing of identity' (Martin 2007a: 213). This hovering of identity, prior to its congealing into a fixed state (historical, personal or narrative), is central to the aesthetic mythology of *The New World*. Malick's 'song of the earth' captures the threshold or origin of a historical myth — the myth of America — one that needs retrieving precisely because of the historical disasters of colonialism; the exploitation, historical conflict, and destruction of nature *and* culture that we have witnessed in its wake.

FROM MYTHIC HISTORY TO CINEMATIC POETRY

Critics have generally tried to resist *The New World*'s romantic naivety (through irony or scepticism) or restricted it to autobiography (see Sinnerbrink 2009b). Here I would like to propose an alternative interpretation of this naivety, and a response to the critical ambivalence it provokes.

First we should reflect on what it means to describe the film as 'naive', which in everyday speech refers to someone who lacks worldly experience, who is ignorant of the way of the world, or perhaps 'otherworldly' in his/her vision of things. In an aesthetic context, however, we can speak of a *naive style*, which refers to a conscious attempt to produce this kind of untutored, spontaneous, child-like or 'primitive' vision of the world. Critics of *The New World,* however, are clearly not intending the term in this sense, despite there being good grounds to describe some aspects of Malick's cinematic aesthetics as a *naive style* in film.

At any rate, the criticism of naivety, understood less as a style than as a way of treating the film's subject-matter, is a charge levelled from the perspective of superior knowledge or judgement tempered by historical experience. It faults the film for unwittingly deploying dubious tropes or reproducing questionable points of view. To (implicitly) criticize *The New World* for romantic naivety is to suggest that it is ignorant of, or remains captured by, a history that it is unable to comprehend; or to suggest that the film reverts to tropes — concerning nature, love and mortality — that have become culturally obsolete. At the same time, the implication is that the film *unwittingly* suffers these historical, moral or aesthetic lapses; otherwise one would have to propose that Malick's film *knowingly* attempts to justify aesthetically one of the more ideologically 'tainted' myths supporting the Colonialist project. Since this alternative would compromise the aesthetic and moral worth of the film, the former alternative provides a means of rationalizing *The New World*'s romanticist gestures.

Malick's bold use of Wagner's *Rheingold* prelude is one such romanticist gesture. To combine Wagnerian opera, *the* tragic art of the modern age, according to Nietzsche, with the Pocahontas myth, is romanticism in full bloom — perhaps even romantic naivety. Yet such criticisms fall into the trap of responding to isolated tropes, figures or scenarios in a film as though these were static tableaux, rather than fragments in becoming, composing an open-ended, fragmentary whole. The opening prelude sequence of *The New World* — much like the opening sequence of *The Thin Red Line* — is deceiving; it could be taken as a romantic and naive depiction of a mythic moment of cultural encounter, an idealized vision of the possibility of another history, a paean to aesthetic transfiguration rather than a tribute to historical documentation. To do so, however, would be to 'essentialize' the film; to arrest its movement to one aspect of its symphonic development, isolating a mutable fragment as though it encompassed the meaning of the whole.

The second time the Wagner prelude appears is to signal the blossoming of love between Pocahontas and John Smith, their nuptials already hinted at or prefigured in the opening sequence of the film.[9] As Martin remarks, love — a constant preoccupation in Malick's films — now becomes 'a full-blown event to which its participants must strive to be faithful'; it is not fidelity to a moral, religious or social order, but rather 'a testimony to the transformative, even utopian power of this emotional entanglement' (2007a: 217). Another voiceover by Pocahontas begins, again evoking or questioning her Mother/Spirit: 'Mother, where do you live? In the sky? The clouds? The sea?' We see images of the interior of a hut, filled with smoke and statues (one of the many varieties of interior dwellings to be found in *The New World*), and another of Pocahontas worshipping the sky. An image of the roof of the hut, open to the sky but framed by a small window-like opening, releasing smoke, inverts the earlier image of Smith's vision of the window-like opening above the hold of the ship. These are portals between worlds but also figures of Malick's cinema, indeed of *The New World* itself, as cinematic portal between mythic-historical worlds.

'Give me a sign', says Pocahontas, 'We rise. We rise.' Like smoke from a fire or clouds from the sea, the spirit rises into the firmament; love takes flight, spanning immeasurable distance, releasing us from the heaviness of earth, but also threatening us with the loss of our grounding in the world. In the extended version of the film, we see an image of Pocahontas' actual mother (played by Irene Bedard), face painted white and reciting a ritual incantation, followed by lyrical and poignant images of Pocahontas and John Smith, their wordless love beginning to flower: 'Afraid of myself. A god he seems to me.' Her growing self-understanding is figured in a moving vignette showing Pocahontas regarding her image in a broken shard of mirror, laughing delightedly at her image. 'What else is life but being near you', the voice asks, as they regard a book together, Smith showing her pictures of that wonder of the Old World, the city of London. Pocahontas' growing recognition of her love for Smith, and for the potential transgression this might entail, is signalled in her reflections on how they appear to others in her community, and her knowledge that this blossoming love is nonetheless fated not to last: 'Do they suspect? Oh, to be given to you. You to me.'

The voiceover here and throughout this sequence is punctuated by images of trees, water, birds soaring; a rapturous fusion of nature, spirit and becoming: 'Two no more. One. One, I am. I am', as images of water appear once again along with treetops reaching for the sky, images of Pocahontas and Smith together. The E flat major 'drone' of the Wagner prelude has swelled to its fullest intensity by this point, as we cut to an image of a Powhatan native calling to one of the pair, at which point Smith now begins to speak, narrating how he was suddenly freed by the King, and told he would be sent back to his own people, to tell them that they could stay until the spring, after which 'they were to go back from where they came'. Against images of Pocahontas taking pleasure in the scent of drying tobacco leaves and giving thanks to the sky, Smith is returned to fortress-like Jamestown, bearing food and gifts for the coming winter. The music fades and finally stops as he is led into the grey, muddy, dispiriting fort, the Wagnerian Prelude replaced by the sound of barking dogs and whistling wind.

The Wagnerian prelude has shifted here from an anthem announcing the encounter between Old and New Worlds, and the linked fates of Pocahontas and Smith, to the accompaniment and expression of their burgeoning love, as well as their realization of the limits and impossibility of this love. It communicates Smith's return from the other world, his idyllic sojourn and rebirth thanks to Pocahontas and his life within the Powhatan community — 'there's only this, nothing else is real' — to the stark reality of his other life as soon-to-be commander of a derelict and dying colony.[10] Wagner's romantic theme, which first announced the encounter between Old and New Worlds, has shifted into an anthem for a vibrant but impossible love; the irreconcilable clash between worlds that demands that both Smith and Pocahontas sacrifice their love for the sake of community and tradition, conquest and colonization.

Indeed, it is this theme of *marriage* as expressing the possibility of a reconciliation between Old and New Worlds, but also of the discovery — or recollection — of another way of inhabiting the earth, that holds together the various 'movements' of *The New World*. Marriage — or better, remarriage, as is the case with Pocahontas/Rebecca — unites aesthetically the allegorical dimensions of the Pocahontas myth. The 'natural' marriage between Pocahontas and Smith is superseded by the 'cultural' marriage between Rebecca [Kilcher] and John Rolfe [Christian Bale]. Indeed, it is only with Rolfe (farmer and cultivator), rather than Smith (leader and adventurer), that the nuptials between naturalized culture and cultivated nature can be realised, however fleetingly.

'WHAT IS THIS WAR IN THE HEART OF NATURE?'

Although it is principally a love story set within a mythic recounting of the encounter between Old and New Worlds, the film also extends the meditations on the nature of human conflict, in particular of war, that were begun in *The Thin Red Line*. Indeed, there are striking parallels between the two films evident in their depiction of the arrival of Captain Newport's [Christopher Plummer's] ships in the Virginia tidewater region and of the American WWII gunboats landing on the shores of Guadalcanal (Michaels 2009: 81). In both cases the experience of war and conflict is made vivid dramatically and cinematically; how the event of a battle is more than the sum of any particular sequence of individual decisions or violent actions; how a kind of collective will-to-violence sweeps up individuals and groups in its fiery wake; how a malevolent energy begins to envelop the wills and moral agency of particular individuals and begins to feed upon itself in a collective act of self-destruction, going well beyond any material, military or strategic objectives. Although Malick avoids reflection on the broader historical or political forces at play in the fomenting of war, the physical proximity and ferocity of the battles scenes in both films — the arduous close-quarter gun battles to take the grassy mountain-top Japanese stronghold, and the brutal, kinetic hand-to-hand combat between Powhatan warriors and British colonists — suggest an existential pathos and subjective intensity that dramatizes the characters' confrontation with mortality, and their later questioning of the source and meaning of human violence.

Like other flawed leaders in *The Thin Red Line* (Captain Tall [Nick Nolte] and Lieutenant Staros [Elias Koteas]), Captain John Smith [Colin Farrell] is a character in whom conflicting impulses between personal ambition, the desire for love, and duty towards his fellow men compete for dominance. He is torn between an idealized conception of romantic love which expresses his communal belonging with the Powhatan, and his sense of moral and military responsibility for his fellows in the struggling fort-colony of Jamestown. It is clear that his decision to assume responsibility for the colony, and thus to break off his idyllic romance with Pocahontas, is as much a tragic conflict of competing impulses as an expression of the social and cultural 'impossibility' of their romantic love. Pocahontas too is conflicted between her love of Smith, her search for, and appeal to, her Mother/Earth, and her loyalty to her Father/community.[11] Her own 'political' conflict between personal passion and communal duty is less frequently remarked. After symbolically rescuing Smith from death and appealing for his inclusion within the community, she not only develops a tender and playful relationship with him but helps the colonists by giving them corn seeds and issuing a warning that the Powhatan are intending to attack. When her Father/Chief Powhatan discovers that she has defied his will and betrayed her people, she is also banished from the community, only to be taken as a strategic 'hostage' by the colonists in order to stymie further Powhatan attacks. The marriage between Old and New Worlds is predicated on conflict, betrayal and violence. Can it be otherwise or is this tragic denouement the inevitable outcome of Smith and Pocahontas' (or Malick's) romantic utopian dream?

This irresolvable conflict comes to a head in Smith's later choice between becoming the adventurer and explorer he was always groomed for, or pursuing his idealised love of Pocahontas and romantic vision of a rapprochement between his world and hers — an 'impossible' choice, one might say, between a human nature at war with itself and a human community reconciled with both inner and outer nature. In the end, Smith chooses the colony over community, discovery over recovery, honour and duty over love and fulfilment. He lies to her, by proxy, conveying the message to her, before the event, that he tragically 'drowned in the crossing' to England (the Old World). In another symbolic death and rebirth, he dies to her (and to himself) as John Smith, the natural leader and romantic visionary between Old and New Worlds, and is reborn, or perhaps reincarnated, as colonial adventurer and Crown explorer for the Old. Pocahontas, for her part, upon hearing the terrible news that John Smith has perished at sea, also undergoes a symbolic death to the foreign community of Jamestown in which she had made 'a fresh start', wandering forlorn through the settlement, mad with grief, daubing her face and body with ashes and mud, casting herself adrift from any meaningful connection with either form of human community.

Although it is generically a love story, much of the film deals with the difficulty of the nuptials between worlds: the conflicts, corruptions, betrayals and battles that have defined the bloody history of colonial contact. The thwarted relationship between Smith and Pocahontas — a 'natural' union that turned out to be culturally manipulated — cannot survive, let alone flourish, in the harsh world of intercultural contact and political conflict. In a striking sequence in the extended director's cut, Pocahontas' symbolic death and rebirth is enacted in an uncanny encounter in the forest: 'Come death, take me, and set me free. Let me be what I was', she intones, walking trance-like in a forest bathed in almost mystical light. She pauses before a tree, picks an ominous-looking mushroom that she is about to eat, only to be interrupted by trilling birdsong — a song of the earth, a message calling her back to life. She embraces the tree, returns to the water's edge and is symbolically reborn, worshipping the sky and giving thanks for her return to life. Now she reappears in Jamestown as a hybrid figure — between worlds, between life and death, yet still without a home or a life or place of her own. The film pivots on these two symbolic deaths: that of John Smith, in returning to the service of King and the Glory of Empire; and that of Pocahontas, following the loss and 'death' of John Smith, her traumatic limbo state brought to an end thanks to the gentle affection and patient understanding of John Rolfe. 'All this sorrow will give you strength', her kindly tutor and helper tells her, 'and point you to a higher way.' Like a tree whose branches grow around any obstacles, always reaching for the light, her sorrow becomes a source of strength and enlightenment in her new life as Rebecca, 'Princess of the New World', celebrated as a hybrid figure of the successful marriage between worlds.

The film's narrative arc thus enacts a complex chiasmus between Pocahontas' transformation into Rebecca, John Smith's reversion from romantic visionary to explorer of Empire, and John Rolfe's subtle and understated shift from solitary farmer to loyal husband, teacher and widowed father. The figure that embodies the fruit of these mutual transformations is their son — bearer of the fusion or hybrid becoming of worlds, a child of the future marking the possibility of a new beginning. Malick's remarkable aesthetic mythology in *The New World* thus attempts to evoke an aesthetic experience of encounter, a moment of being open to the New, while at the same time evoking the tragedy of history, the destruction of the moment of mutual encounter that was yet to come. In doing so, however, *The New World* does not attempt to sceptically undermine the promise of the New thanks to the tragic experience of the Old. It also tempers our romantic naivety by acknowledging the difficulty and conflict that such a promise necessarily entails. It can do so, however, only in the aesthetic register of mythic history — a romantic longing for an idealized unity not only between cultural worlds and worldviews, but between communities of human beings and the nature upon which both history and culture depend.

IN PRAISE OF CINEMATIC ROMANTICISM

From this point of view, let us consider the extraordinary concluding sequence of the film. In a moving gesture of trust and acknowledgement, Rolfe allows the emotionally conflicted Rebecca (who has learned that Smith is still alive) to meet with Smith and decide for herself whom she truly loves. Accompanied again by Mozart's lyrical piano, Rebecca makes her decision clear in her poignant parting from Smith in the English country gardens and her emotional reconciliation with Rolfe ('my husband', she whispers). The concluding sequence features the film's third recitation of the *Rheingold* prelude, one in which its original mythical meaning in Wagner's opera has now effectively been reversed, renouncing wealth and power in favour of love and grace.

As mentioned above, we first hear the prelude at the beginning of the film, accompanied by underwater images of fish and native figures swimming, followed by images of the arrival of the colonists' ships, to the amazement of the 'naturals' watching from shore. The second time the prelude plays is during Smith's idyllic sojourn with the Powhatan, evoking the flowering of love between Pocahontas and Smith and Smith's profound transformation during his sojourn with her people. When we hear the *Rheingold* prelude a third time, however, its significance has been subtly transfigured. It is no longer an anthem to wonder and possibility opened up by the nascent encounter between worlds; it is also broadened beyond the lyrical expression of love and utopian community that Smith experiences with Pocahontas and the Powhatan. These two rather polarised renditions of Wagner's piece are transfigured in this third rendering, which gives sublime musical expression to Pocahontas/Rebecca's acceptance of death, affirmation of life, and reconciling of Old and New Worlds in a no-longer-human world. This swelling, intensifying musical crescendo suggests nothing less than the self-expression of nature that is here momentarily allowed to 'sing', to bear witness to Pocahontas/Rebecca's spiritual reconciliation and her return to (mother) earth. Wagner's prelude is transfigured through aesthetic repetition in a manner that mirrors Pocahontas/Rebecca's own experience of transformation, which is presented, finally, as of a piece with the becoming of nature itself.

In this final sequence, the music signals a process of reconciliation, of homecoming, Rebecca/Pocahontas' discovery of who she is, and her reconciliation with life and death ('Mother, now I know where you live', she says, answering the question she first posed at the beginning of the film). The sequence is shown first from the perspective of her son, Thomas, playing hide-and-seek with his mother in the gardens, looking for her once she suddenly disappears (after her moment of recognition, her answering of the question that has guided her throughout). We then cut to Pocahontas/Rebecca's unexpected death at Gravesend, just as she and her family were to return home to Virginia. The moving images of her deathbed parting from Rolfe ('All must die,' she reminds him, 'yet 'tis enough that our son should live') are narrated from a letter Rolfe has written to his son that is to be read by him in the future. Images of death, recognizable from other Malick films, punctuate the scene: windows, criss-crossed with grills, opening towards the sky; an empty bed; a powerful, noble spirit departing the room in a bounding rush (one of the most sublime images of death in recent cinema). A glorious montage of images follows, depicting Pocahontas/Rebecca's departure from this life; her joyous worship of earth, sky and water, her cartwheels, her sublime celebration of, and return to, the creaturely life of nature. After its final crescendo, accompanied by images of ships departing from the shore, of Rebecca's cruciform gravestone rhyming with that of the ship's masts, seen from below, silhouetted against the evening sky, the music finally ceases — beyond death — with the film's final images of rushing water and towering treetops swaying in the wind. With the music giving way to birdsong, rushing water and forest sounds, the film is fleetingly transformed into a sublime song of the earth, one in which nature itself poetizes in a breathtaking moment of mythic possibility.

The three renderings of Wagner's *Rheingold* prelude mark a profound transformation between the early, middle and concluding parts of the film. These musically and visually rapturous sequences announce the encounter between worlds, celebrating the couple whose idyllic love and shared destinies mark both the utopian possibility and historical tragedy of this 'impossible' marriage between worlds. Malick's visual symphony combined with Wagner's overture reveals the transformation of the (Western) desire for conquest and domination, transfigured through love, the overcoming of opposition, and the need to acknowledge a deeper (spiritual) unity with nature. It aesthetically discloses the sublimity of nature understood as elemental earth, that which underlies and supports any historical and cultural form of human community. Acknowledging this unity with nature is what makes possible the kind of plural co-existence or marriage between worlds that *The New World* evokes through mythic history and cinematic poetry.

SONG OF THE EARTH

There is still something unsettling, however, about *The New World's* aesthetic mythologizing. In its remarkable fusion of mythic history and poetic reflection, *The New World* is a work of cinematic romanticism that presents the experience of an 'impossible' point of view — that of nature itself. On the one hand, the film immerses us, with careful verisimilitude, in the imagined *experience* of the historical encounter between colonists and natives. On the other, it immerses us within a mythic rendering of this event, within the ahistorical space of myth. Both perspectives are then integrated with the sublime presence of nature in all its elemental splendour. *The New World* thus exemplifies what Stanley Cavell describes as the defining myth of film: 'that nature survives our treatment of it and its loss of enchantment for us, and that community remains possible even when the authority of society is denied us' (Cavell 1979: 214). Nature is both the deeper ground of cultural reconciliation and the hidden source of a utopian community that could found a new world; but this experience of nature remains a poetic evocation, a moment of aesthetic sublimity celebrated fleetingly on film. Malick's inherently unstable song of the earth is thus an enthralling combination of historical detail and aesthetic mythology, intimate subjectivity and 'inhuman' nature. The audacity of *The New World*'s romanticism is to allow, through cinematic poetry, nature to reveal or disclose itself as a 'subject', as a participant in this mythic history. This is a perspective that Malick's cinematic romanticism expresses affectively and sensuously; an experience of cinematic thinking that evokes the possibility of another way of thinking, being and dwelling — if only we are open to this possibility.

Viewed from our historical perspective, this romanticism is knowingly *untimely* (in Nietzsche's sense); acting against the prejudices of the age in favour of a time to come. Indeed, Malick's romantic naivety is a refusal of the 'worldliness' that would presume to know the meaning of the historical and cultural conflict between worlds, or that between human worlds and the earth upon which they depend. This is deftly signalled in the extended version of *The New World,* which is prefaced by a quotation from Captain John Smith warning that those who think they have experienced Virginia 'do not understand or know what Virginia is'. Malick's romantic naivety remains true to Smith's warning against the arrogance of historical worldliness — and Smith should know, having renounced nature and love in favour of history and conquest, but in the process having 'sailed past' his true Indies, as Pocahontas/Rebecca remarks. Indeed, *we* still do not know, as Heidegger once observed, what worlds are, let alone how to understand the birth of worlds, or how to foster their flourishing in a manner consonant with the acknowledgment of human plurality and finitude.

That the *The New World*'s aesthetic mythology is risky seems hard to deny, for it conflicts with our shared scepticism towards 'the New'. This is a scepticism characterizing our historical disappointment following the collapse of Enlightenment hopes — or what Nietzsche famously called 'European nihilism'. Malick rejuvenates this possibility of experiencing the New — an American sublimity, we might say — through the poetic power of myth. We can experience this mythic history, however, only aesthetically, through cinematic poetry, and then only fleetingly. The marriage between Old and New Worlds is, in the end, a tragic romance; there is only an aesthetic redemption, thanks to the power of cinematic myth, from the conflict that this historical encounter continues to engender. *The New World* is thus a cinematic critique of the ways in which the encounter between worlds tragically unfolded. At the same time, it is an aesthetic mythology that opens up the possibility of rethinking this meeting of worlds, and of renewing our relationship with the earth, in the hope that this marriage might endure better in the future.

CODA: 'THE SIX MOST BEAUTIFUL MINUTES IN THE HISTORY OF CINEMA'

The style of the most gifted film-philosophers, such as Stanley Cavell, might be called romantic-reflective. It is a transformative herme-neutics in which film is revealed anew as a medium of thought, while philosophy is opened up to new means of expression. This romantic film-philosophy invites us to consider whether philosophical writing on film can be something other than always explanatory, argumen-tative or theoretical. Such a style, however, has its own rhetorical and conceptual risks. Can we avoid the trap of philosophical allegory that seems to beckon as soon as image meets concept?

Giorgio Agamben's brief text (2007: 93–4) on a forgotten scene from Orson Welles' unfinished film version of *Don Quixote* is a case in point. Like many of Cavell's writings on film, Agamben's piece is also a fragment; a performative piece that attempts to show, even stage, the limits and ambiguities of the film-philosophy relationship. In this sense, both Cavell and Agamben could be described as philo-sophical *ironists*. Here is Agamben on what he calls 'the six most beautiful minutes in the history of cinema':

Sancho Panza enters a cinema in a provincial city. He is looking for Don Quixote and finds him sitting off to the side, staring at the screen. The theatre is almost full; the balcony — which is a sort of giant terrace — is packed with raucous children. After several unsuccessful attempts to reach Don Quixote, Sancho reluctantly sits down in one of the lower seats, next to a little girl (Dulcinea?), who offers him a lollypop. The screening has begun; it is a costume film: on the screen, knights in armor are riding along. Suddenly, a woman appears; she is in danger. Don

Quixote abruptly arises, unsheathes his sword, rushes towards the screen, and, with several lunges, begins to shred the cloth. The woman and the knights are still visible on the screen, but the black slash opened up by Don Quixote's sword grows ever larger, implacably devouring the images. In the end, nothing is left of the screen, and only the wooden structure supporting it remains visible. The outraged audience leaves the theatre, but the children on the balcony continue their fanatical cheers for Don Quixote. Only the little girl down on the floor stares at him in disapproval (Agamben 2007: 93).

The description is spare and poignant. Details are carefully articulated with a deft evocation of mood. The text also plays with the question of allegory, both inviting and refusing such a reading. This is fitting given the ambiguity of the scene itself, which does not appear in the posthumously composed version of the film.[1] To be sure, Welles' placing of Don Quixote and Sancho Panza in a contemporary setting becomes seductively allegorical when they enter an ordinary movie theatre. Sancho allows himself to be taught to suck a lollypop and how to watch the movie by a charming little girl (played by Patty McCormack, from Mervyn LeRoy's *The Bad Seed* (1956)), whom Agamben suggests might be Dulcinea.

One detail worth mentioning is that the girl removes an enormous book (Cervantes' *Don Quixote*?) from the seat next to her in order to allow Sancho to sit. Another detail is that the film being screened in the movie theatre, which appears to be a 1950s Sword and Sandals drama, depicts a crucifixion scene, Don Quixote slashing at the screen with his sword just as the bonds on Christ's (?) wrists are being cut. The self-reflexive and allegorical elements here are hard to miss, yet their significance remains enigmatic. Agamben comments on the scene as follows:

What are we to do with our imaginations? Love them and believe in them to the point of having to destroy and falsify them (this is perhaps the meaning of Orson Welles's films). But when, in the end, they reveal themselves to be empty and unfulfilled, when they show the nullity of which they are made, only then can we pay the price for their truth and understand that Dulcinea — whom we have saved — cannot love us (Agamben 2007: 94).

Agamben renders Welles' scene as though it were a parable by Kafka. He draws attention to the question of imagination and the image — our paradoxical love of images, film's power of imaginative evocation, being also a love that entails destruction, an iconoclasm that shows up the 'nullity' of what film imagines, or makes us imagine. It is only in the destruction of their seductive appearances that 'we pay the price for their truth' (2007: 94): the revelation that the fictional power and wonder of movies, their ever thwarted fables, do not always survive their moral or aesthetic dismemberment. The price of revealing the truth about the 'nullity' of images, exposing their imaginative power, is that we destroy the very object of our love. Should we take this as an ironic allusion to the film-philosophy relationship?

From this point of view, we might call this forgotten Wellesian scene a moving rejoinder to the Platonic scepticism that continues to disenfranchise film art. The golden-braided little girl (a 'bad seed' indeed!) teaches Sancho Panza to suck a lollypop and how to enjoy a movie; but she cannot understand or accept Don Quixote's iconoclastic gesture, his literal destruction of the image, revealing the empty (conceptual) framework behind seductive (cinematic) appearances. The children in the stands cheer uproariously, enjoying his comic gesture of destruction. The girl Dulcinea (like the adults in the theatre) disapproves, looking awry at Don Quixote's misguided act of moral and metaphysical censure, his naive ban on images and their visual poetry. Quixote, the philosopher-knight errant, vainly trying to rescue us (and Dulcinea) from perdition, destroys the very thing that he loves, itself a phantasm of imagination. Is this one of the most beautiful vignettes in the history of cinema because of its staging of the philosophical destruction of the image? Its modest beauty makes us bear witness to how film, in an ironic gesture of self-sacrifice, invites philosophy, which would rather dominate the image, to relinquish its mastery and learn to see.

NOTES

NOTES ON INTRODUCTION

[1] These are of course contested terms. Nonetheless, film theory that opposes itself to the 'old' paradigm (psychoanalytic, semiotic, 'Continental'), has a set of shared problems, arguments and debates, and involves authors who explicitly discuss each other's work, can be called a 'movement' with shared views of what comprises 'philosophy of film'.

[2] I use the terms 'film', 'cinema', and 'moving images' interchangeably throughout this book, mindful of the terminological subtleties attending these different terms (see Carroll 2008).

[3] For a comprehensive overview, see Livingston and Plantinga (2009).

[4] See Wartenberg (2004) for a fine overview of recent work in this field.

[5] A sample of key works would include Bordwell (1989b), Cavell (1979 [1971], 1981, 1996), Carroll (1988a, 1988b), Allen (1995), Currie (1995), M. Smith (1995), Bordwell and Carroll (1996a), Allen and Smith (1997), Plantinga and G. M. Smith (1999).

[6] See Gaut (2010: 2–6) and Smith (2010) for useful summaries of this analytic-cognitivist turn.

[7] Ian Jarvie (1987) was one of the pioneers of the new philosophy of film, publishing articles on Bergman's films in 1959 and the early 1960s and various articles on film and philosophy throughout the 1970s and 80s. In addition to Cavell's *The World Viewed* (1971, first edition), important articles appeared in the 1970s by Alexander Sesonke (1973, 1974) and Francis Sparshott (1975, 1985).

[8] My thanks to Fiona Jenkins and Greg Tuck for their helpful comments on an earlier draft of this chapter.

NOTES ON CHAPTER 1

[1] Carroll defines 'Theory' as 'a classy continental number, centrally composed of elements of Louis Althusser, Jacques Lacan, and Roland Barthes, often with optional features derived, often incongruously, from Michel Foucault, Julia Kristeva, Pierre Bourdieu, Gilles Deleuze, and

(*maybe* sometimes) Jacques Derrida, along with contributions from French cinéphiles like Christian Metz, Raymond Bellour, and Jean-Louis Baudry, although generally filtered, albeit with a difference, through exegetes like Stephen Heath, Kaja Silverman, and Teresa de Lauretis' (1996: 37).

[2] See also Carroll's companion book to this one (1988b).

[3] V. F. Perkins had already made this criticism in 1972: '[Film theory] emerged radically deformed and incapable of useful growth. It could develop only as a sterile orthodoxy, a body of rules and prescriptions whose common features include internal contradiction and irrelevance to critical discussion of actual movies' (1972: 11). Perkins' words are echoed in more recent criticisms of the sterile orthodoxy that film theory has become (see Frampton 2006, 169–182).

[4] Allen and Smith, for example, assert that 'Continental' philosophers such as Theodor Adorno, Jacques Derrida and Michel Foucault have all attempted to demonstrate 'the impossibility of knowledge', and have apparently 'embraced this contradiction as *the* defining feature of philosophy and the only legitimate path that philosophy can take in response to modernity' (Allen and Smith 1997: 10). Apart from a derisory and mocking tone, little argumentative or textual evidence is provided to support such hyperbolic claims. Unfortunately it has become commonplace to uncritically repeat such unargued assertions concerning 'Continental' philosophy in many critiques of 'Grand Theory' (see, for example, Smith 2010).

[5] See Sobchack (2011) for a fascinating discussion of Derek Jarman's *Blue* from a phenomenological perspective.

[6] This is the basis of Carroll's critique of Currie's account of the filmic medium, which is unable to deal with avant-gardist and experimental cinema.

[7] A striking example would be Torben Grodal's bioculturalist analyses of action film, pornography or romance genres as 'illustrating' the biologically grounded propensity, derived from our evolutionary history, for men to prefer sex and violence and women to prefer romance and child-nurturing narratives (2009: 56–78). Grodal assumes that culture reflects biological foundations, much like 'vulgar' Marxists assumed that it reflected the 'economic base'.

[8] I would like to thank Fiona Jenkins for her helpful comments on an earlier version of this chapter.

NOTES ON CHAPTER 2

[1] See David Lynch's remarks on the 'end of film' (2006: 149–50).

[2] Necessary conditions are those which something must have in order to count as a case of X; sufficient conditions are those which, if possessed jointly, ensure that something is X. Being male is a necessary condition of being a bachelor but not a sufficient one (there are married men); whereas being male and unmarried is a sufficient condition of being a bachelor.

[3] This of course is a different sense of 'intentionality' than that used in phenomenology and philosophy of mind, according to which 'intentionality' refers to the directedness of consciousness.

[4] It is true that I cannot orient myself on the basis of the image, but then that is also true of a microscopic or telescopic image. Imagine attending a screening of Sokurov's *Russian Ark* (2002) within St Petersburg's famous Hermitage museum; here I would have phenomenological access to the profilmic space but not to the historical-cinematic 'Russian' world of the film. Although we obviously cannot orient ourselves towards the fictional world of the film, Carroll's insistence on the impossibility, 'save in freak circumstances', of orienting ourselves towards any profilmic space we view on screen seems overstated.

[5] Brian de Palma's *Body Double* (1984), Kieslowski's *A Short Film about Love* (1988) and Jacques Audiard's *Read My Lips* [*Sur mes lèvres*] (2001) are excellent examples of this kind of cinematic use of space, which depends upon our ability to orient ourselves within the diegetic world inhabited by the characters.

[6] I owe this example to Jean-Philippe Deranty.

[7] The flicker fusion threshold is the frequency at which all flicker from an intermittent light source is perceived to disappear (for us, approximately 16 Hertz); cinema projectors typically operate at 24 Hertz (24 frames per second), television monitors at 50 or 60 Hertz, and so on. The phi phenomenon refers to our perception of continuous movement when we view rapidly successive images of an object.

[8] An account that, charitably interpreted, is not far off the 'phi phenomenon'.

[9] As Carroll notes, even animals appear to perceive movement in moving images in the same way that human beings do (2008: 88–9).

[10] Or when a film interrupts our ordinary perception (or expectation) of movement and raises explicitly the question of movement and its relationship with the (moving) image, as is the case with Marker's *La Jetée*.

[11] See Sinnerbrink (2009a) for a criticism of Carroll's (1988c) reading of Münsterberg, and his related critique of the film/mind analogy, which is better understood as an aesthetic analogy rather than an epistemic claim.

[12] Carroll criticizes the film/mind analogy (1988c), arguing that comparing film to the mind is unhelpful because we know more about film than the mind, so the logic of analogy fails to be illuminating in the right way. On the other hand, comparing the mind to film — as philosophers such as Henri Bergson, Edmund Husserl and Bernard Stiegler have done — can be highly illuminating, offering new ways of thinking about the mind.

[13] My thanks go to Havi Carel for her helpful comments on an earlier draft of this chapter.

NOTES ON CHAPTER 3

[1] See, for example, Oliver Sacks' (1985) 'The Lost Mariner', which features a character by the name of Jimmie G. who lost the ability to form short-term memories, hence still believes that it is 1945.

[2] I owe this point to Jane Stadler.

[3] In discussing Chantal Akerman's *Jeanne Dielman* (1975), for example, Gaut comments on the film's (Akerman's) use of a static camera as commenting on the trapped existence of the heroine: 'For Akerman,

employing a stationary camera was a matter of choice, whereas for the Lumière brothers it was not' (2010: 40). Gaut's comment certainly reads like the ascription of authorial intention and artistic responsibility to Akerman as solo author (not to mention the Lumière brothers).

[4] One also has to acknowledge the role of the film industry in this regard, for which the author/director has become another means of marketing a certain 'brand'; the advent of DVD extras, moreover, has added to the prestige of the auteur, offering interviews and other authorial insights that promise to reveal the inner meaning of the film. My thanks to Jane Stadler for this point.

[5] One could argue that the authorship for *The Fog of War* is jointly shared with former US Secretary of State Robert McNamara, whose remarkable autobiographical reflections on his life and on American politics provide the film's fascinating subject-matter.

[6] As Frampton points out (2006: 170–4), the fact that it is easy to conflate critical-technical discourse with narrative description continues to bedevil theoretical discussions of film.

[7] *The Sixth Sense*, which features Shyamalan as writer/director, is a straight-forward case. Films with different screenwriters and directors, however, could presumably also have a single implied author imputed to them, even if this implied authorship is divided between different actual authors who collaborated in the making of the film.

[8] My thanks go to Jane Stadler for her helpful comments on an earlier draft of this chapter.

NOTES ON CHAPTER 4

[1] This is, of course, Bordwell's main complaint against what he dismissively calls 'Interpretation Inc' (1989b: 21–9), and the motivation for proposing his alternative model of film analysis, namely 'historical poetics'.

[2] The famous shots of Kane speechifying in front of the campaign poster of his grotesquely exaggerated face cannot help but recall (given the wartime context) a certain proximity to fascist aesthetics.

[3] For example, as Bordwell and other critics point out, Ozu recast the materials of post-war Japanese Meiji culture, 'mediated by such cinematic factors as Hollywood norms, Japanese cinema's "decorative classicism", and the practices of a commercial film industry' (Bordwell 1988: 30). The point is that one should not immediately assume that Ozu's famous use of low-angle shots has an obviously 'traditional' cultural meaning.

[4] Contra Plantinga, however, consider the new French 'cinema of extremity', which includes films such as Gaspar Noé's *I Stand Alone* (1998), Catherine Breillat's *Romance* (1999), Virginie Despentes and Coralie Trinh Thi's *Baise Moi* (2000), Claire Denis' *Trouble Every Day* (2001), Marina de Van's *In My Skin* (2002), Noé's *Irreversible* (2002), Breillat's *Anatomy of Hell* (2004), and so on. See Quandt (2004) and Palmer (2006) for contrasting discussions of this trend.

[5] Carroll uses the nauseating example of Dario Argento's *Creepers* (*Phenomena*) (1985): 'As the heroine thrashes about in the pool — full of

decomposing bodies, sewerage, and insect larvae — and quaffs down viscous gobs of liquidy, brownish stuff, one's feeling of nausea is surely not quasi-nausea nor pretend disgust; it is indiscernible from real disgust' (1990: 78).

[6] A keen gamer, however, might find *Inception*'s lack of 'character engagement' paradoxically engaging precisely because it simulates a computer game, thus allowing the viewer to identify with 'Cobb' in a manner similar to his or her own gaming avatar. I owe this point to Tarja Laine.

[7] See Laine (2010) for an excellent film-philosophical reading of this film as 'emotional event', which explores the phenomenological dimensions of being-with, reversibility between body and world, and intercorporeal relationality that make the film so emotionally engaging.

[8] Interestingly, this Mexican song, written by Tomas Mendez, and intro-duced by Lola Betran in a film of the same name, also appears in Robert Aldrich's Western *The Last Sunset* (1961) and in Wong Kar-wai's queer love story, *Happy Together* (1997).

[9] My thanks go to Tarja Laine for her helpful comments on an earlier draft of this chapter.

NOTES ON CHAPTER 5

[1] As Deleuze remarks in a 1986 interview for *Cahiers du cinéma*: 'The brain is the screen. I don't believe that linguistics and psychoanalysis offer a great deal to the cinema. On the contrary, the biology of the brain — molecular biology — does. Thought is molecular' (2000: 366).

[2] I cite these as authored by Bergson/Deleuze since Deleuze deploys an idiosyncratic and contestable interpretation of Bergson. See Mullarkey for a critique (2009: 97–100).

[3] Or, in the case of digital images, as Mullarkey points out, Bergson's critique would refer to screen refresh rates rather than frame projection rates, with 'the apparent movement of the cinema images being parasitic upon real physical movement existing elsewhere (ultimately, of whatever generates the power for an electrical device …)' (2009: 236).

[4] Bordwell is critical of Deleuze's dualistic schema dividing film history into a pre-War movement-image phase and a post-War time-image phase. Deleuze, Bordwell claims, 'echoes Burch, Ropars, and the *Cahiers* writers, who claimed that the classical cinema was succeeded by a modern one that manipulated time in such ways. Deleuze's unquestioning reliance upon our research tradition is further revealed in his belief that a cinematic essence unfolds across history' (1997: 117). Bordwell's complaint is more to do with Deleuze's reliance on particular historiographical accounts than with the substance of his conceptual analyses.

[5] In addition to films that Deleuze cites (such as *Citizen Kane*), we might mention, among others, Sturges' *Sullivan's Travels* (1941), Wilder's *Sunset Boulevard* (1950), Huston's *The Misfits* (1961) and Kubrick's *Lolita* (1962) as examples of post-War Hollywood films that also move between movement-image and time-image narrative.

[6] Kovács (2000) makes the interesting argument that Deleuze's *Cinema* books, with their historical break between movement-image and time-image cinema, should be read as a cinematic version of the history of thought.

[7] Rancière makes the same point about Jean-Luc Godard's *Histoire(s) du cinéma* (2006: 5).

[8] Among many examples one might cite here, consider Takeshi Kitano's *Hana-bi*, (1997), Apichatpong Weerasethakul's *Blissfully Yours* (2002), Gus Van Sant's *Elephant* (2003), Catherine Breillat's *Anatomy of Hell* (2004), Wong Kar-wai's *2046* (2004), Gavin Hood's *Tsotsi* (2005), Jean-Pierre and Luc Dardenne's *The Child* (2005), Alejandro González Iñárritu's *Babel* (2006), Alfonso Cuáron's *Children of Men* (2006), Rolf de Heer's and Peter Djigirr's *Ten Canoes* (2006), the Coen Brothers' *No Country for Old Men* (2007), Warwick Thornton's *Samson and Delilah* (2009), Gaspar Noé's *Enter the Void* (2009), and so on.

[9] A number of Deleuzian film theorists have also questioned Deleuze's historical and aesthetic assumptions about cinema, and have taken Deleuzian film-philosophy into new and exciting theoretical territory (see Marks 2000 and Martin-Jones 2006).

[10] See Mulhall (1999) for a fine discussion of Cavell, scepticism and film. See Klevan (2011) for an exemplary engagement with Cavell and philosophical film criticism.

[11] Deleuze makes a very similar point concerning the 'frame' in his discussion of the movement-image (1986: 12–18).

[12] This is why cinematic remakes are usually disappointing. It is impossible to substitute one actor for another when we are dealing with an iconic actor/character combination (like Vince Vaughn as Norman Bates in Gus Van Sant's shot-for-shot remake of *Psycho* (1998)).

[13] See Klevan (2005) for an original Cavellian-inspired engagement with screen performance.

[14] See Trahair (2007) for a fine film-philosophical discussion of Keaton's cinematic philosophy of comedy.

[15] This aspect of film, as cinematic mythmaking, has been elaborated, in elegant Cavellian fashion, by Irving Singer (2008).

[16] I cannot deal with these exemplary works in film-philosophy here. Suffice to say that it is where Cavell's film-philosophy finds its fullest expression.

[17] Cf. 'It requires belief, relation to one's past, conviction that one's words and conduct express oneself, that they say what one means, and that what one means is enough to say' (Cavell 1979: 62).

[18] Mullarkey thus criticizes Deleuze for using film examples 'as stand-ins for concepts' (2009: 108).

NOTES ON CHAPTER 6

[1] Bergman's Johan and Marianne seem to have been reincarnated in von Trier's *Antichrist* (2009): He [Willem Dafoe] is also a cognitive therapist, whereas She [Charlotte Gainsbourg] remains similarly lost for words in their 'therapeutic' relationship that is also dominated by marital/sexual trauma.

[2] As Joshua Shaw points out (2009), this is Julian Baggini's (2003) main criticism of Mulhall's *On Film*: not that films cannot philosophize (Baggini mentions that philosophers' favourite, Kurosawa's *Rashomon*) but that the *Alien* films do not.

[3] See http://video.google.com/videoplay?docid=7936414602517427743# Strictly speaking, the philosophy in this case would be occurring in the context of the interview situation, rather than anything cinematic, which raises the question to what extent media interviews, whether written or filmed, can serve as media of philosophical expression. I thank Tom Wartenberg for alerting me to this point.

[4] Bergman writes in a 1957 Preface to the English translation of the screenplay of *Wild Strawberries* (1957): 'Philosophically, there is a book which was a tremendous experience for me: Eino Kaila's *Psychology of the Personality*. His thesis that man lives strictly according to his needs — negative and positive — was shattering to me, but terribly true. And I built on this ground' (quoted in Livingston 2009a: 562).

[5] Smuts overlooks the possibility that *The Matrix* does offer this kind of demonstration within the narrative itself; the viewer undergoes the kind of sceptical experience of radical uncertainty precisely by watching and engaging with the film's fictional simulation of worlds (within the film). From this point of view, the philosopher is providing a commentary on something that the film does cinematically, rather than an interpretation that supplies a demonstrative element absent from the film.

[6] Shaw also discusses this sequence, along similar lines (2008: 9–10).

[7] In *The Well-Wrought Urn*, Cleanth Brooks famously criticized the 'heresy of paraphrase', arguing that poetry should not be 'paraphrased' into its propositional content, for this would destroy the literary and aesthetic qualities of the work. For philosophers like Livingston, by contrast, paraphrase is the properly philosophical response to a work of art, whose aesthetic qualities should be translated into the idiom of philosophical discourse in order to extract their philosophical content for the purposes of engaging in argument. Such approaches, however, ignore the question whether something significant — such as aesthetic meaning — is 'lost in translation', which is precisely what is at stake in the debate over the idea of film as philosophy: are there ways of thinking that cinema can express, but which philosophy fails to address or to communicate?

[8] This is the real merit of Livingston's study (2009b): the philosophically original readings of Bergman's films, which carry the argument that Bergman is a cinematic philosopher far more successfully than Livingston's attempt to philosophically anchor his films in Kaila's theories.

[9] My thanks go to Tom Wartenberg for his helpful comments on an earlier draft of this chapter.

NOTES ON PART III

[1] See Mullarkey (2009, 4 ff.; 2011) for versions of this line of criticism applied to advocates of the 'film as philosophy' thesis.

[2] The fact that the philosophical 'canon' remains overwhelmingly masculinist and Anglo/Eurocentric is a case in point. Here one can only gesture to the possibility of expanding and pluralizing the kinds of films, traditions and auteurs who are at the forefront of philosophical filmmaking (Catherine Breillat, Alejandro González Iñárittu, Claire Denis, Abbas Kiarostami, Apichatpong Weerasethakul, Wong Kar-wai, to name a few).

NOTES ON CHAPTER 7

[1] Guy Debord (1955) defined psychogeography as 'the study of the precise laws and specific effects of the geographical environment, consciously organized or not, on the emotions and behavior of individuals'. This term resurfaces in Patrick Keiller's remarkable Benjaminian reflection on history, memory, and the city, *London* (1994).

[2] As Schaffner remarks, *INLAND EMPIRE* seems to invite a 'psychotopological reading'. Having broached this possibility, however, Schaffner reverts to the familiar psychoanalytic reading of Lynch's work, linking this with the questionable reception of Lynch as 'postmodernist' ironist (2009: 283).

[3] Although Lynch never really explains what he means, I take cinematic ideas to mean visual and aural sequences that combine images and sounds liberated from a purely narrative function with images evincing a complex cinematic reflexivity. This striking conjunction of sensuous immediacy and complex reflection is the hallmark of Lynch's cinematic world.

[4] The opening images of a gramophone needle and spinning record disc illuminated by a spotlight appear to be a visual reference to Germaine Dulac's experimental film *Disque 957* (1928). Dulac, a pioneering woman avant-garde filmmaker, influenced American avant-gardist Maya Deren, whose *Meshes of the Afternoon* (1943) is an important film for Lynch (see Totaro, Rist and Jordan 2009).

[5] We should note that the Rabbits are voiced by Naomi Watts, Laura Elena Harring and Scott Coffey, who all appeared in *Mulholland Drive*.

[6] Frampton (2006) introduces the term 'filmind' to express the (impersonal) animating intentionality of a film; not the intentions of a director or implied author but the global or encompassing intentionality of a filmind expressing a distinctive film-world.

[7] I owe this insight to enlightening discussions with Greg Hainge (see Hainge 2010).

[8] The film seems haunted by the ghost of Billy Wilder (born in Poland), director of the ultimate Hollywood meta-fiction, *Sunset Boulevard* (1950), an obsessive reference point for both *Mulholland Drive* and *INLAND EMPIRE*. Grace Zabriskie, as Visitor #1, references Norma Desmond's [Gloria Swanson's] hairstyle, exaggerated expressions and facial tics in her portentous conversation with Nikki Grace. The Lost Girl, moreover, praying and wearing a veil, also quotes a line (in Polish) from *Sunset Boulevard*, Norma Desmond's famous plea: 'Cast out this wicked dream that has seized my heart' — an intertitle from one of Norma's silent films

(actually von Stroheim's Queen Kelly (1932) starring Gloria Swanson) watched by Norma and screenwriter/lover Joe Gillis (see Mactaggart 2010: 150). Von Stroheim, of course, played Desmond's 'butler' and former director in *Sunset Boulevard*. The Lost Girl's prayer, which appears just before an enigmatic scene in which it is suggested that her character in *47* murders her husband's lover, thus suggests that 'the curse' afflicts *Sunset Boulevard* as much as *OHiBT* (and *INLAND EMPIRE*).

⁹ Haneke's references in *Hidden* [*Caché*] to Lynch's *Lost Highway* — the mysterious videotapes, and the Lynch-Haneke 'Laurent' cross-reference ('Dick Laurent is dead') — are intriguing. For his part, Lynch quotes the number '47' (in German!) as the title of the Polish film within a film in *INLAND EMPIRE*, which is also the number of the mysterious Rabbits' room. Curiously, it is the number of the apartment belonging to the Algerian father and son confronted by Georges Laurent [Daniel Auteuil] in *Hidden* [*Caché*].

¹⁰ The image of Mr K. [Erik Crary] standing in the blue-lit entrance to the theatre stairway recalls Edward Hopper's atmospheric painting, *New York Movie* (1939), which shows a blonde theatre attendant, not unlike Laura Dern, standing near the exit stairs, a pensive look on her face.

¹¹ Visitor #2 [Mary Steenburgen], who conveys the same message to Sue Blue as Visitor #1 ('there's an unpaid debt that needs paying') is seen sporting the mysterious watch, marking her as one of the messengers or 'seers' with temporal access between (cinematic) worlds.

¹² In *Mulholland Drive*, this portal is the Blue Box into which the camera plunges, just before Betty disappears, marking the transition from the Betty/ Rita story to the Diane/Camilla story (see Sinnerbrink 2005).

NOTES ON CHAPTER 8

¹ For Carroll (1990), a 'monster' is defined as any creature not held to exist according to contemporary science. As Aaron Smuts remarks, however, this should mean the science accepted within the world of the film (since there may be cases, for example genetics or cloning, where actual science may come to match what a fictional world posits as scientific fact) (2009b: 505).

² Carroll defends a version of the 'thought theory' of affect in response to fictional characters: I do not believe in the literal existence of Dracula; rather, I entertain the (unasserted) thought of a vampire with the dreadful compulsion to suck its victims' blood. The 'thought theory', however, tends to ignore the visceral nature of horror, experienced as a bodily affective response.

³ One should acknowledge, however, that Cynthia Freeland (2002) has argued that a cognitivist approach can be brought to feminist analysis of (horror) film, Dan Flory (2009) has developed a critical analysis of race within popular film drawing on cognitivist insights, while Carl Plantinga maintains that cognitivism can help illuminate a neutral (non-normative) concept of ideology operating within popular film genres (2009a: 200–18).

[4] Smuts complains, however, that despite their interpretive and explanatory power, psychoanalytic theories of horror remain 'typically unparsimonious, have difficulty explaining the attraction of horror to female audiences, and rest on the suspect foundation of psychoanalysis' (2009b: 513).

[5] Von Trier, resplendent in tuxedo and bow tie, signed off each episode with a cryptic and ironic speech, concluding his enigmatic précis of each episode with the tag: 'And remember to take the Good with the Evil'.

[6] As John Waters quipped (2009): 'If Ingmar Bergman had committed suicide, gone to hell, and come back to earth to direct an exploitation/art film for drive-ins, this is the movie he would have made.'

[7] I mean by 'supernaturalism' both an excessive naturalism and a beyond of naturalism, which covers both the horror of excessive life in nature (the rotting plant roots, insect sounds, dead trees), and a 'beyond' of nature (occult forces that defy rational explanation).

[8] As Rob White notes (White and Power, 2009), a homage to the famous coffin point-of-view shots in Carl Dreyer's 1932 horror classic, *Vampyr*.

[9] Von Trier mentions in an interview that this particular image was originally intended for a film version of Wagner's *The Ring* (2010: 7).

[10] As She intones during a particularly disturbing 'breakthrough' moment in her therapy, one that deeply shakes her husband/therapist: 'Nature is Satan's Church'.

[11] My thanks to Magdalena Zolkos for her thoughtful comments on an earlier version of this chapter.

NOTES ON CHAPTER 9

[1] As Adrian Martin notes, this verse is an example of Malick's remarkable use of pre-existing versions of the Pocahontas tale, in this case echoing and reworking 'a poem by that great on-the-spot theorist of silent film, Vachel Lindsay (1917)' entitled 'Our Mother/Pocahontas' (2007a: 215). Lines from Lindsay's poem — 'We rise from out of the soul of her' and 'Because we are her fields of corn' — are directly cited in the voiceover to Malick's film (Martin 2007a: 215). Malick, however, submits it to a subtle rewriting: Lindsay takes Pocahontas to be the 'sacred mother' figure, whereas in *The New World* Pocahontas is a seeker *searching* for her Mother, the 'spirit' whom she invokes in order to sing 'the story of our land' (2007a: 215).

[2] See Millington (2010) for an interesting analysis of the difficulty of attributing the plural chorus voiceovers to particular characters in *The Thin Red Line*.

[3] The film also features a suitably romantic-aquatic signature piece, 'Aquarium', from Saint-Saëns' *Le Carnaval des Animaux*.

[4] The prelude to Wagner's *Das Rheingold* begins with three Rhine maidens swimming beneath the surface of the water. They mock the ugly Alberich, a Nibelung dwarf, who steals the famous Rhine gold they are guarding, a treasure that can only be acquired by abandoning love in favour of wealth and power. He then fashions a magic ring out of the gold that gives its bearer the power to rule the world. It is not difficult to discern the parallels in Malick's recasting of this mythic scene to the Virginian tidewater region,

with its Native American water maidens contrasting with the arriving colonists, who embody Alberich's rejection of nature and love in favour of power and wealth. It is also used, to quite different effect, in Werner Herzog's *Nosferatu* (1979).

5 *The New World* exists in three versions: a 150-minute version screened at the 2006 Berlinale and then withdrawn; a 135-minute general international release version; and a recent, extended 'Director's Cut' DVD version (172 minutes), which might be called the most 'romantic' version of the film

6 As Adrian Martin remarks: 'The time that Malick takes, and the time that he makes, that he hollows and stretches out on the screen, give us a sense of expansiveness: an epic and lyric feeling' (2007b).

7 A 'Philosophers on Film' volume has been published dedicated to *The Thin Red Line* (Davies 2009a), and Malick has also been honoured with an entry in Livingston and Plantinga's volume on *Philosophy and Film* (Davies 2009b: 569–80).

8 All of which appear to be taken up, with a cosmic-religious undertone, in Malick's latest, and much anticipated film, *The Tree of Life* (2011).

9 The other piece of music used to express the blossoming relationship between Pocahontas/Rebecca and Smith is from the poignant second movement of Mozart's Piano Concerto No. 23 in A major (K. 488).

10 In a crucial scene from Smith's historical account and the Pocahontas legend, Smith is about to be killed by the Powhatan when Pocahontas throws herself upon his breast and begs that his life be spared. Malick's version of this scene suggests that he undergoes a symbolic 'ritual' death and rebirth that inducts him into the Powhatan community.

11 Pocahontas' prayers, conversations, and entreaties to her 'Mother' resonate richly throughout the film, alluding to her actual mother (who appears in the extended cut), the Mother goddess and Spirit of the Earth.

NOTES ON CODA: 'THE SIX MOST BEAUTIFUL MINUTES IN THE HISTORY OF CINEMA'

1 This unhappily recomposed version of the film, edited by Jesus Franco (one of Welles' collaborators on *Chimes At Midnight* (1965), was recently released on DVD. Although omitted from the DVD version, the scene Agamben discusses can be viewed on YouTube. See http://www.youtube.com/watch?v=GU9xJVnFy9M (with an introduction by Jonathan Rosenbaum); or http://www.youtube.com/watch?v=cHQEViM3QYU (a better quality image but with an added soundtrack).

APPENDIX: FURTHER READING, FILMOGRAPHIES, WEBSITES

FURTHER READING

There is now an extensive and expanding literature on diverse aspects of the relationship between film and philosophy. The following are some important and influential texts, organised into relevant topics, which the reader may find interesting and enlightening.

Anthologies and Reference Texts

Carroll, Noël and Jinhee, Choi (eds). (2006), *Philosophy of Film and Motion Pictures*. Malden: Blackwell Publishing.

Colman, Felicity (ed). (2009), *Film, Theory and Philosophy*. Durham: Acumen Publishing.

Livingston, Paisley and Plantinga, Carl (eds). (2009), *The Routledge Companion to Philosophy and Film*. London/New York: Routledge.

Wartenberg, Thomas E. and Angela Curran (eds). (2005). *The Philosophy of Film: Introductory Text and Readings*. Malden: Blackwell Publishing.

Essay Collections

Allen, Richard and Smith, Murray. (1997), *Film Theory and Philosophy*. Oxford: Oxford University Press.

Bordwell, David and Carroll, Noël (eds). (1996), *Post-Theory:*

Reconstructing Film Studies. Madison: University of Wisconsin Press.

Carel, Havi and Tuck, Greg (eds). (2011), *New Takes in Film-Philosophy*. New York: Palgrave Macmillan.

Freeland, Cynthia A. and Wartenberg, Thomas E. (eds). (1995), *Philosophy and Film*. New York: Routledge, 1995.

Read, Rupert and Goodenough, Jerry (eds). (2005), *Film as Philosophy: Essays on Cinema After Wittgenstein and Cavell*. London: Palgrave Macmillan.

Smith, Murray and Wartenberg, Thomas E. (2006). 'Thinking through cinema: Film as philosophy'. *The Journal of Aesthetics and Art Criticism* 64, (1), Winter. Reprinted as Murray Smith and Thomas E. Wartenberg (eds). (2006), *Thinking Through Cinema: Film as Philosophy*. Malden MA./Oxford: Basil Blackwell.

Classic Texts

Arnheim, Rudolf. (1957 [1932]), *Film as Art*. Berkeley: University of California Press.

Balázs, Béla. (2010), Erica Carter (ed), *Béla Balázs: Early Film Theory – Visible Man and The Spirit of Film*, translated by Rodney Livingstone. London: Berghan Books.

Bazin, André. (1967, 1971), *What is Cinema? Volume I and Volume II*, trans. Hugh Gray. Berkeley: University of California Press.

Eisenstein, Sergei. (1942), *The Film Sense*, New York: Harcourt, Brace.

Eisenstein, Sergei (1949), *The Film Form*. New York: Harcourt, Brace.

Kracauer, Siegfried. (1960), *Theory of Film: The Redemption of Physical Reality*. New York: Oxford University Press.

Mitry, Jean. (1990 [1963]). *The Aesthetics and Psychology of the Cinema*, 2 volumes, trans. C. King. Bloomington: University of Indiana Press.

Morin, Edgar. (2002 [1956/1978]), *The Cinema, or The Imaginary Man*, trans. Lorraine Mortimer. Minneapolis: University of Minnesota Press.

Münsterberg, Hugo. (2002 [1916]), *The Photoplay: A Psychological Study* in Allen Langdale (ed), *Hugo Münsterberg on Film*. London: Routledge.

Panofsky, Erwin. (1997 [1934]), 'Style and Medium in the Motion

Pictures', in J. Harrington (ed), *Film and/as Literature*. New York: Prentice Press, pp. 283–294.

Perkins, V. F. (1972), *Film as Film: Understanding and Judging Movies*. New York: Penguin Books.

Stanley Cavell

Cavell, Stanley. (1979), *The World Viewed: Reflections on the Ontology of Film*. Enlarged Edition. Cambridge, MA./London: Harvard University Press.

Cavell, Stanley. (1981), *Pursuits of Happiness: The Hollywood Comedy of Remarriage*. Cambridge, MA.: Harvard University Press.

Cavell, Stanley. (1996), *Contesting Tears: the Melodrama of the Unknown Woman*. Chicago: University of Chicago Press.

Cavell, Stanley. (2005), William Rothman and Marian Keane (eds), *Cavell on Film*. Albany: State University of New York Press.

Eldridge, Richard (ed). (2003), *Stanley Cavell*. Cambridge: Cambridge University Press.

Mulhall, Stephen. (1999), *Stanley Cavell: Philosophy's Recounting of the Ordinary*. Oxford: Oxford University Press.

Rothman, William and Keane, Marian. (2000), *Reading Cavell's The World Viewed: A Philosophical Perspective on Film*. Detroit: Wayne State University Press.

Cognitivism

Anderson, J. D. (1996), *The Reality of Illusion: An Ecological Approach to Cognitive Film Theory*. Carbondale: Southern Illinois University Press.

Bordwell, David. (1985), *Narration in the Fiction Film*. Madison: University of Wisconsin Press.

Bordwell, David. (1989), 'A case for cognitivism'. *Iris* 9, 11–40.

Currie, Gregory. (1995), *Image and Mind: Film, Philosophy, and Cognitive Science*. New York: Cambridge University Press.

Grodal, Torben. (2009), *Embodied Visions: Evolution, Emotion, Culture, and Film*. Oxford: Oxford University Press.

Plantinga, Carl and Smith, Greg M. (1999), *Passionate Views: Film, Cognition, and Emotion*. Baltimore: Johns Hopkins University Press.

Plantinga, Carl. (2002). 'Cognitive Film Theory: An Insider's Appraisal', *Cinémas: review d'etudes cinematographiques/Cinémas: Journal of Film Studies*, 12, (2), 15–37.

Plantinga, Carl. (2009), *Moving Viewers: American Film and the Spectator's Experience*. Berkeley: University of California Press.

Critique of 'Grand Theory'

Bordwell, David. (1989), *Making Meaning: Inference and Rhetoric in the Interpretation of Cinema*. Cambridge, MA.: Harvard University Press.

Carroll, Noël. (1988), *Mystifying Movies: Fads and Fallacies in Contemporary Film Theory*. New York: Columbia University Press.

Carroll, Noël (1988), *Philosophical Problems of Classical Film Theory*. Princeton: Princeton University Press.

Carroll, Noël. (1996), 'Prospects for Film Theory: A Personal Assessment', in David Bordwell and Noël Carroll (eds), *Post-Theory: Reconstructing Film Studies*. Madison: University of Wisconsin Press, pp. 37–68.

Gilles Deleuze

Bogue, Ronald. (2003), *Deleuze on Cinema*. London: Routledge.

Deleuze, Gilles. (1986 [1983]), *Cinema I: The Movement-Image*, trans. Hugh Tomlinson and Barbara Habberjam. Minneapolis: University of Minnesota Press.

Deleuze, Gilles. (1989 [1985]), *Cinema II: The Time-Image*, trans. Hugh Tomlinson and Robert Galatea. Minneapolis: University of Minnesota Press.

Gregory Flaxman (ed) (2000), *The Brain is the Screen: Deleuze and the Philosophy of Cinema*. Minneapolis: University of Minnesota Press.

Kennedy, Barbara. M. (2003), *Deleuze and Cinema: The Aesthetics of Sensation*. Edinburgh University Press, Edinburgh.

Marks, Laura U. (2000), *The Skin of the Film: Intercultural Cinema, Embodiment, the Senses*. Durham: Duke University Press.

Marrati, Paola. (2008), *Gilles Deleuze: Cinema and Philosophy*, trans. Alisa Hartz. Baltimore: Johns Hopkins University Press.

Martin-Jones, David. (2006), *Deleuze, Cinema, and National Identity*. Edinburgh: Edinburgh University Press.

Pisters, Patricia. (2003), *The Matrix of Visual Culture: Working with Deleuze in Film Theory*, Stanford: Stanford University Press.

Powell, Anna. (2005), *Deleuze and Horror Film*, Edinburgh: Edinburgh University Press.

Powell, Anna. (2009), *Deleuze, Altered States and Film*, Edinburgh: Edinburgh University Press.

Rodowick, D. N. (1997), *Gilles Deleuze's Time Machine*. Durham: Duke University Press.

Rodowick, D. N. (ed). (2009), *Afterimages of Gilles Deleuze's Film Philosophy*. Minneapolis: University of Minnesota Press.

Film and Emotion

Carroll, Noël. (1990), *The Philosophy of Horror; or, the Paradoxes of the Heart*. London/New York, Routledge.

Choi, Jinhee. (2003), 'Fits and startles: cognitivism revisited.' *Journal of Aesthetics and Art Criticism*. 61: 149–157.

Coplan, Amy. (2006), 'Catching character's emotions: emotional contagion responses to narrative fiction film'. *Film Studies: An International Review* 8, 26–38.

Laine, Tarja. (2011), *Feeling Film: Emotional Dynamics in Film Studies*. London/New York: Continuum.

Plantinga, Carl and Smith, Greg M. (1999), *Passionate Views: Film, Cognition, and Emotion*. Baltimore: Johns Hopkins University Press.

Plantinga, Carl (2009), *Moving Viewers: American Film and the Spectator's Experience*. Berkeley: University of California Press.

Smith, Greg M. (2003), *Film Structure and the Emotion System*. Cambridge: Cambridge University Press.

Smith, Murray. (1995), *Engaging Characters: Fiction, Emotion, and the Cinema*. Oxford: Oxford University Press.

Sobchack, Vivian. (2004), *Carnal Thoughts: Embodiment and Moving Image Culture*. Berkeley: University of California Press.

Tan, Ed. S. (1996), *Emotion and the Structure of Narrative Film: Film as an Emotion Machine*. Mahwah NJ: Lawrence Erlbaum.

Ethics and Politics

Beller, Jonathan. (2006). *The Cinematic Mode of Production: Attention Economy and the Society of the Spectacle*. Lebanon NH: Dartmouth College Press.

Kellner, Douglas. (2010), *Cinema Wars: Hollywood Film and Politics in the Bush-Cheney Era*. Malden MA/Oxford: Wiley-Blackwell.

Marks, Laura U. (2000), *The Skin of the Film: Intercultural Cinema, Embodiment, the Senses*. Durham: Duke University Press.

Marrati, Paola. (2008), *Gilles Deleuze: Cinema and Philosophy*, trans. Alisa Hartz. Baltimore: Johns Hopkins University Press.

Martin-Jones, David. (2006), *Deleuze, Cinema, and National Identity*. Edinburgh: Edinburgh University Press.

Rancière, Jacques. (2004), *The Politics of Aesthetics*, trans. Gabriel Rockhill. London: Continuum.

Rancière, Jacques. (2006), *Film Fables*, trans. Emiliano Battista. Oxford/New York: Berg Books.

Rancière, Jacques. (2009). *The Emancipated Spectator*, trans. Gregory Elliott. London/New York: Verso.

Stadler, Jane. (2008), *Pulling Focus: Intersubjective Experience, Narrative Film, and Ethics*. New York/London: Continuum.

Wartenberg, Thomas E. (1999), *Unlikely Couples: Movie Romance as Social Criticism*. Boulder: Westview Press.

Žižek, Slavoj. (1999). *The Fright of Real Tears: Krzystof Kieślowski Between Theory and Post-Theory*. London: British Film Institute.

Film and Philosophy/Philosophy of Film

Carroll, Noël. (1996), *Theorizing the Moving Image*. Cambridge: Cambridge University Press.

Carroll, Noël. (2008), *The Philosophy of Motion Pictures*, Malden MA.: Blackwell Publishing.

Gaut, Berys. (2010), *A Philosophy of Cinematic Art*. Cambridge: Cambridge University Press.

Jarvie, Ian. (1987), *Philosophy of the Film: Epistemology, Ontology, Aesthetics*. London: Routledge.

Mullarkey, John. (2009), *Refractions of Reality: Philosophy and the Moving Image*. Basingstoke: Palgrave Macmillan.

Rancière, Jacques. (2006), *Film Fables*, trans. Emiliano Battista. Oxford/New York: Berg Books.

Sesonske, Alexander. (1974), 'Aesthetics of film, or a funny thing happened on the way to the movies'. *Journal of Aesthetics and Art Criticism*, 33, (1), 51–7.

Smith, Murrary. (2001), 'Film' in Berys Gaut and Dominic McIver Lopes (eds), *The Routledge Companion to Aesthetics*. London: Routledge.

Thompson-Jones, Katherine. (2008), *Aesthetics and Film*. London/ New York: Continuum.

Wartenberg, Thomas E. (2004), 'Philosophy of Film'. *Stanford Encyclopaedia of Philosophy*, http://plato.stanford.edu/entries/film/ (accessed April 3, 2009).

Film as Philosophy/Film-Philosophy

Bersani, Leo and Dutoit, Ulysse. (2004), *Forms of Being: Cinema, Aesthetics, Subjectivity*. London: BFI Books.

Constable, Catherine. (2009), *Adapting Philosophy: Jean Baudrillard and the Matrix Trilogy*. Manchester: Manchester University Press.

Frampton, Daniel. (2006), *Filmosophy*. London: Wallflower Press.

Mulhall, Stephen. (2002), *On Film*. New York: Routledge.

Mulhall, Stephen. (2008), *On Film*, Second Edition. New York: Routledge.

Mullarkey, John. (2011), 'Films Can't Philosophise (and Neither Can Philosophy): Introduction to a Non-Philosophy of Cinema' in Havi Carel and Greg Tuck (eds), *New Takes in Film-Philosophy*. Basingstoke: Palgrave Macmillan, pp. 86–100.

Peretz, Eyal. (2009), *Becoming Visionary: Brian de Palma's Cinematic Education of the Senses*. Stanford: Stanford University Press.

Phillips, James (ed.) (2009), *Cinematic Thinking: Philosophical Approaches to the New Cinema*. Stanford: Stanford University Press.

Livingston, Paisley. (2009), *Cinema, Philosophy, Bergman: On Film as Philosophy*. Oxford: Oxford University Press.

Singer, Irving. (2007), *Ingmar Bergman, Cinematic Philosopher: Reflections on His Creativity*. Cambridge, MA./London: The MIT Press.

Singer, Irving. (2008), *Cinematic Mythmaking*. Cambridge MA./ London: The MIT Press.

Sinnerbrink, Robert. (2011), 'Re-Enfranchising Film: Towards a Romantic Film-Philosophy', in Havi Carel and Greg Tuck (eds),

New Takes in Film-Philosophy. London: Palgrave Macmillan, pp. 25–47.

Smuts, Aaron. (2009), 'Film as philosophy: in defence of a bold thesis'. *The Journal of Aesthetics and Art Criticism*, 67, (4), Fall, 409–420.

Wartenberg, Thomas E. (2007), *Thinking on Screen: Film as Philosophy*. New York/London: Routledge.

Wartenberg, Thomas. E. (2011), 'On the Possibility of Cinematic Philosophy' in Havi Carel and Greg Tuck (eds), *New Takes in Film-Philosophy*. Basingstoke: Palgrave Macmillan, pp. 9–24.

Horror

Carroll, Noël. (1990), *The Philosophy of Horror; or, the Paradoxes of the Heart*. London/New York, Routledge.

Clover, Carol. (1992), *Men, Women, and Chainsaws*. Princeton: Princeton University Press.

Freeland, Cynthia A. (2000), *The Naked and the Undead: Evil and the Appeal of Horror*. Boulder: Westview Press.

Schneider, S.J. and Shaw, Daniel (eds). (2003), *Dark Thoughts: Philosophical Reflections on Cinematic Horror*. Lanham, MD: Scarecrow Press.

Shaw, Daniel. (2001), 'Power, horror, and ambivalence'. *Film and Philosophy*, 6 [Special Issue on Horror], 1–12.

Smuts, Aaron. (2009), 'Horror', in Paisley Livingston and Carl Plantinga (eds), *The Routledge Companion to Film and Philosophy*. London/New York: Routledge, pp. 505–514.

Wood, Robin. (1986), 'The American Nightmare: Horror in the 70s', in *Hollywood from Vietnam to Reagan*. New York: Columbia University Press, pp. 70–94.

Narrative

Bordwell, David. (1985), *Narration in the Fiction Film*. Madison: University of Wisconsin Press.

Branigan, Edward. (1984), *Point of View in the Cinema: A Theory of Narration and Subjectivity in Classical Film*. Berlin/New York: Mouton.

Branigan, Edward. (1992), *Narrative Comprehension and Film*. London: Routledge.

Buckland, Warren (ed). (2009), *Puzzle Films: Complex Storytelling in Contemporary Cinema*. Wiley-Blackwell.

Chatman, Seymour. (1990), *Coming to Terms: The Rhetoric of Narrative in Fiction and Film*. Ithaca: Cornell University Press.

Gaut, Berys. (2004), 'The Philosophy of the Movies: Cinematic Narration' in Peter Kivy (ed). *The Blackwell Guide to Aesthetics*. Oxford: Blackwell Publishing, 230–253.

Smith, Murray. (1995), *Engaging Characters: Fiction, Emotion, and the Cinema*. Oxford: Oxford University Press.

Wilson, George M. (1986), *Narration in Light: Studies in Cinematic Point of View*. Baltimore/London: The Johns Hopkins University Press.

Wilson, George M. (1997), '*Le grand imagier* steps out: the primitive basis of film narration'. *Philosophical Topics*, 25, 295–318.

Pedagogical Texts

Falzon, Christopher. (2002), *Philosophy Goes to the Movies*. London/New York: Routledge.

Fumerton, Richard and Jeske, Diane. (2009). *Introducing Philosophy Through Film: Key Texts, Discussion, and Film Selections*. Malden MA/Oxford: Wiley-Blackwell.

Gilmore, Richard A. (2005), *Doing Philosophy at the Movies*. Albany: SUNY Press.

Kupfer, Joseph H. (1999), *Visions of Virtue in Popular Film*. Boulder: Westview Press.

Litch, Mary. (2002), *Philosophy through Film*. New York: Routledge.

Rowlands, Mark. (2004), *The Philosopher at the End of the Universe: Philosophy Explained through Science Fiction*. New York: St Martin's Press.

Phenomenology

Casebier, Allan. (1991), *Film and Phenomenology: Towards a Realist Theory of Cinematic Representation*. Cambridge: Cambridge University Press.

Merleau-Ponty, Maurice. (1964), *Sense and Non-Sense*, trans. Patricia Allen Dreyfus. Evanston: Northwestern University Press.

Merleau-Ponty, Maurice (2002 [1945]), *Phenomenology of Perception*, trans. Colin Smith. London: Routledge.

Sobchack, Vivian (1992). *The Address of the Eye: A Phenomenology of Film Experience*, Princeton: Princeton University Press.

Sobchack, Vivian. (2004). *Carnal Thoughts: Embodiment and Moving Image Culture*. Berkeley: University of California Press.

Sobchack, Vivian. (2011), 'Fleshing Out the Image: Phenomenology, Pedagogy, and Derek Jarman's *Blue*' in Havi Carel and Greg Tuck (eds), *New Takes in Film-Philosophy* Basingstoke: Palgrave Macmillan, pp. 191–206.

FILMOGRAPHIES

David Lynch Filmography

Eraserhead (1977)
The Elephant Man (1980)
Dune (1984)
Blue Velvet (1986)
Wild at Heart (1990)
Twin Peaks: Fire Walk with Me (1992)
Lost Highway (1997)
The Straight Story (1999)
Mulholland Drive (2001)
INLAND EMPIRE (2006)

Selected Literature on Lynch

Barney, Richard A. (ed). (2009), *David Lynch Interviews*. Jackson: University Press of Mississippi.

Gleyzon, Francois-Xavier (ed). (2010), *David Lynch in Theory*. Prague: Charles University Press.

Lynch, David. (2006), *Catching the Big Fish: Meditation, Consciousness, and Creativity*. New York: Tarcher Penguin.

MacGowan, Todd. (2007), *The Impossible David Lynch*. New York: Columbia University Press.

Mactaggart, Allister. (2010), *The Film Paintings of David Lynch: Challenging Film Theory*, Bristol/Chicago: Intellect Books.

Sheen, Erica and Davison, Annette. (2004), *The Cinema of David Lynch: American Dreams, Nightmare Visions*. London/New York: Wallflower Press.

Wilson, Eric G. (2007), *The Strange World of David Lynch:*

Transcendental Irony from Eraserhead *to* Mulholland Drive. New York/London: Continuum.

Terrence Malick Filmography

Badlands (1973)
Days of Heaven (1978)
The Thin Red Line (1998)
The New World (2005)
The Tree of Life (2011)

Selected Bibliography on Malick

Chion, Michel. (2004), *The Thin Red Line*. London: British Film Institute.

Clewis, Robert. (2003), 'Heideggerian wonder in Terrence Malick's *The Thin Red Line*'. *Film and Philosophy* 7, 22–36.

Critchley, Simon. (2005), 'Calm—On Terrence Malick's *The Thin Red Line*,' in Rupert Read and Jerry Goodenough (eds), *Film as Philosophy: Essays on Cinema after Wittgenstein and Cavell.* Basingstoke: Palgrave Macmillan, pp. 133–148.

Davies, David (ed). (2009), *The Thin Red Line*. London: Routledge.

Kendall, Stuart and Tucker, Thomas Deane (eds). (2011), *Terrence Malick: Film and Philosophy*. London: Continuum.

Michaels, Lloyd. (2009), *Terrence Malick*. Urbana: University of Illinois Press.

Paterson, Hannah (ed). (2007), *The Cinema of Terrence Malick: Poetic Visions of America,* 2nd edition. London: Wallflower Press.

Lars von Trier Filmography

The Element of Crime (1984)
Epidemic (1987)
Medea (1988)
Europa [*Zentropa*] (1991)
The Kingdom I (1994)
Breaking the Waves (1996)
The Kingdom II (1997)
The Idiots (1998)
Dancer in the Dark (2000)

Dogville (2003)
The Five Obstructions (2003)
Manderlay (2005)
The Boss of It All (2006)
Antichrist (2009)
Melancholia (2011)

Selected Bibliography on von Trier

Badley, Linda. (2010), *Lars von Trier*. Urbana: University of Illinois Press.

Bainbridge, Caroline. (2007), *The Cinema of Lars von Trier: Authenticity and Artifice*. London: Wallflower Press.

Hjort, Mette and MacKenzie, Scott (eds). (2003). *Purity and Provocation: Dogme 95*. London: British Film Institute.

Hjort, Mette. (2008). *Dekalog 1: On The Five Obstructions*. London/ New York: Wallflower Press.

Von Trier, Lars. (2010), 'An interview with Lars von Trier' (Peter Schepelern). *Projections: The Journal for Movies and Mind*, 4, (1), 1–15.

WEBSITES

Cinema Journal: http://www.utexas.edu/utpress/journals/jcj.html
Film and Philosophy: http://www.lhup.edu/dshaw/journal.htm
Film-Philosophy: http://www.film-philosophy.com/index.php/f-p
Journal of Aesthetics and Art Criticism: http://www.wiley.com/bw/journal.asp?ref=0021-8529
New Review of Film and Television Studies: http://www.tandf.co.uk/journals/titles/17400309.asp
Rouge: http://www.rouge.com.au/
Screen: http://screen.oxfordjournals.org/
Screening the Past: http://screeningthepast.com/
Senses of Cinema: http://www.sensesofcinema.com/

David Bordwell's Website: http://www.davidbordwell.net/
Film Studies For Free: http://filmstudiesforfree.blogspot.com/
David Lynch's website: http://davidlynch.com/
Philosophical Films: http://www.philfilms.utm.edu/ and http://www.philfilms.utm.edu/2/filmlist.htm

BIBLIOGRAPHY

Abell, Catherine (2010), 'Cinema as representational art'. *British Journal of Aesthetics*, 50, (3), 273–86.

Agamben, Giorgio (2007), *Profanations*, trans. Jeff Fort, New York: Zone Books.

Allen, Richard (1995), *Projecting Illusion: Film Spectatorship and the Impression of Reality*. Cambridge: Cambridge University Press.

Allen, Richard and Smith, Murray (1997), *Film Theory and Philosophy*. Oxford: Oxford University Press.

Andrews, Dudley (2009), 'Edgar Morin' in Paisley Livingston and Carl Plantinga (eds), *The Routledge Companion to Philosophy and Film*. London/New York: Routledge, pp. 408–21.

Aristotle (1996), *Poetics*, trans. M. Heath. London: Penguin Books.

Arnheim, Rudolf (1957 [1932]), *Film as Art*. Berkeley: University of California Press.

Badiou, Alain (2005), 'The False Movements of Cinema', in *Handbook of Inaesthetics*, trans. Alberto Toscano. Stanford: Stanford University Press, pp. 78–88.

Baggini, Julian (2003), 'Alien Ways of Thinking: Mulhall's *On Film*'. *Film-Philosophy*, 7, (24). August. http://www.film-philosophy.com/vol-2003/n24baggini (accessed May 1, 2008).

Barthes, Roland (1972 [1957]), *Mythologies*, trans. Annette Lavers. New York: Hill and Wang.

Baudry, Jean-Louis (2004a), 'Ideological Effects of the Basic Cinematographic Apparatus', in L. Braudy and M. Cohen (eds), *Film Theory and Criticism: Introductory Readings*, Sixth Edition. New York: Oxford University Press, pp. 355–65.

— (2004b), 'The Apparatus: Metapsychological Approaches to the Impression of Reality in the Cinema', in L. Braudy and M. Cohen (eds), *Film Theory and Criticism: Introductory Readings*, Sixth Edition. New York: Oxford University Press, pp. 206–23.

Bazin, André (1967 [1958/59]), *What is Cinema? Volume I*, trans. Hugh Gray. Berkeley: University of California Press.

Benjamin, Walter (2006), 'The Work of Art in the Age of its Technical Reproducibility: Third Version', Howard Eiland and Michael W. Jennings (eds), *Selected Writings Volume 4: 1938–1940*. Cambridge MA./London: Belknap Press.

Bergson, Henri (1998 [1896]), *Matter and Memory*, trans. Nancy Margaret Paul and W. Scott Palmer. New York: Zone Books.

— (2005 [1907]), *Creative Evolution*, trans. Peter A. Y. Gunter. New York: Barnes and Noble Publishing.

Bersani, Leo and Dutoit, Ulysse (2004), *Forms of Being: Cinema, Aesthetics, Subjectivity*. London: BFI Books.

Bordwell, David (1985), *Narration in the Fiction Film*. Madison: University of Wisconsin Press.

— (1988), *Ozu and The Poetics of Cinema*. London/Princeton: BFI Books/Princeton University Press.

— (1989a), 'A case for cognitivism'. *Iris* 9, 11–40. http://geocities. com/david_bordwell/caseforcog.1.htm?200914 (accessed May 14, 2009).

— (1989b), *Making Meaning: Inference and Rhetoric in the Interpretation of Cinema*. Cambridge, MA.: Harvard University Press.

— (1990), 'A case for cognitivism: further reflections'. *Iris,* 11, 107–112. http://www.davidbordwell.net/articles/Bordwell_Iris_ no11_summer1990_107.pdf (accessed May 14, 2009).

Bordwell, David and Carroll, Noël (eds) (1996a), *Post-Theory: Reconstructing Film Studies*. Madison: University of Wisconsin Press.

Bordwell, David (1996b), 'Contemporary Film Studies and the Vicissitudes of Grand Theory', in D. Bordwell and N. Carroll (eds), *Post-Theory: Reconstructing Film Studies*. Madison: University of Wisconsin Press, pp. 3–36.

— (1997), *On the History of Film Style*. Cambridge, MA.: Harvard University Press.

— (2008), *Poetics of Cinema*. New York: Routledge.

Branigan, Edward (1984), *Point of View in the Cinema: A Theory of Narration and Subjectivity in Classical Film*. Berlin/New York: Mouton.

— (1992), *Narrative Comprehension and Film*. London: Routledge.

Brown, William (2010), 'Claiming interdisciplinary studies. Review of James Phillips (ed.) *Cinematic Thinking: Philosophical Approaches to the New Cinema* (Stanford: Stanford University Press, 2009)'. *Film-Philosophy*, 14, (1), 337–9.

Buckland, Warren (ed.) (2008), *Film Theory and Contemporary Hollywood Movies*. New York/London: Routledge.

Buckland, Warren (2009), 'Introduction: Puzzle Plots', in Warren Buckland (ed.), *Puzzle Films: Complex Storytelling in Contemporary Cinema*. Wiley-Blackwell, 2009, pp. 1–12.

Carroll, Noël (1985), 'The power of movies'. *Daedalus* 114, (4), Fall, 79–103.

— (1988a), *Mystifying Movies: Fads and Fallacies in Contemporary Film Theory*. New York: Columbia University Press.

— (1988b), *Philosophical Problems of Classical Film Theory*. Princeton: Princeton University Press.

— (1988c), 'Film/mind analogies: The case of Hugo Münsterberg', *Journal of Aesthetics and Art Criticism*, 46, (4), Summer, 489–99.

— (1990), *The Philosophy of Horror; or, the Paradoxes of the Heart*. London/New York, Routledge.

— (1996), 'Prospects for Film Theory: A Personal Assessment', in David Bordwell and Noël Carroll (eds), *Post-Theory: Reconstructing Film Studies*. Madison: University of Wisconsin Press, pp. 37–68.

— (2003), *Engaging the Moving Image*. New Haven/London: Yale University Press.

— (2006), 'Defining the Moving Image', in Noël Carroll and Jinhee Choi (eds), *Philosophy of Film and Motion Pictures: An Anthology*. Malden, MA./Oxford: Blackwell Publishing, pp. 113–33.

— (2008), *The Philosophy of Motion Pictures*, Malden, MA.: Blackwell Publishing.

Casebier, Allan (1991), *Film and Phenomenology: Towards a Realist Theory of Cinematic Representation*. Cambridge: Cambridge University Press.

Cavell, Stanley (1979), *The World Viewed: Reflections on the Ontology of Film*, Enlarged Edition. Cambridge, MA./London: Harvard University Press.

— (1981), *Pursuits of Happiness: The Hollywood Comedy of Remarriage*. Cambridge, MA.: Harvard University Press.

— (1996), *Contesting Tears: the Melodrama of the Unknown Woman*. Chicago: University of Chicago Press.

— (1999), 'An interview with Stanley Cavell'. *Harvard Journal of Philosophy*, VII, 19–28.

— (2005), William Rothman and Marian Keane (eds) *Cavell on Film*. Albany: State University of New York Press, pp. 11–40.

— (2008), 'On Eyal Peretz's *Becoming Visionary*,' in Eyal Peretz, *Becoming Visionary: Brian de Palma's Cinematic Education of the Senses*. Stanford: Stanford University Press, pp. xi–xvii.

Chatman, Seymour (1990), *Coming to Terms: The Rhetoric of Narrative in Fiction and Film*. Ithaca: Cornell University Press.

Cholodenko, Alan (2008), 'The animation of cinema', *The Semiotic Review of Books*, 18, (2), 1–10.

Clewis, Robert (2003), 'Heideggerian wonder in Terrence Malick's *The Thin Red Line*'. *Film and Philosophy* 7, 22–36.

Clover, Carol (1992), *Men, Women, and Chainsaws*. Princeton: Princeton University Press.

Colman, Felicity (ed.) (2009), *Film, Theory and Philosophy*. Durham: Acumen Press.

Constable, Catherine (2009), *Adapting Philosophy: Jean Baudrillard and the Matrix Trilogy*. Manchester: Manchester University Press.

Coplan, Amy (2006), 'Catching characters' emotions: emotional contagion responses to narrative fiction film'. *Film Studies: An International Review* 8, 26–38.

Cousins, Mark (2007), 'Praising *The New World*', in Hannah Paterson (ed.) *The Cinema of Terrence Malick: Poetic Visions of America*. London: Wallflower Press, pp. 192–8.

Critchley, Simon (1997), *Very Little … Almost Nothing: Death, Philosophy, Literature*, Revised Edition. London and New York: Routledge.

— (2005), 'Calm — On Terrence Malick's *The Thin Red Line*,' in Rupert Read and Jerry Goodenough (eds), *Film as Philosophy: Essays on Cinema after Wittgenstein and Cavell*. Basingstoke: Palgrave Macmillan, pp. 133–48.

Critchley, Simon and Webster, Jamieson (2010), 'What is the hole inside the hole? On David Lynch's *INLAND EMPIRE*'. *Bedeutung* I, (3), http://www.bedeutung.co.uk/?page_id=1921 (accessed July 13, 2010).

Currie, Gregory (1993), 'The long goodbye: the imaginary language of film'. *British Journal of Aesthetics* 33, (3), July: 207–219.

— (1995), *Image and Mind: Film, Philosophy, and Cognitive Science*. New York: Cambridge University Press.

— (1999), 'Cognitivism', in Toby Miller and Robert Stam (eds), *A Companion to Film Theory*. Malden MA/London: Blackwell, pp. 105–22.

Danto, Arthur C. (1979), 'Moving Pictures'. *Quarterly Review of Film Studies*, 4, (1), Winter, 1–21.

— (1986), *The Philosophical Disenfranchisement of Art*. New York: Columbia University Press.

Davies, David (ed.) (2009a), *The Thin Red Line*. London: Routledge.

Davies, David (2009b), 'Terrence Malick', in Paisley Livingston and Carl Plantinga (eds), *The Routledge Companion to Philosophy and Film*, London/New York: Routledge, pp. 560–80.

Debord, Guy (1955), 'Introduction to a Critique of Urban Geography'. *Les Lèvres Nues* #6, http://library.nothingness.org/articles/SI/en/display/2 (accessed December 30, 2010).

Deleuze, Gilles (1986 [1983]), *Cinema I: The Movement-Image*, trans. Hugh Tomlinson and Barbara Habberjam. Minneapolis: University of Minnesota Press.

— (1989 [1985]), *Cinema II: The Time-Image*, trans. Hugh Tomlinson and Robert Galatea. Minneapolis: University of Minnesota Press.

— (2000), 'The Brain is the Screen. An Interview with Gilles Deleuze', trans. Marie Therese Guirgis, in Gregory Flaxman (ed.), *The Brain is the Screen: Deleuze and the Philosophy of Cinema*. Minneapolis: University of Minnesota Press, pp. 365–73.

de Sousa, Ronald (1987), *The Rationality of Emotion*. Cambridge, MA.: The MIT Press.

Elsaesser, Thomas and Buckland, Warren (2002), *Studying Contemporary American Film: A Guide To Movie Analysis*. New York: Oxford University Press.

Elsaesser, Thomas (2009), 'The Mind-Game Film', in Warren Buckland (ed.), *Puzzle Films: Complex Storytelling in Contemporary Cinema*. Chichester: Wiley-Blackwell, pp. 13–41.

Flanagan, Martin (2007), '"Everything a Lie": The Critical and Commercial Reception of Terrence Malick's *The Thin Red Line*', in Hannah Patterson (ed.), *The Cinema of Terrence Malick: Poetic Visions of America*, Second Edition. London: Wallflower Press, pp. 125–40.

Flory, Dan (2009), 'Race' in P. Livingston and C. Plantinga (eds), *The Routledge Companion to Philosophy and Film*. London: Routledge, pp. 227–36.

Frampton, Daniel (2006), *Filmosophy*. London: Wallflower Press.

Freeland, Cynthia (2002), *The Naked and the Undead*. Boulder, CO.: Westview Press.

Furstenau Marc and MacEvoy, Leslie (2007), 'Terrence Malick's Heideggerian Cinema: War and the Question of Being in *The Thin Red Line*', in Hannah Paterson (ed.) *The Cinema of Terrence Malick: Poetic Visions of America*. London: Wallflower Press, pp. 179–91.

Gadamer, Hans-Georg (2004), *Truth and Method*, Second Edition. London/New York: Continuum.

Gaut, Berys (2002), 'Cinematic art'. *Journal of Aesthetics and Art Criticism*, 60, (4), 299–312.

— (2010), *A Philosophy of Cinematic Art*. Cambridge: Cambridge University Press.

Gilmore, Richard A. (2005), *Doing Philosophy at the Movies*. Albany: State University of New York Press.

Grodal, Torben (2009), *Embodied Visions: Evolution, Emotion, Culture, and Film*. Oxford: Oxford University Press.

Hainge, Greg (2010), 'Red Velvet: Lynch's Cinemat(ograph)ic Ontology', in Francois-Xavier Gleyzon (ed.), *David Lynch in Theory*. Prague: Charles University Press, 2011, pp. 24–39.

Heidegger, Martin (1982), *On the Way to Language*, trans. Peter D. Hertz. San Francisco: Harper Books.

Hjort, Mette (2009), *'The Five Obstructions'*, in P. Livingston and C. Plantinga (eds), *The Routledge Companion to Philosophy and Film*. London/New York: Routledge, pp. 631–40.

Hume, David (1965 [1757]), 'Of Tragedy', in *Of the Standard of Taste and Other Essays*, John W. Lenz (ed.). Indianapolis: Bobbs-Merrill.

Jarvie, Ian (1987), *Philosophy of the Film: Epistemology, Ontology, Aesthetics*. London: Routledge.

Klevan, Andrew (2005), *Film Performance: From Achievement to Appreciation*. London: Wallflower Press.

— (2011), 'Notes on Stanley Cavell and Philosophical Film Criticism', in Havi Carel and Greg Tuck (eds), *New Takes in Film-Philosophy*. New York: Palgrave Macmillan, pp. 48–64.

Kovács, András Bálint (2000), 'The Film History of Thought' in Gregory Flaxman (ed.), *The Brain is the Screen: Deleuze and the Philosophy of Cinema*. Minneapolis: University of Minnesota Press, pp. 153–70.

— (2009), 'Andrei Tarkovsky', in P. Livingston and C. Plantinga (eds) *The Routledge Companion to Philosophy and Film.* London/ New York: Routledge, pp. 581–90.

Lacan, Jacques (2006), 'The Mirror Stage as Formative of the *I* as Revealed in Psychoanalytic Experience', in *Écrits: The First Complete Edition in English*, trans. B. Fink. New York: Norton Books, pp. 75–81.

Laine, Tarja (2010), '*The diving bell and the butterfly* as an emotional event', Midwestern *Studies in Philosophy*, XXXIV, 295–305.

— (2011), *Feeling Film.* London/New York: Continuum.

Litch, Mary (2002). *Philosophy through Film.* New York: Routledge.

Livingston, Paisley (2006), 'Theses on Cinema as Philosophy', in Murray Smith and Thomas E. Wartenberg (eds), *Thinking through Cinema: Film as Philosophy.* Malden, MA./Oxford: Blackwell Publishing, pp. 11–18.

— (2008), 'Recent work on cinema as philosophy'. *Philosophy Compass* 3, (4), 590–603.

Livingston, Paisley and Plantinga, Carl (2009), *The Routledge Companion to Philosophy and Film.* London: Routledge.

Livingston, Paisley (2009a), 'Ingmar Bergman', in P. Livingston and C. Plantinga (eds) *The Routledge Companion to Philosophy and Film.* London: Routledge, pp. 560–8.

Livingston, Paisley (2009b), *Cinema, Philosophy, Bergman: On Film as Philosophy.* Oxford: Oxford University Press.

Lopes, Dominic McIver (2005), 'Aesthetics of photographic transparency'. *Mind* 112, 335–48.

Lynch, David (2006), *Catching the Big Fish: Meditation, Consciousness, and Creativity.* New York: Tarcher Penguin.

Macdonald, Iain (2009), 'Nature and the Will to Power in Terrence Malick's *The New World,* in David Davies (ed.), *The Thin Red Line.* London/New York: Routledge, pp. 87–110.

Mactaggart, Allister (2010), *The Film Paintings of David Lynch: Challenging Film Theory*, Bristol/Chicago: Intellect Books.

Marks, Laura U. (2000), *The Skin of the Film: Intercultural Cinema, Embodiment, the Senses.* Durham: Duke University Press.

Marrati, Paola (2008), *Gilles Deleuze: Cinema and Philosophy*, trans. Alisa Hartz. Baltimore: Johns Hopkins University Press.

Martin, Adrian (2006), 'Laura Mulvey, Death at 24x a second: stillness and the moving image' (Book Review), *Cineaste*, Winter, 75–6.

— (2007a), 'Approaching *The New World*', in Hannah Paterson (ed.), *Poetic Visions of America: The Cinema of Terrence Malick*, Second Edition. London: Wallflower Press, pp. 212–21.

— (2007b), 'Things to look into: The cinema of Terrence Malick'. *Rouge*, 10, http://www.rouge.com.au/10/malick.html (accessed January 19, 2007).

Martin-Jones, David (2006), *Deleuze, Cinema, and National Identity*. Edinburgh: Edinburgh University Press.

Merleau-Ponty, Maurice (1964), *Sense and Non-Sense*, trans. Patricia Allen Dreyfus. Evanston: Northwestern University Press.

— (2002 [1945]), *Phenomenology of Perception*, trans. Colin Smith. London: Routledge.

Metz, Christian (1974), *Film Language: A Semiotics of the Cinema*, trans. Michael Taylor. New York: Oxford University Press.

— (1982), *The Imaginary Signifier: Psychoanalysis and Cinema*, trans. C. Britton, A. Williams, B. Brewster and A. Guzzetti. Bloomington: Indiana University Press.

Michaels, Lloyd (2009), *Terrence Malick*. Urbana: University of Illinois Press.

Millington, Jeremy (2010), 'Critical voices: points of view in and on *The Thin Red Line*'. *Cineaction*, June 22.

Morin, Edgar (2002 [1956/1978]), *The Cinema, or The Imaginary Man*, trans. Lorraine Mortimer. Minneapolis: University of Minnesota Press.

Morrison, James (2007), 'Making Worlds, Making Pictures: Terrence Malick's *The New World*', in Hannah Patterson (ed.), *Poetic Visions of America: The Cinema of Terrence Malick*, Second Edition. London: Wallflower, pp. 199–211.

Mulhall, Stephen (1999), *Stanley Cavell: Philosophy's Recounting of the Ordinary*. Oxford: Oxford University Press.

— (2002), *On Film*. New York: Routledge.

— (2008), *On Film*, Second Edition. New York: Routledge.

Mullarkey, John (2009), *Refractions of Reality: Philosophy and the Moving Image*. Basingstoke: Palgrave Macmillan.

— (2011), 'Films Can't Philosophise (and Neither Can Philosophy): Introduction to a Non-Philosophy of Cinema', in Havi Carel and Greg Tuck (eds), *New Takes in Film-Philosophy*. Basingstoke: Palgrave Macmillan, pp. 86–100.

Mulvey, Laura (1975), 'Visual Pleasure and Narrative Cinema'. *Screen*, 16, (3), 6–18.

Münsterberg, Hugo (2002 [1916]), *The Photoplay: A Psychological Study* in Allen Langdale (ed.), *Hugo Münsterberg on Film*. London: Routledge.

Nietzsche, Friedrich (1967 [1872]), *The Birth of Tragedy and the Case of Wagner*. New York: Vintage Books.

Orr, John (2009), 'A cinema of parallel worlds: Lynch and Kieslowski + INLAND EMPIRE. *Film International*, 7, (11), February, 28–43.

Palmer, Tim (2006), 'Style and sensation in the contemporary French cinema of the body'. *Journal of Film and Video*, 58, (3), Fall, 22–32.

Panofsky, Erwin (1997 [1934]), 'Style and Medium in the Motion Pictures', in J. Harrington (ed.), *Film and/as Literature*. New York: Prentice Press, pp. 283–94.

Peretz, Eyal (2008), *Becoming Visionary: Brian de Palma's Cinematic Education of the Senses*. Stanford: Stanford University Press.

Perkins, V. F. (1972), *Film as Film: Understanding and Judging Movies*. New York: Penguin Books.

Plato (1987), *The Republic*, trans. Desmond Lee. London: Penguin.

Plantinga, Carl and Smith, Greg M. (1999), *Passionate Views: Film, Cognition, and Emotion*. Baltimore: Johns Hopkins University Press.

Plantinga, Carl (2002), 'Cognitive film theory: An insider's appraisal', *Cinémas: revue d'etudes cinematographiques/Cinémas: Journal of Film Studies*, 12, (2), 15–37.

— (2009a), *Moving Viewers: American Film and the Spectator's Experience*. Berkeley: University of California Press.

— (2009b), 'Emotion and Affect', in P. Livingston and C. Plantinga (eds), *The Routledge Companion to Philosophy and Film*. London: Routledge, pp. 86–96.

Prince, Stephen (1996), 'Psychoanalytic Film Theory and the Case of the Missing Spectator', in D. Bordwell and N. Carroll (eds), *Post-Theory: Reconstructing Film Studies*. Madison: University of Wisconsin Press, pp. 71–86.

Prinz, Jesse (2004), *Gut Reactions: A Perceptual Theory of Emotions*. New York: Oxford University Press.

Quandt, James (2004), 'Flesh and blood: Sex and violence in recent French cinema', *Artforum*, 42, (6), February: 24–47.

Radford, Colin (1975), 'How can we be moved by the fate of Anna Karenina?'. Proceedings of *the Aristotelian Society*, Supplemental Volume, 49, 67–80.

Rancière, Jacques (2004), *The Politics of Aesthetics*, trans. Gabriel Rockhill. London: Continuum.

— (2006), *Film Fables*, trans. Emiliano Battista. Oxford/New York: Berg Books.

Rhym, John (2010), 'The paradigmatic shift in the reception of Terrence Malick's *Badlands* and the emergence of a Heideggerian cinema'. *Quarterly Review of Film and Video*, 27, 255–66.

Roberts Robert C. (2003), *Emotions: An Essay in Aid of Moral Psychology*. Cambridge/New York: Cambridge University Press.

Robinson, Jenefer (2005), *Deeper than Reason: Emotion and its Role in Literature, Music, and Art*. Oxford: Clarendon Press.

Rodley, Chris (ed.) (2005), *Lynch on Lynch*, Revised Edition. London: Faber and Faber.

Rodowick, D. N. (1997), *Gilles Deleuze's Time Machine*. Durham: Duke University Press.

— (2007a), 'An elegy for theory'. *October*, 122, Fall, 91–109.

— (2007b), *The Virtual Life of Film*. Cambridge, MA./London: Harvard University Press.

Rothman, William and Keane, Marian (2000), *Reading Cavell's The World Viewed: A Philosophical Perspective on Film*. Detroit: Wayne State University Press.

Rowlands, Mark (2004), *The Philosopher at the End of the Universe: Philosophy Explained through Science Fiction*. New York: St Martin's Press.

Russell, Bruce (2006), 'The Philosophical Limits of Film', in Noël Carroll and Jinhee Choi (eds), *Philosophy of Film and Motion Pictures: An Anthology*. Malden, MA./Oxford: Blackwell Publishing, pp. 387–90.

Sacks, Oliver (1986), *The Man Who Mistook His Wife for a Hat*. London: Picador Books.

Schaffner, Anna Katharina (2009), 'Fantasmatic splittings and destructive desires: Lynch's *Lost Highway, Mulholland Drive,* and *INLAND EMPIRE*'. *Forum for Modern Language Studies*, 45, (3), 270–91.

Scruton, Roger (1981), 'Photography and representation'. *Critical Inquiry*, 7, (3), Spring, 577–601.

Sesonske, Alexander (1973), 'Cinema Space', in David Carr and Edward S. Casey (eds), *Explorations in Phenomenology*. The Hague: Martinus Nijoff, pp. 399–409.

— (1974), 'Aesthetics of film, or a funny thing happened on the way to the movies'. *Journal of Aesthetics and Art Criticism*, 33, 51–7.

Shaw, Daniel (1997), 'A Humean definition of horror'. *Film-Philosophy*, 1, (4), August. http://www.film-philosophy.com/vol1–1997/n4shaw (accessed November 18, 2010).

— (2001), 'Power, horror, and ambivalence'. *Film and Philosophy*, 6 [Special Issue on Horror], 1–12.

— (2008), *Film and Philosophy: Taking Movies Seriously*. London: Wallflower Press.

Shaw, Joshua (2009), 'A second look at Mulhall's *On Film*, 2nd edn' *Film-Philosophy*, 13, (1), 187–98. http://www.film philosophy. com/2009v13n1/shaw.pdf (accessed November 18, 2010).

Silverman, Kaja (2003), 'All Things Shining', in David L. Eng and David Kazanjian (eds), *Loss: The Politics of Mourning*. Berkeley: University of California, pp. 323–42.

Singer, Irving (2007), *Ingmar Bergman, Cinematic Philosopher: Reflections on His Creativity*. Cambridge, MA./London: The MIT Press.

Sinnerbrink, Robert (2005), 'Cinematic Ideas: on David Lynch's *Mulholland Drive*', *Film-Philosophy*, 9, (4), June. http://www.film-philosophy.com/index.php/f-p/article/view/847/759 (accessed July 1, 2005).

— (2006), 'A Heideggerian cinema? On Terrence Malick's *The Thin Red Line*'. *Film-Philosophy*, 10, (3), December, http://www.film-philosophy.com/2006v10n3/sinnerbrink.pdf (accessed December 24, 2006).

— (2009a), 'Hugo Münsterberg', in Felicity Colman (ed), *Film, Theory and Philosophy*. Durham: Acumen Press, pp. 20–30.

— (2009b), 'From Mythic History to Cinematic Poetry: Terrence Malick's *The New World* Viewed'. *Screening the Past*, 26, [Issue on Early Europe], December. http://www.latrobe.edu.au/screeningthepast/26/early-europe/the-new-world.html (accessed December 20, 2009).

— (2010), 'Disenfranchising Film? On the Analytic-Cognitivist Turn in Film Theory', in Jack Reynolds, Ed Mares, James Williams and James Chase (eds), *Postanalytic and Metacontinental: Crossing Philosophical Divides*. Continuum, pp. 173–89.

— (2011), 'Re-Enfranchising Film: Towards a Romantic Film-Philosophy', in Havi Carel and Greg Tuck (eds), *New Takes in Film-Philosophy*. London: Palgrave Macmillan, pp. 25–47.

Smith, Greg M. (2003), *Film Structure and the Emotion System*. Cambridge: Cambridge University Press.

Smith, Murray (1995), *Engaging Characters: Fiction, Emotion, and the Cinema*. Oxford: Oxford University Press.

— (2006), 'Film Art, Argument, and Ambiguity', in Murray Smith and Thomas E. Wartenberg (eds), *Thinking Through Cinema: Film as Philosophy*. Malden/Oxford: Blackwell Publishing.

— (2010), 'Film theory meets analytic philosophy; or, *l'affaire Sokal* and film studies'. *Cinema: The Journal of Philosophy and the Moving Image*, 1, 111–17.

Smith, Richard (2001), 'The philosopher with two brains'. *Film-Philosophy*, 5, (34), November. http://www.film-philosophy.com/index.php/f-p/article/view/655/568 (accessed January 4, 2010).

Smuts, Aaron (2003), 'Haunting the House from Within: Disbelief Mitigation and Spatial Experience', in S. J. Schneider and D. Shaw (eds), *Dark Thoughts: Philosophical Reflections on Cinematic Horror*. Lanham, MD: Scarecrow Press.

— (2007), 'The paradox of painful art'. *Journal of Aesthetic Education*, 41, 59–77.

— (2009a), 'Film as philosophy: in defence of a bold thesis'. *The Journal of Aesthetics and Art Criticism*, 67, (4), Fall, 409–20.

— (2009b), 'Horror', in Paisley Livingston and Carl Plantinga (eds), *The Routledge Companion to Philosophy and Film*. London/New York: Routledge, pp. 505–14.

Sobchack, Vivian (1992), *The Address of the Eye: A Phenomenology of Film Experience*. Princeton: Princeton University Press.

— (2011), 'Fleshing Out the Image: Phenomenology, Pedagogy, and Derek Jarman's *Blue*', in Havi Carel and Greg Tuck (eds), *New Takes in Film-Philosophy*. Basingstoke: Palgrave Macmillan, pp. 191–206.

Sparshott, Frances E. (1975), 'Vision and dream in the cinema'. *Philosophic Exchange*, Summer, 111–22.

— (1985), 'Basic Film Aesthetics', in Gerald Mast and Marshal Cohen (eds), *Film Theory and Criticism*, Third Edition. New York: Oxford University Press.

Stadler, Jane (2008), *Pulling Focus: Intersubjective Experience, Narrative Film, and Ethics*. New York/London: Continuum.

Thompson-Jones, Katherine (2008), *Aesthetics and Film*. London/New York: Continuum.

Totaro, Donato; Rist, Peter; and Jordan, Randolph (2009), 'Roundtable on David Lynch's *INLAND EMPIRE*, Part 2'. *Offscreen*, 13(9), September 30. http://www.offscreen.com/ index.php/pages/essays/roundtable_inland_empire_pt2/ (accessed November 30, 2010).

Trahair, Lisa (2007), *The Comedy of Philosophy: Sense and Nonsense in Early Cinematic Slapstick*. Albany: State University of New York Press.

Von Trier, Lars (2010), 'An interview with Lars von Trier' (Peter Schepelern). *Projections: The Journal for Movies and Mind*, 4, (1), 1–15.

Walton, Kendall L. (1984), 'Transparent pictures: on the nature of photographic realism'. *Critical Inquiry*, 11, (2), December, 246–77.

— (1990), *Mimesis as Make-Believe: On the Foundations of the Representational Arts*. Cambridge, MA.: Harvard University Press.

Wartenberg, Thomas E. (2004), 'Philosophy of Film'. *Stanford Encyclopaedia of Philosophy*, http://plato.stanford.edu/entries/ film/ (accessed April 3, 2009).

— (2007), *Thinking on Screen: Film as Philosophy*. New York/ London: Routledge.

White, Rob and Power, Nina (2009), '*Antichrist*: a discussion', *Film Quarterly*, Web Exclusives, December, http://www.filmquarterly. org/2009/12/antichrist-a-discussion/ (accessed November 16, 2010).

Wilson, Eric G. (2007), *The Strange World of David Lynch: Transcendental Irony from* Eraserhead *to* Mulholland Drive. New York/London: Continuum.

Wilson, George M. (1986), *Narration in Light: Studies in Cinematic Point of View*. Baltimore/London: The Johns Hopkins University Press.

Wilson, George M. (1997), '*Le grand imagier* steps out: the primitive basis of film narration', *Philosophical Topics*, 25, (1): 295–318.

Wood, Robin. (1986), 'The American Nightmare: Horror in the 70s', in *Hollywood from Vietnam to Reagan* New York: Columbia University Press, pp. 70–94.

FILMOGRAPHY

Adaptation (Spike Jonze/Charlie Kaufman, 2002)

Alien (Ridley Scott, 1979)

Aliens (James Cameron, 1986)

*Alien*³ (David Fincher, 1992)

Alien Resurrection (Jean-Pierre Jeunet, 1997)

All About Eve (Joseph L. Mankiewicz, 1950)

All About My Mother [*Todo Sobre Mi Madre*] (Pedro Almodóvar, 1999)

American Beauty (Sam Mendes, 1999)

An Andalusian Dog [*Un Chien Andalou*] (Luis Buñuel, 1929)

Anatomy of Hell [*Anatomie de l'enfer*] (Catherine Breillat, 2004)

Antichrist (Lars von Trier, 2009)

Au hasard Balthazar (Robert Bresson, 1966)

Babel (Alejandro González Iñárritu, 2006)

Badlands (Terrence Malick, 1973)

The Bad Seed (Mervyn LeRoy, 1956)

Baise Moi (Virginie Despentes and Coralie Trinh Thi, 2000)

Band of Ninja [Ninja bugei-cho] (Nagisa Oshima, 1967)

Being John Malkovich (Spike Jonze, 1999)

The Big Sleep (Howard Hawks, 1946)

Blade Runner (Ridley Scott, 1982)

Blissfully Yours [*Sud sanaeha*] (Apichatpong Weerasethakul, 2002)

Blue (Derek Jarman, 1993)

Body Double (Brian de Palma, 1984)

The Canterbury Tales [*I raconti di Canterbury*] (Pier Paolo Pasolini, 1972)

Carrie (Brian de Palma, 1976)

Casablanca (Michael Curtiz, 1942)

The Child [*L'enfant*] (Jean-Pierre Dardenne and Luc Dardenne, 2005)

Children of Men (Alfonso Cuáron, 2006)

Chimes At Midnight (Orson Welles, 1965)

Citizen Kane (Orson Welles, 1941)

City Lights (Charlie Chaplin, 1931)

Contempt [*Le mépris*] (Jean-Luc Godard, 1963)

Creepers (*Phenomena*) (Dario Argento, 1985)

Dark Water [*Honogurai mizu no soko kara*] (Hideo Nakata, 2002)

Days of Heaven (Terrence Malick, 1978)

Disque 957 (Germaine Dulac, 1928)

Don Quixote (Orson Welles [unfinished])

Do the Right Thing (Spike Lee, 1989)

Don't Look Now (Nicolas Roeg, 1973)

Double Indemnity (Billy Wilder, 1944)

Dr Strangelove (Stanley Kubrick, 1964)

Duck Soup (Leo McCarey, 1933)

8 ½ (Federico Fellini, 1963)

Elephant (Gus Van Sant, 2003)

Element of Crime [*Forbrydelsens element*] (Lars von Trier, 1984)

Empire (Andy Warhol, 1964)

Enter the Void (Gaspar Noé, 2009)

Eraserhead (David Lynch, 1977)

Eternal Sunshine of the Spotless Mind (Michel Gondry/Charlie Kaufman, 2004)

Europa (Lars von Trier, 1991)

The Exorcist (William Friedkin, 1973)

Farinelli (Gérard Corbiau, 1994)

Fight Club (David Fincher, 1999)

Finding Nemo (Andrew Stanton and Lee Unkrich, 2003)

The Five Obstructions (Lars von Trier, 2003)

The Flicker (Tony Conrad, 1965)

The Fog of War: Eleven Lessons from the Life of Robert S. McNamara (Errol Morris, 2003)

Funny Games (Michael Haneke, 1997/2007)

The Great Dictator (Charlie Chaplin, 1940)

Hana-bi (Takeshi Kitano, 1997)

Happy Together [*Chun gwong cha sit*] (Wong Kar-wai, 1997)

Hidden [*Caché*] (Michael Haneke, 2005)

Hour of the Wolf [*Vargtimmen*] (Ingmar Bergman, 1968)

I Stand Alone [*Seul contre tous*] (Gaspar Noé, 1998)

The Idiots (Lars von Trier, 1998)

Inception (Christopher Nolan, 2010)

In the Mood for Love [*Fa yeung nin wa*] (Wong Kar-wai, 2000)

In My Skin [*Dans ma peau*] (Marina de Van, 2002)

INLAND EMPIRE (David Lynch, 2006)

Irréversible (Gaspar Noé, 2002)

Kiss Me Deadly (Robert Aldrich, 1955)

Jeanne Dielman, 23 Quai du commerce, 1080 Bruxelles (Chantal Akerman, 1975)

The Kingdom I and II [*Riget I and II*] (Lars von Trier, 1994 and 1997)

The Lady Eve (Preston Sturges, 1941)

La guerre est finie (Alain Resnais, 1966)

La Jetée (Chris Marker, 1962)

The Last Sunset (Robert Aldrich, 1961)

Last Year at Marienbad [*L'année dernière à Marienbad*] (Alain Resnais, 1961)

Letter to Jane (Jean-Luc Godard and Jean-Pierre Gorin, 1972)

Lolita (Stanley Kubrick, 1962)

London (Patrick Keiller, 1994)

Lost Highway (David Lynch, 1997)

Magnolia (P. T. Anderson, 1999)

The Maltese Falcon (John Huston, 1941)

The Matrix (Larry Wachowski and Andy Wachowski, 1999)

Medea (Lars von Trier, 1987)

Memento (Christopher Nolan, 2000)

Meshes of the Afternoon (Maya Deren, 1943)

Minority Report (Stephen Spielberg, 2002)

Mirror [*Zerkalo*] (Andrei Tarkovsky, 1975)

The Misfits (John Huston, 1961)

Mission: Impossible (Brian de Palma, 1996)

Mission: Impossible II (John Woo, 2000)

Mission: Impossible III (J. J. Abrams, 2006)

Modern Times (Charlie Chaplin, 1936)

Mouchette (Robert Bresson, 1967)

Mulholland Drive (David Lynch, 2001)

My Fair Lady (George Cukor, 1964)

Nashville (Robert Altman, 1976)

The New World (Terrence Malick, 2005)

Nightwatching (Peter Greenaway, 2007)

No Country for Old Men (Ethan Coen and Joel Coen, 2007)

North by Northwest (Alfred Hitchcock, 1959)

Nosferatu the Vampyre (Werner Herzog, 1979)

Notorious (Alfred Hitchcock, 1946)

October: Ten Days that Shook the World [*Oktyabr*] (Sergei Eisenstein, 1928)

One Second in Montreal (Michael Snow, 1969)

The Passion of Joan of Arc [*La passion de Jeanne d'Arc*] (Carl Theodor Dreyer, 1928)

The Perfect Human [Det perfekte menneske] (Jørgen Leth, 1967)

Persona (Ingmar Bergman, 1966)

Pickpocket (Robert Bresson, 1959)

Poetic Justice (Hollis Frampton, 1972)

Psycho (Alfred Hitchcock, 1960)

Psycho (Gus Van Sant, 1998)

Queen Kelly (Erich von Stroheim, 1932)

Rashomon (Akira Kurosawa, 1950)

Read my Lips [*Sur mes lèvres*] (Jacques Audiard, 2001)

Rear Window (Alfred Hitchcock, 1954)

Reservoir Dogs (Quentin Tarantino, 1992)

Ring [*Ringu*] (Hideo Nakata, 1998)

Romance (Catherine Breillat, 1999)

Rome, Open City [*Roma, città aperta*] (Roberto Rossellini, 1945)

Rosemary's Baby (Roman Polanski, 1968)

The Rules of the Game [*La règle de jeu*] (Jean Renoir, 1939)

Russian Ark [*Russkiy kovcheg*] (Alexander Sokurov 2002)

Samson and Delilah (Warwick Thornton, 2009)

Scenes from a Marriage [*Scener ur ett äktenskap*] (Ingmar Bergman, 1973)

The Searchers (John Ford, 1956)

The Seventh Continent [*Die siebente Kontinent*] (Michael Haneke, 1989)

The Seventh Seal [*Det sjunde inseglet*] (Ingmar Bergman, 1957)

The Shining (Stanley Kubrick, 1980)

Shirin (Abbas Kiarostami, 2008)

A Short Film About Love (Krzysztof Kieslowski, 1988)

The Silence of the Lambs (Jonathan Demme, 1991)

The Sixth Sense (M. Night Shyamalan, 1999)

Stage Fright (Alfred Hitchcock, 1950)

Sullivan's Travels (Preston Sturges, 1941)

Summer with Monica [*Sommaren med Monika*] (Ingmar Bergman, 1953)

Sunset Boulevard (Billy Wilder, 1950)

Talk to Her [*Hable con ella*] (Pedro Almodóvar, 2002)

Taxi Driver (Martin Scorsese, 1976)

Ten Canoes (Rolf de Heer and Peter Djigirr, 2006)

That Obscure Object of Desire [*Cet obscur objet du désir*] (Luis Buñuel, 1977)

The Thin Red Line (Terrence Malick, 1998)

The Third Man (Carol Reed, 1949)

Tokyo Story [*Tôkyô monogatari*] (Yasujiro Ozu, 1953)

The Tree of Life (Terrence Malick, 2011)

Trouble Every Day (Claire Denis, 2001)

Tsotsi (Gavin Hood, 2005)

Twin Peaks (David Lynch and Mark Frost, 1990–1991)

2001: A Space Odyssey (Stanley Kubrick, 1968)

2046 (Wong Kar-wai, 2004)

The Unknown (Tod Browning, 1927)

The Usual Suspects (Bryan Singer, 1995)

Vampyr (Carl Theodor Dreyer, 1932)

The Vanishing [*Spoorloos*] (Georges Sluizer, 1988)

Vertigo (Alfred Hitchcock, 1958)

Vivre sa vie: Film en douze tableaux (Jean-Luc Godard, 1962)

Wild Strawberries [*Smultronstället*] (Ingmar Bergman, 1957)

Winter Light [*Nattvardsgästerna*] (Ingmar Bergman, 1963)

Wittgenstein (Derek Jarman, 1993)

The Wizard of Oz (Victor Fleming, 1939)

INDEX